Other Avon books by
Leon Edel

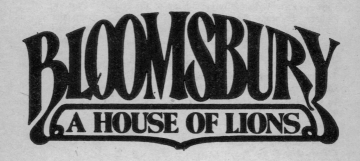

BLOOMSBURY
A HOUSE OF LIONS

LEON EDEL

 AVON
PUBLISHERS OF BARD, CAMELOT AND DISCUS BOOKS

The portraits of Virginia Woolf, from the collection of Mrs. Ian Parsons, are reproduced by permission of Mrs. Parsons. The portraits of Vanessa Bell, Leonard Woolf, Lytton Strachey, Roger Fry, Clive Bell, Desmond MacCarthy and Maynard Keynes are reproduced by permission of the National Portrait Gallery, London; the portrait of Duncan Grant from the Devonshire Collection, Chatsworth, reproduced by permission of the Trustees of the Chatsworth Settlement; and the portrait of Franklin Delano Roosevelt by permission of the National Portrait Gallery, Smithsonian Institution, Washington, D.C. The two drawings by Carrington in Part IV are reproduced from *Carrington: Letters and Extracts from Her Diaries,* edited by David Garnett, by permission of the Sophie Partridge Trust and Jonathan Cape Ltd.

The J. B. Lippincott edition carries the following Library of Congress Cataloging in Publication Data:
Bibliography: p.
Includes index.
1. London—Intellectual Life. 2. London—Biography. 3. Bloomsbury group. I. Title.

AVON BOOKS
A division of
The Hearst Corporation
959 Eighth Avenue
New York, New York 10019

Copyright © 1979 by Leon Edel
Published by arrangement with
Lippincott & Crowell, Publishers
Library of Congress Catalog Card Number: 79-4341
ISBN: 0-380-50005-1

First Avon Printing, May, 1980

AVON TRADEMARK REG. U.S. PAT. OFF. AND IN
OTHER COUNTRIES, MARCA REGISTRADA, HECHO EN
U.S.A.

Printed in the U.S.A.

Contents

Contents

Preface

A House of Lions was planned by me some fifteen or twenty years ago as a series of biographical essays on the principal figures in the "Bloomsbury Group"—writers, painters, critics, economic and political activists who came together during the Edwardian period and flourished beyond the Second World War. I was then in the midst of my long, difficult and multiple-volumed life of Henry James, and I told my publishers I would never again undertake so large a work. I would confine myself, I said, to the biographical essay—a beautiful literary form requiring brevity, lucidity, selective detail and, above all, a light ironic touch. I would emulate Strachey's *Eminent Victorians* but would avoid his satire, and my book would be about "Eminent Bloomsberries," some of whom were the children of eminent Victorians. I remember saying, in the Strachey manner, "In Bloomsbury there are nine characters in search of an author."

I little dreamed, when I made these lighthearted remarks, that I still had a dozen years' work on my life of James, or that after a while there would be such an outpouring of Bloomsbury biographies, letters, memoirs, diaries, posthumous papers, bedroom histories and critical writings—a veritable deluge. Faced with an entire library about my nine figures (not to speak of new and massive archives), I gradually altered my plan. Instead of a series of essays, I decided to tell the story of Bloomsbury and how it came to be. I would try to answer Clive Bell's question of long ago, "What *was* Bloomsbury?" My answer is *A House of Lions.*

They would have denied they were lions even as they kept insisting that they were never a group. This growing legend describes them as "loving friends," a parcel of snobs, eccentric, insolent, arrogant, egotistical, preoccupied with neurotic personal relations—that is, with sex in its varied androgynous manifestations. Certainly there was some arrogance, and some insolence, and perhaps a certain amount of snobbishness (though a snob is hard to define in other than the Thackerayan terms). But I also discovered that they were a group of rational and liberal individuals with an arduous work ethic and an aristocratic ideal. Each labored in his separate vineyard. They had a passion for art; they liked the fullness of life; they knew how to relax when their day's work was done. They wrote. They painted. They decorated. They built furniture. They sat on national committees. They achieved a large fame. With success came a certain amount of power. One of them became a peer. Another was knighted. Others refused honors. They were damnably critical. They criticized the Establishment but, unlike most critics, they worked to improve it. They hated war. Some refused to fight; others believed they had to see the 1914–18 conflict through to the end. All actively worked for peace. People who knew them were irritated, and some found them rude and abrasive. One eminent lady with a splendid critical pen said to me, when I told her I was writing this book, "Bloomsbury bores me." I cannot reproduce her tone. To others they were the least boring people in the world, for they had intelligence and charm, though no doubt a certain high and gentry view of civilization.

My nine characters include the economist Maynard Keynes, whose theories have affected the lives of millions, and Leonard Woolf, the influential writer and publisher, a considerable power in Labour Party politics. There were two literary figures: Virginia Woolf, the novelist, with her lyrical imagination and her fictional inventions, whose writings establish her as a larger kind of George Eliot in our century; and Lytton Strachey, the scholar-eccentric, who altered the course of modern biography. There were two critics: Clive Bell in painting, Desmond MacCarthy in letters. And there were three painters: Roger Fry, an influential theorist who also painted, and Vanessa Bell and Duncan Grant, who absorbed brilliantly for English painting the influences of Cézanne and Matisse. The three took part in the modern revolution that brought Post-Impressionism into general awareness.

Bloomsbury had other members, who led quiet lives and played marginal roles in its annals. There are some who have been labeled "Bloomsbury" but were simply "friends of the friends." Was E. M. Forster really Bloomsbury? I think not, for his life did not become intertwined with the nine originals. Was Lady Ottoline Morrell? Many think so—but she was in reality running a salon of her own: her lions were D. H. Lawrence, Aldous Huxley, Bertrand Russell, painters such as Mark Gertler and, briefly, dancers such as Nijinsky. Hers was a celebrity salon. Bloomsbury, on the other hand, was a committed group of friends whose interrelated lives made for an interrelated achievement—even though they all worked and lived as individuals. The only imagination allowed a biographer (I said this long ago) is the imagination of form. He is not allowed to imagine his facts. But I should have added that a biographer has a responsibility toward his facts; they must be interpreted. As Strachey put it, "Uninterpreted truth is as useless as buried gold" (a very Keynesian remark). Having abandoned the idea of writing nine essays, what form was my book to have? I resolved to seek my truths in both an episodic structure and a psychological interpretation of Bloomsbury's past. My episodes are strung together as one strings beads—and when the string is complete and harmonious, each bead has a relation to the other beads on the string. My Bloomsbury personages met in youth; they became friends; they struggled into maturity; they courageously faced the world's turmoil; their lives became intertwined. There are many novels which tell such a story—the story of an *Entwicklung*, an unfolding. To tell it in biographical form, as if it were a novel, and be loyal to all my materials was the delicate and amusing task I set myself. I can register at least one personal satisfaction. After writing five volumes about one character, I have written one volume about nine characters. My story takes these characters into middle age, to the time when they began searching their memories and writing their own histories. That seems an appropriate place to leave them. The later years of the elderly lions is another story.

LEON EDEL

Honolulu 1973–78

Illustrations

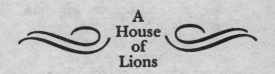

A
House
of
Lions

Clive Bell	1881–1964
Vanessa Bell	1879–1961
Roger Fry	1866–1934
Duncan Grant	1885–1978
Maynard Keynes	1883–1946
Desmond MacCarthy	1877–1952
Lytton Strachey	1880–1932
Leonard Woolf	1880–1969
Virginia Woolf	1882–1941

Gordon Square is like nothing so much
as the lions house at the Zoo.
One goes from cage to cage.
All the animals are dangerous,
rather suspicious of each other,
and full of fascination and mystery.
VIRGINIA WOOLF

... lions are sophisticated,
are blasé, are brought up from the first
to prowling and mauling ...
HENRY JAMES

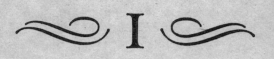

I

Thoroughly

If we seek the beginnings of our story, we might start in various parts of England or Scotland or Wales, or in Cambridge, where the Bloomsbury males were educated, or even in some ghetto of Europe. But we might as well start in Bloomsbury itself and with a Jew named Benjamin Woolf. He was born in London in 1808; that is, in the time of Napoleon. He learned the tailor's trade, a trade to which so many lower-middle-class and working-class Jews found themselves harnessed by history, as it were. Benjamin Woolf was very good at his trade. He had a shop in Regent Street and another in Piccadilly. He tried other ventures. He prospered. When Victoria came to the throne, he was living in a comfortable house in or near Tavistock Square in Bloomsbury, a friendly quarter of London. Prosperity went hand in hand with fertility. Benjamin's wife, Isabella Phillips, bore seven sons and three daughters. His death certificate listed him as a "gentleman." His sons accordingly avoided trade. Grandfather Benjamin, said Leonard Woolf, "educated his sons out of their class."

The status of the Jews had changed considerably in England by the time one of Benjamin's sons, Solomon Rees Sidney Woolf, became a solicitor and then a barrister and a Queen's Counsel. With the continuing enlightenment, the Jews, persecuted during the old cruel centuries, were finally emancipated, and with their characteristic resourcefulness they had produced an eloquent, ornately verbose prime minister, Benjamin Disraeli, who was the delight of Queen Victoria. Solomon Woolf, the man of law, was slight, dapper, studious, a barrister of dignity and courage. Some said he had "an eager and nipping air" as he went about his duties. His son remembered that "he practically never stopped working" save in the moments when he presided

3

over the bountiful family table, the Sunday roast beef in Lexham Gardens. He had purchased a big house and extravagantly added a large wing, for he had married a Dutch woman who bore him ten children. This family, with its servants, nursemaids, governesses, needed a great deal of space. Slight, his face masklike, especially when framed by its legal wig, with sunken, shadowed, melancholy eyes, he suggested soft speech and hardheadedness. His second son, Leonard Sidney Woolf, born in 1880, grew up with this sense of wisdom, space and affluence. He remembered his father vividly. Once, when he was six, he was taken to court and saw his parent exchange icy legal words with another man of law, fighting out a case before a solemn judge. Then they went off to lunch in the friendliest manner. The boy thought there was no logic in this. Could acrimony and friendliness live side by side? Could two men be at each other's throats with polite, nasty legal language and then sit at soup afterward in such amity? They should have slugged it out. It made the court scene unreal, like a play. It made life seem strange and contradictory. This was but one of the world's anomalies Leonard Sidney Woolf noticed and tried to live with and to change.

His father was unorthodox, although he did go on high feast days to the synagogue. He loved his family and his work. And then, with terrible suddenness, everything changed. The energetic lawyer, so full of life and earnest fun, became ill one day and in a few days he was dead—at forty-eight—leaving his large family, many debts and the big house. The family buried Solomon Woolf in a London cemetery. On the stone they engraved words from Micah which he had always quoted: "To do justly, and to love mercy, and to walk humbly with thy God." Leonard Woolf, aged eleven, found the words bewildering. God expected too much. He was not always merciful. "I've always been sure," he would say in his maturity, "that the heat of hell is preferable to the cold of heaven." For there is no hurt among all the human hurts deeper and less understandable than the loss of a parent when one is not yet an adolescent. The mystery of death, the sense of separation and cruel abandonment, the deep-seated anger which one is forced to control—all this is accompanied in a small boy of Leonard's alertness by a feeling of discrimination and injustice. His

playmates had their fathers. He had lost his. Solomon
Woolf had walked humbly with God. In court he had
seemed proud and almost like a god himself. Was this the
way the walk ended? Although Leonard Woolf has not
documented this, we can discern in the later patterns of his
life how profound were the insecurities and the rage
created by sudden loss in the midst of an otherwise happy
boyhood. Much later Leonard would write a passionate
novel about the life of primitive people eking out a starved
existence in clearings on the edge of a creeping jungle that
always threatened to engulf them. The intensity of this
novel contains within it the intensities of Leonard's actual
as well as racial memories. It was curious, this deep fund
of insecurity and anger in one who is growing up among
the fine old middle-class securities of Victoria's time.

II

A photograph of Leonard Woolf, probably taken a year or
two after Solomon's death, shows us a face not unlike his
father's. The eyes of childhood look directly at us. The
nose is straight, like the parent's; the full, sensuous lips
form a severe line below. There is a touch of deep melancholy in the eyes, a kind of immediate as well as ancestral
hurt.

One can hear the schoolboy asking straight questions
and wanting straight answers. Leonard was a young Spar-
tan in the heart of chaotic London. Behind him were centuries of persecution, violence, death. No more, I suppose,
than the centuries behind the Irish or the Huguenots—or
the Puritans, before these also became persecutors. Yet
with important differences. Leonard's people had a longer
history of dispersal, an ingrained learned toughness, a
curious mixture of inferiorities and stubbornness, pride and
consciousness of race and status. They had seemed at first
"outlandish" in England; this was a grave handicap in a
society with strong boundaries, cultivated stratifications.
Leonard Woolf's heritage was strong: a Biblical ethic, a
sense of the importance of work, a built-in discipline of
strength, of control. One had to be proof against life's
insults. For the centuries had piled insults on the Jews and

made them prize tenaciously a heritage of righteousness that is the world order imposed on chaos by the Old Testament—which itself is a record of chaos, crime, rapacity, persecution and privilege.

Leonard Woolf combined Old Testament virtues with an ingrained English sense of "fair play," even though he soon learned that individuals did not always play fair. Leonard's father had disliked stupidity and injustice, and Leonard followed him in this with an impatience and a hot temper which he always struggled to subdue. The family moved from the big house in Lexham Gardens to an ugly Victorian house on Colinette Road in Putney. This was a bitter rite of passage, a descent from affluence into poverty. "I know all there is to know about security and insecurity," he would say.

He must at all cost continue his schooling, his mother said. He had been educated by tutors and governesses; at ten he had been sent to school in Brighton. Like Bloomsbury, Brighton would be a landscape for the mature years of Leonard Woolf. In the Arlington House preparatory school he learned all the necessary and stable things that made his generation thoroughly educated even if learning came by a rough process, by rote, from uneasy masters teaching the savage young. Leonard and his elder brother, Herbert, applied themselves to their work; unlike some Jewish boys they also liked games. This was the saving grace. They were not simply Jewish "swots." Here also Leonard was initiated into the world of boy-sex by "a small boy who had probably the dirtiest mind in an extraordinarily dirty-minded school." Obviously, among the Jewish virtues taken to school by Leonard had been a great innocence and, as he came to recognize, an unawareness of sin. However, the small, prattling, dirty-minded little boy who associated sex with the female navel was not so much a sinner as simply a crude and offensive member of the human race.

As important in Leonard's rearing as the Old Testament sense of virtue and goodness were large chunks of diluted Baptist doctrine imparted by his favorite nurse some years earlier. The nurse was a Somersetshire woman, with straight-parted black hair and a smooth, oval farm-girl face. She read to him in the nursery at Lexham Gardens out of the *Baptist Times* and, curiously, out of De Quincey's *Confessions of an English Opium Eater*. One suspects that Leonard got very little of the Baptist faith, either the Calvinism or the Evangelism; but he became "quite an authority on the politics and polemics of the Baptist sect." Then Miss Vicary nursed him to sleep with "the voluptuous rhythm of de Quincey's interminable sentences whose baroque ornamentations must have been embellished by the nurse's mispronunciations and her Somerset accent." Leonard got from her both the pleasures and fear of public events, "the horrors and inequities of the great world of society and politics as recorded in the *Baptist Times*, about the year 1885." And all this in the untroubled atmosphere of the Lexham Gardens third-floor nursery, where the boy felt snug and safe. The fire blazed behind the tall guard; the kettle sang musically, and the music mingled with the nurse's reading of serious things, not least the story of De Quincey's struggle between his dangerous opium habit and his powerful will. Far off, the other music of the Victorian age could be heard in the *clop-clop* of hansoms in the street. Small wonder that Leonard "never again found any safety and civilization to equal that of the gas-lit nursery."

III

By the time Leonard Woolf got to his school at Brighton, he had learned how limited was the safety of the nursery. He saw with childlike wonder and horror a brawling London whose violence and ginmill sordidness were visible at all times. At night he heard a woman's shrieks; or he saw a drunken, tattered man staggering about with a policeman violently hitting him; he also glimpsed inferno-slums filled with strange human shapes. They made the small boy sick with terror. Rude initiations were common to little London boys, and the real and the unreal of animosity and fraternity, of safety and cruelty, of smiling policemen and brutal policemen, of his father in court and out—all these were prime discoveries for the future socialist and member of the Labour Party's "elite." The other part of Leonard's education was as Victorian as any we read about in old novels—"desiccation, erosion, mouldiness, frustration. . . . Before I went to Cambridge, I must have spent at least 10,000 hours of my short life sitting in some class-room, smelling of ink and boys, being taught by a gowned schoolmaster usually Latin, Greek, or mathematics, and occasionally French or history." Fortunately, not all tutors were incompetent. There was one whose passion for literature was imparted to the small boy. Mr. Floyd made Leonard "dimly aware that lessons—things of the mind—could be exciting and even amusing." Floyd had for some books the same kind of insatiable love as Leonard's nurse had for De Quincey.

Leonard was at Brighton from 1890 to 1894. He learned to play cricket. His master taught it as an art, almost as if he were teaching the ballet. Most of the masters, however, were bored and consequently boring. Leonard got a solid grounding in Greek and Latin. His greatest satisfaction— testimony to his puritanism—was his use of his power, when he became a senior boy, to put an end to offensive sexual practices in the school. "When I left for St. Paul's in 1894," he wrote with a note of distinct pride years later, "the atmosphere had changed from that of a sordid brothel to that more appropriate to fifty fairly happy small boys under the age of fourteen." Leonard was a reformer from the first.

He had a scholarship at St. Paul's, and during his five years there he acquired a belief in sane rules, precepts, disciplines. No lapses were tolerated. The students were trained strictly for the university. Leonard learned to be serious, moral, ethical; and because he was ambitious and determined, he applied rules to himself as well as to others. He left St. Paul's for Cambridge carrying an invisible outer shell, a carapace, that was his permanent shield against life.

IV

What was this carapace which Leonard Woolf carried for seventy years as if his nerves were sheathed in armor? He had above all an unusual capacity to control his feelings—

to suppress them if necessary. He was "defended" largely by his intellect. The mind could cage his emotions. He learned how to stand "a little to one side of my environment"—something which had been forced upon his Jewish ancestors. He also describes how he learned to be the kind of "I" who watches himself as if he were double—"not I." This kind of self-awareness has been sketched by many others, not least Emerson and William James in their "me" and "not-me." In Leonard it seemed as if he were both actor and observer: "I cannot avoid continually watching myself playing a part on the stage." This is much less true of one to the manner born. Insecurity and anxiety breed a quest for other selves. Sometimes this becomes schizoid and troublesome; sometimes it creates nerves of steel. Leonard's will was iron. He could be severe with others and always was with himself. He nourished a fantasy of becoming "His Excellency, Sir Leonard Woolf K.C.M.G."—the kind of fantasy James Joyce imparts to his Dublin Jew, Leopold Bloom, who in the drunken haze of night-town thinks himself Lord Mayor and later King–Emperor–Chairman. Leonard's ambition and tenacity, his law-enforcing character, his ability to treat his emotions as an army treats its recruits—all this was a measure of an anxious man who clings to cleared land beside a jungle. He accepted the law of reason; he freely committed himself to rational movements and mainly to socialism. If his emotions were rebellious, his reason could accept both immediacies and conformities—insofar as they were necessary. Conformity was better than anarchy. For years Leonard knew how *not to feel*—how to distance himself from intimacy. This made for an uneasy calm, a tremor of the soul, but it was better than tempests of feeling. Animals were easier to love than humans. He found the affection they inspired "of a purity and simplicity." Humans were much more difficult. Leonard's love of animals rested in part on his need to be absolute master of himself so as to cope with the violences of life, such as presiding at a hanging in the colonies or rescuing his wife from the abyss of madness. Leonard tells us that in Ceylon he was thought "too severe and too opinionated." Without that severity, that dry yet often charismatic power, Leonard Woolf would have been a bundle of nerves, the fallible human he sought to transform into the role-playing "not-me." He held on tightly all his life. And he did so with a simple strength through which shone an essential goodness, a love of life, an unshakable sincerity of belief.

What Leonard learned in developing his carapace, as his father had done before him, was that men could be mean, cowardly, untruthful, nasty, cruel—as he felt himself to be along with other boys, filled with the submerged stuff of life. The "gentle, eager, inquisitive, generous, vulnerable guest and companion of our bodies," the acquired ego and the social ego, had to learn to live together with primitive impulses and instinct. Hyde and Jekyll were always there. Sometimes one was more real than the other. These were the internal shadows of civilized man. The lapses from civilization could be considerable, with serious consequences for man's future. Leonard saw these as a "series of psychological curtains which one interposed between oneself and the outside world of 'other people.'" It was all a part of the process of growing up and also a means of self-concealment and self-defense. Particularly valuable in this process was his learning of a peculiar ecstasy which comes from "*feeling* the mind work smoothly and imaginatively upon difficult and complicated problems." In the philosophical stumblings of youth, the world seemed filled with strange contradictions: one believed, and yet at moments felt there was nothing one could believe. Things mattered —intensely—and then it seemed as if nothing mattered. Teachers themselves seemed to have contempt for what they taught. Still, persuading, arguing, being logical mattered above all. Leonard remembered an old boy of St. Paul's named G. K. Chesterton, an ardent debator; Chesterton was Catholic and would later be militantly anti-Semitic. He was standing upright at the table tearing sheets of paper into little pieces as he talked; his hands were nervous, but his mind was cold and logical regarding bimetallism, taxation, the Irish question.

Leonard Woolf had his own kind of nervousness. It was a shaking of the hands. All male members of the Woolf family had it. He had seen his father's hands shaking so that his morning paper rustled and trembled. A peculiar hereditary trait, so the doctors told him, for he tried to find a cure. Virginia Stephen's brother Thoby told his sister that Leonard was "a man who trembled perpetually all over." Why did he tremble? Virginia asked. It was a part of his nature, the brother replied—he was so violent, so savage, he despaired of the human race. That was the way Virginia Woolf told it years later in her mocking way. Perhaps she was right: or perhaps the Woolfs, possessing the name of so predatory a creature in the animal kingdom, had to control and subdue, and the trembling was as of a man lifting a weight, staggering under a heavy burden. Was it the price they paid for their high civilization? Leonard's father had been proud of the implications of his name. His emblem was a wolf's head. Underneath this emblem he had written a single word: *Thoroughly*. It was his motto. Leonard would discard the motto and keep the emblem. But he lived the motto all his life. "Thoroughly" included stubbornness, unyielding, unswerving tenacity. The rule of the jungle was fear—and Leonard knew the twin demons of fear and rage. It gave him towering strength over his own weaknesses and uncertainties. He was a man of deep depression—and he defeated melancholy by the inscrutable willpower of his being.

Leonard Woolf sat for the scholarship examination at Trinity College—the college of Isaac Newton—in Cambridge in March 1899, when he was almost nineteen. He was adept at passing exams. In October of that year, when the century had reached an extremity of old age, the right-thinking and stoical-skeptical young Jew went up to the university, to the elaborate ancient Christian college that bore a name so much at war with the essence of the Jewish faith. The Jews had one God. Here was a celebration of a Trinity. This, we may be sure, was far from Leonard's thoughts. He arrived, in spite of his different heritage, ostensibly as an equal among equals. He looked at the Great Court, the Great Gate, the spread of lawn, the romantic medieval. It was "a new strange jungle, full of unknown enemies, pitfalls, and dangers." He also had the usual feeling boys have on arriving at a college—a sense of loneliness and isolation. Mixed with this, however, was "the splendour of the adventure." This was the third stage in the family pilgrimage from ancestral Bloomsbury and Judaism through middle-class Brighton to the seat of England's elite, the university which trained "a large proportion of those destined to guide public opinion and to execute policy."

Here began the adult life of Leonard Sidney Woolf—"thoroughly."

The Hunter's Eye

Clive Bell's blue eyes looked at times like an animal's—dark and shiny. His face was pink and round, at times sanguine. He was short and inclined to stoutness or thickness—thick shoulders, thick sensuous lips, the face of a country boy, with a high forehead and a mop of ginger hair. His laughter was an explosive spasm or guffaw, and in his youth he possessed distinct crudities that made him seem like some young rural squire out of Fielding rather than a sensitive poetry-conscious undergraduate at an ancient college. Leonard Woolf's early environment had been that of a middle-class intellectual and of a city-bred boy. Arthur Clive Heward Bell's was middle-class hunting and fishing. He grew up in a Regency villa converted into a Tudor mansion, with a baronial hall, paneling and a minstrel's gallery. It was filled with stuffed animals and a board groaning with game. "Animals dominated the conversation, yielding only occasionally to lawn tennis, hockey or the weather." So Clive's son tells us. Clive himself boasted that he had a game license from the age of sixteen and "walked with guns" from childhood. Virginia Stephen, visiting Cleeve House ("rich and illiterate") in Wiltshire, found herself dipping her pen into an inkpot fashioned out of the hoof of a favorite hunter, with the name and date of the animal's death engraved on it—a form of piety and sentimentality not generally visible among her hosts. At table presided William Heward Bell, light and simple, gruff, cordial; and his spouse Hannah Cory, "a little rabbit-faced woman, craning forward and attentive," with strong religious principles. Her eyes were blue and eager, yet abstract. There were two sisters, the oldest and youngest of the children, in pale blue satin with satin bows in their hair, altogether "a parcel of clever children"—an older brother, bright, good-humored and assertive, named Cory (later a soldier and a member of parliament), and Clive, the third child, comfortably placed between the older brother he could look up to and the younger sister, who probably looked up to him. The family derived its comparatively newfound wealth from a productive coal mine. The crisis in the life of Leonard Woolf had been one of loss and insecurity. Clive Bell grew up materially secure in Wiltshire landscapes he could claim as his own. But he had his personal malaise, for he had too strong a sensibility and too good a mind to be content with game and his shotgun, deeply satisfying though he found the sportsman's world— the proximity to nature and the soil. One could not sport all the time. Clive's mind asked questions.

He never gave us the story of his childhood; he was impatient with "those indefatigable searchers after truth who concern themselves with the small beginnings of things." This was natural. Clive believed in the seized moment. His mind was only broadly historical. Like most hedonists, he preferred to look neither backward nor forward. The here and now, the picture in front of him, the woman he was with, the bird in flight—this was life: the rest was history. The future could assuredly take care of itself. He found himself at one with Proust in the thought that "the only certainty in life is change." One hunted— one didn't have to write about it. One made love—one didn't have to—one couldn't—set down the sounds of love. The hunting sufficed. Sex sufficed. Love—*that* was a particular state of being, and the growing boy had no particular thoughts about it. Only later did he feel that romanticism in general was a "delicious distemper of intellectual puberty." We are forced to deduce his childhood, to extrapolate from hints. The single fact that looms large is Clive Bell's use of his eyes.

The young Bell possessed (besides the Latin and Greek he learned at his middle-class public school of Marlborough) the lore of a huntsman and fisherman, and this lore could be applied to other fields of human experience. Indeed, his quest for art, his discovery of an aesthetic world, was an outgrowth of his discovery of the life of the field, the pursuit of the chase. "Art," he wrote, "rarely catches us," but, he added, "we hunt it down."

Indeed yes, Clive's life became a splendid hunting party in the galleries of the Western world, in the art shops, in the great houses. He first saw life in the power of the aimed bullet, the blood on the plumage, the plummet of a doomed bird. The commonplaces of the shoot can produce stubborn subterranean thoughts. One had to have a special eye, a trained eye, to see the gyre and to place the pattern of shot; one had to smell the land, to know the field, to know one's horse, to understand how animals and birds respond to heat and cold, sun and haze. Above all, one was a sportsman. One shot one's quarry only when it was on the move. The hunter with his gun had an advantage of weapon and human speed and coordination and a mind behind the act: the dumb beasts and arching birds had to be allowed their slender advantage, their brute chance in a strange, unequal gamble between a grouse or a partridge and a gun. We can see the patterns of later things, the skills of the aesthetic world to which Clive transferred his skills of the physical world—that of the galloping horse, the yelping dogs, the desperate animal, the bird in flight.

In later life Clive Bell used to summon up his poetical namesake, Peter Bell, to whom

> A primrose by a river's brim
> A yellow primrose was to him,
> And it was nothing more.

Peter Bell was the *alter ego* of his youth. There would be a great difference, of course, for Clive would come to know more than the mere "real." Yet this seems to have been the way in which life began for him. In the midst of the excitement of the hunt, the pride in its trophies, the head of the stag, the handsomely mounted fish, the stuffed birds —the frozen effigies of brute conquest—Clive Bell first saw reality and only reality: yes, a partridge was a partridge, a grouse a grouse, and the excitement of the hunt a delightful fleeting moment. The primrose was a primrose.

His later friends made much of the Peter Bell buried within Clive Bell. They nicknamed him Peter. They thought it a bit of a joke—this country squire, this rough rural youth, bucolic in his tastes, concerned with horses and dead birds. Why did he read so much? Why was he so hungry for art? A curious mixture of sport and reading, said Lytton Strachey, whose own effete being could accept the good-natured and hearty Clive while looking at him with eyes of mockery. And Strachey's biographer echoes his subject, "If [Clive] had been content with the part for which his nature had so palpably intended him—the country magistrate, destined to marry an ugly wife and die at the age of 84, having spent his life doing excellent work prodding up his turnips in Wiltshire. But no; he *would* be an art critic!" A "buzzing bluebottle," said Virginia Woolf. She had her own special kind of mockery, but also much affection for both Peter Bell and Clive Bell. Thoby Stephen, Virginia's brother, looking at the Cambridge Clive, saw "a sort of mixture." Clive Bell never triumphed altogether over Peter Bell; but the two lived harmoniously together. Wordsworth's Peter enabled Clive to see that the emperor did not always wear clothes.

The thoughtful young exposed to the sportsman's life— as we can see in Turgenev's sketches or in Tolstoy's early pictures of the leisure occupations of the aristocracy—live with certain deaths of their own making. They assert their advantages, but they can also learn that one doesn't shoot at humans as if they were animals. They sometimes become concerned with what man is, what strange existential gamble can place a bullet at a given point where life suddenly ends. Clive would be a pacifist. The sportsman's eye became the critic's eye, and also the humanist's. In a letter written when revisiting the stuffed family house in Wiltshire, Clive spoke of being "out of the pale of civilization." He worried about the nature of civilization. Leonard Woolf had no such concern. His concern was with men who refused to be civilized. Lytton Strachey had no such concern. He took civilization for granted. He played its particular games and chose its particular historical moments— and laughed at its failures. But the strange conversion of the family *parvenu* spirit in Clive made him want to write a treatise on civilization, on the "new renaissance," on art— very much as Tolstoy, a rough nobleman with the smell of the fields and manure about him, encountering life's subjects, wanted to write great essays: What was philosophy? What was art? What was life? Tolstoy would leave many treatises and sets of rules, feeling within himself so much disorder and such lack of control. (I do not compare Clive with Tolstoy as figures in literature but simply note that similar concretions of experience can occur in individuals as different as a Russian nobleman and an English bourgeois.)

What we often see in the gifted young is a need for order, a desire for comformity mixed with an enthusiasm for things which others take for granted. Did Clive have a feeling that life was chaos except when it could have the order of the gyre? Man and prey; man as hunter; man and animal: the step from this to the question of "civilization" is logical enough. We know little what kind of experience Clive had at Marlborough, but if the cruelties and rigidities of the British school system gave him his Latin and Greek, it also fed his sensitivities. Many English lads learned—or had learning flogged into them—but they were not sensitive. There is a passage in Clive Bell's book *Civilization* which suggests his center of conflict, the part of him that makes him much more than the gadfly and hedonist of so many pages of Virginia's diaries and Lytton's and Leonard's condescensions. It is distinctly autobiographical. He begins by saying that an English boy, born with a fine sensibility for art, an absolutely first-rate intelligence, "finds himself from the outset at loggerheads with the world in which he is to live." He cannot accept churchgoing (we might say the churchgoing of Hannah Cory)—although, Clive adds significantly, "it might be different were it a question of going to Mass." Then there are "the hearty conventions of family life." These we know: the groaning board, the neutral talk, the sisters dressed in satin, the older brother's cultivated stance of man of the world. How escape? And into what—and where? "He will be reared," wrote Clive about his young man (who so resembled himself), "probably in an atmosphere where all thought that leads to no practical end is despised, or gets, at most, a perfunctory compliment." As for artists, unless they acquired "big" names in the public prints, they "are pretty sure to be family jokes."

Clive went on to say that "all of his finer feelings"—those of his young English boy—"will be constantly outraged; and he will live a truculent, shamefaced misfit."

John Bull would be under his nose, *Punch* his standard reading. At some public school, compulsory games, the Thomas Arnold tradition, muscular Christianity would either break his spirit "or make him a rebel for life." In this singular passage Clive Bell praises the French and their acceptance of both the physical side of life and the mind of art. What is relevant, in attempting to arrive by induction at the young Clive (who was but a few months younger than Leonard), is his eagerness, his willful enthusiasm, his delight and wonder. Clive Bell learned early how to look at pictures. Lytton would look at a picture and turn it into Lytton—that is, make it the subject for a sally of Lyttonian wit. Clive looked and thought about pictures through his ambivalence of conformity and rebellion, often tinged also with unconscious pomposity in his endeavor to be "serious"—seeing what the painter had done in his own effort (like Clive's) to make something out of the world, to give life some shape other than the patterned shapes of convention. He had, said Virginia Woolf, an odd gift for making one talk sense. All Clive's life was a quest for a superior "civilization." Clive needed answers to questions that occurred neither to Leonard nor Lytton, nor to the Stephen girls, since they had been bred from the first to possess the answers.

Much of this seems to have been latent in the boy, who in a good-natured way accepted and rebelled against his mother's religious precepts and his father's concrete world. And yet he wanted approval. He wanted to be right, gentlemanly, proper; the improprieties would come later. Virginia, in her continuing remarks about him, said he had the mind of "a peculiarly prosaic and literal type"—Peter Bell, of course. She could also see that Clive Bell was "sensitive, honest, kindly"—a mixture of vanity and decorum. He was for her "a little too carefully polished, a little too conscious of his social gifts." Lady Ottoline Morrell, who had the shrewd worldly eyes of the tutored aristocracy, recognized "the sipper, the taster, the professional connoisseur." She added with insight, "His sensitivity, of which he is so proud, is stimulated by his vanity."

What his friends could not understand was the depth of the discovery—given Clive's background—that there was a world of meaning beyond Cleeve House. Clive Bell found this world an endless joy, as if he had embraced a new religion, one that would survive. It made him a perpetual evangelist, an explainer, an ideal critic. His discovery is told in moving terms as a story out of ancient Greece. Clive had been saying that he was not content with simple aesthetic experience; from art he brought away "enriched and purified emotion." He found in it an expression of his "most intimate and mysterious feelings." And he told how in the days of Alexander Severus there lived in Rome a freed Greek who had a craft, a full belly, and security of body. His hands and brain were pleasantly busy, and "he awoke each morning to a quiet day of unexacting labour, a little sensual pleasure, a little rational conversation, a cool argument, a judicious appreciation of all that the intellect apprehended." This apparently had happened to Peter Bell: he had become educated to this extent; he had freed himself like the Greek. But it was not enough. He discovered what was lacking when one day a cranky fanatic (was it Roger Fry?) burst into the Greek's calm proclaiming a religion: "To the Greek it seemed that the breath of life had blown through the grave, imperial streets. Yet nothing in Rome was changed, save one immortal, or mortal soul. The same waking eyes opened on the same objects; yet all was changed; all was charged with meaning. New things existed. Everything mattered."

Somewhere in Clive Bell's life there had been a transcendent experience in which Peter Bell's yellow primrose became "charged with meaning." From that moment life became "a miracle and an ecstasy." Clive goes on to tell us in this passage (which we can read only as autobiography, so closely does it fit what we know): "He had learnt to feel; and, because, to feel a man must live, it was good to be alive. I know an erudite and intelligent man, a man whose arid life had been little better than one long cold in the head, for whom the madman, Van Gogh, did nothing less." This his closest friends apparently did not grasp. The vain little "name-dropper" Clive Bell had had a revelation.

The youth whose name was Woolf, prowling in the Great Court on his arrival at Trinity, saw a sportsman in full regalia, sturdy, obviously a young "blood" such as he had never known in Putney, dressed in his rig-out, swinging a whip and—so Leonard seemed to remember—carrying a hunting horn. The huntsman was oblivious, on his side, that a Woolf was watching him. He was happily lost in his own well-being, in his sense of freedom, a youth among other young bloods at the largest college in the great English university, the "epitome" of England.

Caliban in Different Voices

Leonard Woolf was in a distant emotional way a Jewish "outsider" in a world in which he felt himself to be "inside." Clive Bell had the assurance of his philistine world but aspired to subtler forms of experience. Giles Lytton Strachey, who was born eight months before Leonard—on the first of March in 1880—and was a year older than Clive, was divided in quite another way. He spoke, as all his friends have testified, with two voices. One was deep and manly; the other was tiny and a squeak. One had warm baritone notes filled with emotion; the other was somehow the piping voice of childhood, perhaps learned from a bevy of sisters who filled the Strachey home. It has been said that the entire Strachey family possessed this kind of squeak. Leonard Woolf remarked that after being with a Strachey one somehow went away squeaking a little inside.

However that may be, the two voices of Lytton Strachey were the voices of the masculinity to which he generally aspired—but without real struggle—and the femininity that was his by virtue of his rearing and environment, the streak of juvenility that seemed to remain with him all his life and led to his ultimate ménage with a female juvenile. He had an excellent mind, a well-nourished mind, but one that was highly specialized. His world had been from the first that of an omnipresent mother and innumerable sisters who apparently counted for so much more than his brothers: in the actual family hierarchy he was flanked by two sisters, one born before him and one after. Jane Maria Strachey overstimulated her children in the massive Victorian house in which they lived, Lancaster Gate, a macabre architectural pile. In fact, there is a Gothic note in the entire aspect of the house and the boy who grew up in it. The famous portrait by Henry Lamb shows an elongated Lytton, with an elongated beard in a high palatial elongated room containing elongated furniture. Lytton spent his boyhood, adolescence and youth, and indeed his young manhood, in Lancaster Gate. In the background was his father, whom Leonard remembered as "a little man with a very beautiful head." He was a general—a British general who had been in India. But no man looked less like a general. He did not clank; he did not pace. A sedentary stooping man, he resembled a studious college professor. He had been heroic in the Army when young; the Army could testify to this. Then he had become an administrator. He used the scientific knowledge of the age of Darwin and Huxley and botanized; he was meteorological and geological, and an engineer. He married late and lost his wife soon afterward. At forty-two he tried again. This time he married a sturdy Scotswoman with all the hardihood and endurance of the north—and of her race. Year after year she bore him children—thirteen in all (two dying in infancy). Giles Lytton was the eleventh. The general was sixty-three when Lytton was born; his mother was thirty-nine.

"The most ridiculous boy," said Lady Strachey when Lytton reached the age of speech, for he spoke his fantasies aloud. In the babbling tower of Lancaster Gate the houseful of children read and wrote verses, played games, acted plays. A verbal world, an eternal nursery. The mother, surrounded by her numerous progeny, kept alive the sense of the nursery in herself, even though her height and bearing were queenly. She could be elegant in black satins. She dressed Lytton in petticoats, which she thought less absurd than knickerbockers. The consequence was that Lytton in his earliest years was all the little girl. A splendid photograph testifies to this—an arresting photograph of a three-year-old in velvet dress, with lace collar, little feet crossed like a ballerina's, standing, one ankle over the other, wearing little girl's shoes and socks, a lace cuff, long hair, dark eyes looking out at the world—very straight and cutting—the posture of a self-assured child, a loved child on the verge of making a speech. It is an uncanny picture of youth and age; but one expects only a tiny voice, the voice of childhood, in spite of the baritone pose.

II

Lytton grew up with less assurance than his early picture suggests. He shot up, spindly, fragile, delicate in health, nimble in mind—"a distinctly unusual and original kind of boy." Decidedly. For under those petticoats there was a proud and active phallus, even if the child looked increasingly as if he would be a Victorian spinster. He considered himself an ugly duckling; certainly he was "odd." He recognized that he was "a funny man" and the logical thing was to play the part—with style. Very early he found that his best claim to masculinity lay in conquering young boys, in giving them love, and in being motherly as his mother had been with him. The double identification of himself as man, and himself as mother, was of a piece with the baritone and the squeak. He would be in the end a busy, ardent, oversexed homosexual with an androgynous mind. He had no conflict or inhibition about this. His juvenile verses, given to us in excessive abundance, show the witty, feline personality that was Lytton Strachey. His mother's father had been a knight, Sir John Peter Grant, and she grew up in a solid, mentally strong British upper middle class filled with hardheaded administrators—tough-minded, like her husband, but also men of feeling and some refinement, capable of pursuing study and hobbies. There were paradoxes in this world, large ones, which Lytton recognized—"paradox and pederasty," Lytton summed up his Cambridge and personal world. He would be a wag, a mocker; he might be a misfit (Alexander Pope was misshapen); but he could be both a Pope and a Voltaire, or at the least an English version of the latter.

An individual so mothered and sistered, so constantly stimulated in the literary and dramatic arts, made feminine by the femininity of his environment, fluttered over when ill, indulged, rooted in a family and an English-Scottish past, with a mother presiding like the queen over the destinies of this country, could be sickly and agile, mental and intellectual, and also a stinging wasp, a bee, loved and disliked. His desire was to cast off his past, to find big men with big voices, to melt his spindly body into them so that he might feel himself less physically absurd. Yet he felt, also, in his emotions, queenlike—like his mother, Jane

Maria Strachey, or like Victoria, or Elizabeth, or even Florence Nightingale, who made herself mother of an entire army.

III

Lytton Strachey was the most eccentric, and at times the least likable, member of Bloomsbury—shallower, in some ways, than Clive, although more brilliant; certainly shallower than Leonard, who was his very good friend. Lytton was in reality an unusual mosaic and a "mosaicist," as Clive called him, a human pastiche who later turned his craft of biography into the art of pastiche, into imitation of voices he found in documents, larded over with seasoned generalizations of wit and psychological insight, as well as psychological asperity. But his childhood, the records of which are surfeiting, shows him a creature of oddity and caprice, with a vein of hysteria and a fund of rage that for a time was so bottled up in him that he suffered from those forms of irregular heartbeat known as paroxysmal tachycardia—his heart rhythms, like his voice, went off their prescribed track. Living in a house "afflicted with elephantiasis" (as he said), with its spiral staircase leading up high, high to a pink dome, up and down which ran a household force of servants and romping children (a house in which there was only one—very audible—bathroom for parents and children), it is small wonder that his mind crept into the century nearest to that of his youth in time —the eighteenth century, with its smells and earthiness. It established a kind of mental order for the chaos of Lancaster Gate.

Lytton acquired over the years, aided by Cambridge discipline, a need to summarize, to find in the French way the inevitable *formule saisissante*. When it came to mothering the boys he loved, he had an abundance of feeling. "Oh how dreadful to be a mother," he once exclaimed to Maynard Keynes, voicing a sudden emotion. "How terrible to love so much and know so little." One cannot say what kind of knowledge he was invoking. The statement has in it distinct passion: Lytton knew how much a mother could love, how much *he* loved when at one of his schools, after a boyish orgy (ten times! he boasted in his diary), he wrapped a comforter around his sleepy love-object in an armchair. School for Lytton was erratic as well as erotic: his mother worried about his health; she was determined to ease his life. Unlike Leonard, unlike Clive, who were hearty, healthy boys, who loved games and learned their Latin and Greek well, and were heterosexuals, Lytton was not subjected to formal public schools. Illness had become a way of gaining privileges. First there was Mr. Henry Forde at Parkstone, Poole Harbour, in Dorset, where Lytton read widely and was considered "a most admirable boy." At thirteen he was sent to the New School, Abbots-holme, in Derbyshire, where manual labor was demanded. The fragile Lytton collapsed. He went on then to Leamington College, where he was bullied because of his oddities, but in due course his capacity for mothering the boys made him school prefect and head of his house. The boys here called him "Scraggs," his legs and arms were so thin. In preparation for university he was sent to Liverpool University College, where he studied with Walter Raleigh, who greatly prized his intelligence. Lytton took long bicycle rides, browsed in bookshops, and tried for Balliol—a college considered suitable for an administrator and political scientist. He failed. He then tried for Trinity in Cambridge.

Everywhere we look during his young years we see signs of a comparatively happy childhood in spite of his long thin legs, his nearsightedness, his lack of physical vitality. He was a prisoner of his odd physique who lived vicariously in the physiques of others. Had he been a woman, he would have become a Victorian invalid, with smelling salts, a corner chair, a pile of novels. In a diary of a journey to Gibraltar and Egypt (*aetat* 12) we see an observant, quick, lively boy. Facing the Sphinx, he has a *frisson* —there on the desert sands is a massive man-woman, and he feels himself in the androgynous present to be a cat— feline, yet worshiped. His journey to these foreign parts was made on a troopship. The company of so much military masculinity was exhilarating. As his chronicler puts it, Giles Lytton Strachey wanted to be a "superman" but thought he was a kind of freak. And yet he was not a shrinking boy: he was capable of mental assertion; he

possessed a good deal of natural warmth, not to speak of
the sexual vitality which helped to compensate for certain
shortcomings. One solution was to mock himself and thus
laugh with the world. He could cultivate his eccentricity—
the English world makes large allowance. His life search
was for the ordered beauty that he hoped existed somewhere, the imagined exquisite of the Age of Reason and
the writings of Voltaire.

IV

Thanks to an early initiation, there was ordered beauty for
Lytton Strachey in the literature of France. The country
itself might seem chaotic; to an Englishman, the French
people have distinct limitations; but in the French language
and in the literature of France, Lytton Strachey found
exquisite order. He could speak the language with the
mimicry and pantomime of his nature; and when one
emerged from the chaos of Lancaster Gate and the huge
nursery of life, what a pleasure to encounter the divine
lucidity, the compactness of the French *art de dire!* Lytton
found this first in a Frenchwoman who bore his mother's
middle name, Marie Souvestre. She had set up a school in
England for the daughters of upper-class families like the
Stracheys. Daughter herself of a distinguished father, Marie
Souvestre had a queenly bearing and an administrative
sense; she served almost as a kind of second queen mother
in the young years of Lytton's education. She brought him
her language, a sense of a recent past, a hardheaded femininity, all the masculine-feminine of France verbalized in a
strong Latin language, uttered in the noble accents of a
proud woman. England was the maternal nursery of Lytton, the nurture of his anachronistic mind. France was his
intellectual mistress—and he loved her brevity of speech.
He could encompass entire provinces in a few sentences;
he could offer sweeping generalizations that might make
English philosophers weep. The young boy learned much
in the school of Madame Souvestre, not as her pupil, but
as his sisters' brother—and the teacher must be accounted
a very strong influence on his later work. He knew French
as only an Englishman can learn it—that is, with precision

and classical resonance often not found in the more currently colloquial French. Clive Bell would learn it with all its colloquialisms and in his own way became an adoptive son of Paris—but the Paris of his own time. Lytton's speech was filled with the rhetoric of the past. He knew his Rousseau; he knew his Voltaire; he even knew his Président de Brosses! It will perhaps offer us some guide to the reputation of Marie Souvestre if we mention that Eleanor Roosevelt studied with her and that Henry James sought (unsuccessfully) to induce his brother William to place his daughter—Henry's niece—under her tutelage.

At nineteen, Lytton Strachey was admitted as Pensioner to Trinity College. A diary note tells us, "As I walk through the streets I am agonized by the thought of my appearance. Of course it is hideous, but what *does* it matter? I only make it worse by peering into people's faces to see what they are thinking. . . . The truth is I want *companionship*." The nineteen-year-old who came to Cambridge was a ribald, stoop-shouldered youth, possessing a good deal of priggishness, ruthlessness, energy, a mixture of liveliness and lassitude, a supercilious manner, an arrogant style; he affronted this college of more than six hundred conforming or rebellious youths, some full of aspiration (Leonard) or in quest of freedom and "class" (Clive).

Clive Bell, always sociable, stopped to talk with the head porter of the Great Gate during his first days at Trinity. The porter pointed to a youth who wore pince-nez and what would later be described as a "dismal" moustache. Lytton's hair was lank and dark; he had a long chin; he seemed a clumsy bag of bones; he had a kind of "flexible endlessness." "You wouldn't think," said the porter ruminatively, addressing the young newcomer Clive Bell, "you wouldn't think he was a general's son."

Very Serious Young Men

They met in the casual way students at colleges meet. Leonard found himself reading a notice board next to an erudite prodigy named Saxon Sydney-Turner, who lived on Clive's stair; through him Leonard met Clive. The ubiquitous Saxon also struck up a friendship with Lytton. The real common denominator, we might say, was that these youths were each—spiritually, mentally, and, in the case of Lytton, physically—outside the common run of students, the undistinguishable stereotypes of young England who accept and conform and know they are simply going through certain rituals of learning-and-living before settling into a British stability.

Presently the young intellectual "outsiders" were visiting in each other's rooms, discovering writers, playing with ideas. The world seemed freshly made—as it always is for first-year students. Each moment was unpredictable. "On one side of us," Leonard would say half a century later, "we were, in 1901, very serious young men." Why 1901? Because by then the three had reached their coming-of-age. They had had the opportunity to be (as Leonard would say) clever, arrogant, supercilious, cynical, sarcastic—and then Lytton "always looked very queer and had a squeaky voice." Doubtless it was a bit queer also at Trinity at that time to come from a *parvenu* family that owned a coal mine, or to belong to the tribes of Israel. To college intellectuals, who always form a nucleus in dormitory or pub or dining hall, the "bloods" and athletes are a world apart. Thoby Stephen called the athletes "little men in waistcoats" —big Thoby, who himself towered more than six feet, and to whom Lytton was drawn because he looked the Apollo Lytton wished to be. Thoby was also the son of a man destined to be a knight, but not a general. Leslie Stephen won his nighthood by remaining a Cambridge literary intellectual—out of Trinity Hall—and sticking to his guns as an eminent agnostic Victorian. Number 69 Lancaster Gate knew 22 Hyde Park Gate, and Thoby found Lytton's new friend Leonard interesting and Clive companionable— Thoby and Clive had much in common: cigars and horses and the out-of-doors. In his own Olympian way, Thoby was one of them. They called him "the Goth." His sister Virginia confided to a friend that he should have stood naked in the Louvre like a Greek god—he was really too massive, she felt, for ordinary rooms. He had a small head set on very large shoulders; he was good-natured, as "easy" as one's old glove; he could dissolve a high-flown flight of Lytton's with a good natured "Nonsense, my good fellow!" Leonard Woolf had never known such personal charm. And then there were others—H. T. J. Norton, who was scientific; a chap named A. J. Robertson; and Saxon, who had served as a sort of needle and thread and had sewn them all together. Saxon had then a bloom of precocity (later, in the big wide world, his student talents would seem very dull): he kept a list of the operas he had heard; he knew who had sung which role; he played the piano and wrote verses; he possessed endless "useful knowledge"; he would be a paragon of the crossword puzzle. They liked him even when he had crawled into his hole-and-corner in the Treasury, for they remembered his compulsions, his queerness and brightness.

II

We know all this from fugitive records and the more colored memories of later years, but the rest we can readily deduce. Did they dine in Hall together? What kind of high jinks did they invent? We do know they formed their Midnight Society in February of 1900—during the last year of the old century. It met for the first time in Clive's rooms properly at midnight on Saturday. This group, which they all remembered, was formed at the end of their first term; by then they considered themselves friends. Lytton's letter to his mother identifies them. He saw dull Sydney-Turner as "very distinguished and with immense knowledge of English literature." Bell was "a curious mixture of sport and reading"—something which, we might remark, was "curious" only to Lytton, for Lytton did not indulge in sport. Woolf was casually dismissed—their friendship had not yet become intimate—as "nothing particular." But Thoby—the godlike Thoby—had irresistible physical appeal. Thoby was "a charmer"—rather strange—looking very much like a Stephen; that is, handsome, "sensible and the best I have yet met." Clive tended to sit at the feet of Lytton, relishing all the bold things that issued out of his two-toned mouth.

Lytton would continue to think Clive "rather a mystery." One was either an intellectual or a sportsman: in Lytton's logic one couldn't be both. How could someone who read Surtees and dressed so well in all his roles be interested in the arts? "Why the dickens," said Lytton to Leonard, as usual a bit condescendingly, "should he imitate *us?*" What, asked Lytton, lapsing into his gallic nature, was Clive's *raison d'être?* Clive unconsciously gave his answer in a derived poem of that significant year of 1901. He wanted "not to mean anything, but to be." There was no *raison d'être*—there was simply *être!* That was a Wordsworthian stance. Deep down he did want to "mean"—and to understand—what art was. Why did it move him?

Leonard described his friends at Cambridge as consisting of two quite distinct circles: the intimate intellectual companions, Sydney-Turner, Lytton, Thoby, and later Keynes; and a kind of satellite group, slightly outside the aura of intimacy. Among these he put Clive. Leonard described Clive as having "a very attractive face, particularly to women, boyish good-humored, hair red and curly, and what in the eighteenth century was called I think, a sanguine complexion." Clive had a Degas reproduction (even then) pasted or nailed to the wall of his room, or was it his door? For him this was a fine nude and a fine painting; to Lytton, who was much less sensitive to visual art—and the female sex—it was simply a naked woman. Why else would he wonder "what the uninitiated would think about it?" Leonard, we might add, is much less described by his peers; perhaps unconsciously, in spite of the liberal and open minds of these young (Thoby from Clifton, Sydney-Turner from Westminster, Lytton from his assorted schools), the little "Jew-boy" from St. Paul's was outside their common experience. Even Lytton's biographer, in his two massive volumes, includes photographs, a veritable album, of all the Cambridge friends of Lytton—a splendid image of Thoby, a living one of Clive—but Leonard is not there: no image is given. One gets a hint of Leonard's own dilemma, his inability to keep pace with his new friends. They had as much money as they needed; by Leonard's standards they were "really well-off." They spent considerably more than he did. Leonard had gained his exhibition of £75 a year; and he increased this to £100 by taking a scholarship examination. His family gave him another £20. This provided him with the equivalent at that time of $600 a year. Out of his cautious assets, Leonard is telling us that he had enough not to feel he was a poor relation among his peers.

Thoby's stories about Leonard—for he talked freely of his college life with his sisters—were recorded by Virginia Stephen in her high mocking style much later in life (and read in Leonard's presence). Leonard, said Thoby, was as eccentric and as remarkable in his way as were Bell and Strachey. And he told how (as we have seen) he was a man whose hands trembled. But not all Jews trembled. One night Leonard had dreamed he was choking a man—dreamed it with such violence that he awoke to find he had pulled his thumb out of joint! Thoby's jokes, and Virginia's mockeries, in reality reveal the strong controls Leonard had imposed upon his feelings—his impatience and indignation with irrationality, his particular logic which he could never reconcile with the errors of society. Virginia, looking back on what was then Leonard's future, concluded that the "misanthropic" young Jew shook his fist at civilization—and decided to disappear into the tropics. The act was more complicated. At Cambridge he had less of a formed self than the assured young sons of the Establishment, or the wealthy and indulged young, like Clive. Leonard would have to make his own world within their ready-made world.

III

We renew the question: What did these vibrant young do? They read a great deal, wrote a great deal, formed societies, charged into the Great Court in the rainy dawns declaiming Swinburne; they also quoted Henry James, enchanted with the efflorescence of the Master's mandarin style, his verbal slyness and wit, little grasping his psychological sagacity. Chroniclers have made much of Lytton's and Leonard's (and Saxon's) being elected to the all-university secret society, the Apostles, which went back to the days of Tennyson and before. This was very important to them at the time and afterward in cementing and preserving friendships. Clive was not elected, but it is to be noted that he wasted no time lingering at Cambridge. He went out eagerly into the world. Leonard stayed on long enough to take examinations qualifying him for the Civil Service. Lytton would gladly have remained at Trinity all his life, had he been able to become a don.

What did these fleeting years at Cambridge mean to the young men, much more aware of life and feeling than many of their peers? Leonard, reflecting in his old age on his university past, provided a backward glance. Having come from an unenclosed background, he probed where others took matters for granted. "I have never again been quite so happy or quite so miserable as I was in the five years at Cambridge from 1899 to 1904. One lived in a state of continual excitement and strong and deep feeling. We were intellectuals, intellectuals with three genuine and, I think, profound passions: a passion for friendship, a passion for literature and music (it is significant that the plastic arts came a good deal later), a passion for what we called the truth." Leonard forgets that one of their number, at least, was less musical than plastic. And he goes on to say that these young lived in extremes of happiness and pain, "of admiration and contempt, of love and hate." Then there were books; there were always books—Tolstoy and Dostoevsky, Ibsen and Flaubert, the Elizabethans and G. E. Moore. "The hates, contempts, miseries were as violent—almost as exciting—as the loves, friendships, admirations, ecstasies." There was also the dogmatism of youth, the sense that the world was filled with old people—

all over twenty-five—and as moribund as Victoria. "We were a part of a negative movement of destruction against the past." They had the utopias of their young minds; they still had to confront realities. It was a heady world, filled with exhilarations that belong to this one time of life, its most remembered moment. Nothing later can touch it, for these are always called—and quite rightly—"impressionable years." The truth was, as we know, that the young were in revolt against a lingering past. The Victorian age had ended; it had ended even before Oscar Wilde went to jail; it was ending in Vienna in the explorations of Freud; it had ended, if we really look far enough, with Darwin. However, its residual modes still prevailed. It always takes several new generations to recognize and alter the past. Every age seems an age of "transition."

Leonard Woolf had begun by seeing Cambridge as a "jungle." He would go out into the actual jungles of the world to say that "all jungles are evil." His life at Cambridge taught him that the university was neither a jungle nor evil, but an illumination of existence. For Lytton, Cambridge from the first was a romp, a lark, a phallic universe. "Ho! Ho! Ho!"—he exclaimed—and he told his doting mother, "How proud I was as I swept through the streets arrayed for the first time in cap and gown." No jungle this for Lytton! Clive also put on his cap and gown; but it was raining, and he carried an umbrella. "Anyone can see you're a freshman, sir," the head porter at Trinity said, and he explained that it wasn't customary to carry an umbrella with cap and gown—presumably these were protection enough against fluvial Cambridge. Clive remembered this because he liked to dress properly for all his roles. It would always be important whether the tie was black or white. Lytton, as his chronicler tells us, liked the Cambridge community "with its high proportion of vocational bachelors." Desmond MacCarthy once remarked that Lytton's friendships at Cambridge were more like loves. One thinks of him always as taking possession of his friends. In his letter to Leonard asking about the *raison d'être* of Clive, there is a significant remark: "He's not," said Lytton, "under our control." *Control*, possession, and we might add, manipulation. Lytton loved power. He took hold of the Apostles from the moment he was elected and dominated and controlled; and he even "used" Leonard, for he found him appealing enough to divulge all sorts of intimacies to him; he made him, we might say, into a mother-confessor, which Lytton's real mother could not be. But Lytton could not control Clive's appetite for life. Clive was a hungry-for-experience heterosexual. In Leonard, and perhaps in Clive, there were unknowns of tradition and feeling which they had to discover. Little of this was unknown to Lytton or his friend Thoby or even Saxon. Cambridge was simply a continuation of their well-established worlds. Yet it was a liberation for them all.

IV

They laughed at themselves; they were critical of one another. There were others at Cambridge who would be angry and hurt that these young men, and their later friends, could annihilate so many tried values with a phrase, be sexually ambiguous, treat sacred matters—and particularly the Victorian-sacred—as if they didn't matter at all. It was not altogether unusual for England to *épater les bourgeois*, but one did it, so to speak, in the rhymed couplets of Pope. The art of verbal murder runs deep in England. What was different about these young men—and it would spread to the young women in their circle—was that they simply and often innocently talked about things which were not then supposed to be mentioned. Later generations (of the mid-twentieth century) would behave as if they invented sex, so free did they find themselves; but it is difficult for latecomers to understand what it meant for young liberated Victorians to begin to use four-letter words in mixed company and to question God even more violently than Leslie Stephen or Henry Sidgwick had, or as the Leonards and Lyttons did later; and then, as Leonard admitted, it could rub some people the wrong way to be faced with the cool arrogance of the rebel young. There is a capital document in Leonard's autobiography to remind us just how shocking these neoromantics could be to gentle souls. "I cannot endure the people I meet in your rooms," wrote one unnamed young man whose friendship Leonard prized. "Either they or I had to go, and as I was the newest and alone I waived my claim." He added, "Strachey etc. are to me in their several ways the most offensive people I have ever met. . . . I am not what is known as religious, but I was not going to associate with people who scoffed and jeered at my religion: fair criticism given in a gentlemanly way I do not mind. But the tone of Strachey and even you on matters of religion was not gentlemanly to me. . . . I have never been in your rooms without someone coming in whom I do not like, usually Strachey." This letter, *sancta simplicitas*, concluded, "Silence is then safer."

The document suggests that for many in England gods might be overthrown, but one had to be gentlemanly and polite in one's destruction. We will see that in this way the later "Bloomsbury" also offended; its intellectual ardor and arrogance struck home; its atheism was painful; its rudeness—that is, its inability to tolerate fools—hurt. In some such way we hear, in these preludes to Bloomsbury, notes that would climb to a *fortissimo* of feeling: too many things were galloped over roughshod. The accusations came not only from the bloods, who simply ducked (it was said) a ridiculous object like Lytton in the fountain, but also from the sensitive kind, who consulted their feelings—and chose silent disapproval. Not all would be silent, of course; and a miner's son named Lawrence would characterize our personages as resembling beetles.

Perhaps what hurt the particular young man of Leonard's story was the verbal crudity with which the intellectual young—Lytton's homosexuality apart—espoused their ideal of "telling the truth." Leonard would write that "the young are not only ruthless, they are often perfectionists." In Cambridge the perfectionism ran to philosophical, not political, lines. Gods were demolished in the name of Truth. The meliorism of the three undergraduates of our story comes to us through the annals of the Apostles and the lifeblood received in the *Principia Ethica* of the philosopher G. E. Moore. "Moorism," as they came to call it, amounted to a hardheaded form of subjective Socratic dialogue on Truth and Goodness and Beauty carefully and exigently set forth by the philosopher. In essence he seems to have forced these young men to a logic within a logic, a critical examination of premises and assumptions. Gertrude Stein was perhaps echoing Moorism when she was asked, "What is the answer?" Her reply is well known: "What is the question?" What *was* the question? Moore kept asking. Leonard Woolf and Maynard Keynes, each in his own way, testified to the fresh wind Moore blew into their forming minds with his reasoned examination of given precepts; that is, his search for "the good" and the validity of certain emotions and instincts. Above all, what he seems to have communicated was a passion for veracity. Leonard would guard that passion all his life. He alone among the Bloomsbury characters became a political "activist," while in a sense Maynard Keynes, in the larger sphere of logic and world economics, became a suprapolitical activist and statesman. Keynes, however, was a special case, trained from childhood in the objective examination of problems and usually having the genius to dissociate them from confusions of feeling. Moore, as Leonard remembered, "suddenly removed from our eyes an obscuring accumulation of scales, cobwebs and curtains, revealing for the first time to us, so it seemed, the nature of truth and reality, of good and evil and character and conduct."

"The Age of Reason has arrived," Lytton proclaimed (this was in 1903 when Moore published his *Principia*). How characteristic this was of an Apostle like Lytton—to proclaim the age of reason! In one of his many papers delivered to his fellow Apostles he argued that he preferred "anarchy to the Chinese Empire, for out of anarchy," he said, "good may come, out of the Chinese Empire nothing." With individuals like Lytton (was he not himself a potential mandarin?) one may expect that the reverse of what he says is usually the truth. He actually preferred the Chinese Empire, for he hated anarchy; he wanted the illogical and irrational world—the world that made him into a Caliban instead of a Christ—to be logical, rational, and also clever like himself. He wanted to be a Voltaire. He delivered papers on "Christ or Caliban," or on "Ought the Father to Grow a Beard," and in due course, thinking himself fatherly—although he was motherly—he grew the beard by which we know him. The beard masked Caliban and suggested masculinity. Voltaire had hardly been an Apollo. A maiden on the farm, Lytton wrote in one of his verses, thought him "a dreadful fright" and, said Lytton, to complete the rhyme, "she's right." By our theory of opposites he didn't *really* believe he was a fright, and his young men adored him. Moreover, he felt, in his manipulative power, absurdly strong. To Strachey the philosophy of G. E. Moore provided a frame of the Ideal for the combination of his physical limitations and his mental acerbity. "It's madness of us to dream," he wrote (musing on the *Principia Ethica*), "of making dowagers understand that feelings are good, when we say in the same breath that the best ones are sodomitical." The *Principia* provided a personal ethic: the members of the Midnight Society found Moore reassuring, each in his own way. Perhaps the philosopher, through reason, was arriving at some of the ideas that Freud was proving clinically. The fundamental inquiry was into "the pleasure principle." But the ethical side of Moorism, one feels, touched the young men less than the philosophical sanction given them to assert themselves, to shake off old rigidities, to be homosexual if they wished, to scoff at the dying—the dead—Victorians. Yet some of the Victorian trappings still clung to their young shoulders.

Hands

In 1902, when Leonard Woolf and Lytton Strachey lingered into their fourth year at Cambridge, there came to King's College a young man whose reputation had preceded him from Eton. He had an unusual ability to master difficult and abstract subjects and yet be eternally concrete. He was logical, administrative, "efficient." At the end of his time at Eton, he lived in the school as if it were his own fine country house and cooperated with his friends in running it. Unlike Leonard, Clive and Lytton, sons of suburb, countryside, metropolis, John Maynard Keynes was "all" Cambridge. He was a town boy, the elder son, born at No. 6 Harvey Road, a roomy, servanted Victorian house that would remain the family home throughout his lifetime. He had a sister two years younger and a still younger brother. His mother belonged to Town, his father to Gown. In the Keynes household the politics of academe and the abstractions of academe merged with municipal politics. Maynard's father was an eminent don at Pembroke College, a logician and economist, author of basic works in his subject; his mother was involved in local politics at a time when women were supposed to stay at home. She became a justice of the peace, an alderman and finally Mayor of Cambridge. The theoretical and the practical were present to Maynard's vision from the first. He got his local politics with his meals and his knowledge of economics and logic in his father's study, from which children are often barred. He shared his father's room; he precociously read proofs of his father's books. In his far-ranging life some called Keynes in later years the Newton of economics; he would indeed be concerned with practical economics on an international scale.

He possessed a settled security, an unusual freedom

from anxiety about his own identity. It marked him as different from anxious Leonard and mercurial Lytton, who became his friends (Clive, off to London to do research, did not meet him until four years later). Leonard's life was a constant quest for control. Lytton's mind was feminine and romantic. We may ask whether it is fair to compare such minds with the probing intelligence of a Keynes, its mixture of the salient and the sentimental. Maynard's romanticism lay in personal relations. His hardheadedness and even ruthlessness stemmed from a grasp of reality so great that it frightened others—those who have to hide reality from themselves. As we seek to glimpse some of the mysteries of genius, we discern that Maynard Keynes was endowed with "accepting" parents; they made him aware of disciplines of the mind without falling into the "permissive." This combination is rare. So accepted, a man faces the world unafraid. He doesn't need to listen to authority; he is his own authority. And yet he is sufficiently trained to ponder and even to admit error; if there is error, he promptly seeks corrections and solutions. There are "side effects" in such types, to be sure. Strength of ego can sometimes lead to presumption and cruelty. And Keynes had such abrasive moments, painful to those who knew him. He could be—and his biographer several times repeats it—"devastatingly rude." E. M. Forster called him "a curious mixture of benevolence and schoolboy selfishness." Leonard spoke of his "intellectual wilfulness and arrogance which often led him into surprisingly wrong and perverse judgments." Privately, Leonard in the earlier time also called him "a mental hermaphrodite."

The nurturing of the mind without forcing it, and in the very lap of academe—Cambridge academe—yet also in the lap of the "practical," made Maynard in some ways a spiritual "outsider" and an emotional kin of the young "outsiders" at Trinity. Genius is always "outside." An intelligence that leaps, soars and ruthlessly cuts a swath, if necessary, through the world's clutter, is particularly unpopular with the less gifted, for commonplace is usually irrational. Mankind plods along, trying to do what it can within an arbitrary and disordered world. Someone like Keynes leaps above it and around it. Such men have difficulty finding their peers; and then they feel they live in a rarefied atmosphere which they want to escape. How can such an intelligence have patience with the sleepy wool-gatherers, the eternal fumblers? What democracy can a Newton or an Einstein find in the region of the imagination, where the mind is alone, always winding itself around a new truth? Keynes, looking at the young Einstein in Berlin—long before the venerable Princetonian figure in loose clothes, shambling walk and crown of white hair—saw "a naughty boy, a naughty Jew-boy, covered with ink, pulling a long nose as the world kicks his bottom, a sweet imp, pure and giggling." What can genius do with genius? —"I had a little flirt with him," said Maynard, looking across the years. They had met on a silent homoerotic level. This was rather like Henry James writing—with much greater solemnity—to Whistler one day in the 1890s (a day on which he was destined to meet Joseph Conrad), "With the artist, the artist communicates." Minds that soar, art that transcends the commonplace—for when was art common?—can never be egalitarian.

II

Maynard was a decorous little boy with certain delightful signs of future precocity. Aged four and a half, he had imbibed enough economics from his father to answer that "if I let you have a halfpenny and you kept it for a very long time, you would have to give me back that halfpenny and another too. That," explained little Maynard, "is interest." At six (so the father's diary shows) Maynard was wondering how his brain worked. Aged seven, he is in the kindergarten, but he has had elementary instruction at home. Then there comes a day school and there is much reading aloud of evenings in the family. Maynard has more than the usual quota of colds, coughs, temperatures, headaches—the delicate machinery of mind and body never quite in harmony: but mind forges ahead, especially in mathematics and algebra; and young Maynard has a large vocabulary. He begins to work in bed in the mornings and will do so all his life. Yet when it comes to games he is a fairly hearty boy—he likes cricket and compulsively keeps a record of all the scores. He makes "commercial treaties" with his little peers at school. As he grows, school reports begin to use words like "brilliant"—and suddenly he is "head and shoulders above all the other boys." And always his intimacy with his father. The boy does some of his homework in his father's study. Before the entrance examination at Eton he is all nerves and unwell; he qualifies midway—tenth of twenty scholars elected. But he feels himself on equal terms with the world.

What is interesting about his life at Eton is not only his ascendancy among his fellows, analogous to Leonard's ascendancy at St. Paul's. The important element was his continuing intimacy with his father. Instead of the usual casual life-in-a-hurry letters home, Maynard reports regularly, discusses his problems, confides: and here there must have been forged in the young man a closeness to the masculine which played a larger role than usual in his later life, for it provided a "conditioned" homoeroticism. The accepting mother and the loved father committed Maynard's libido in two directions. The stronger seems inspired by the maternal intimacy. Where other brilliant young revolt against both fathers and mothers, Maynard finds himself nurtured and fulfilled. He is an exception to the "Oedipal"—it has been dissolved. He derives from his father not only systematic logic and economic wisdom, but also, it seems, personal warmth, closeness, respect, love. Roy Harrod speaks of Maynard and his siblings as "carefully cherished in the home." The boy was made aware of androgynous comfort; he was never "driven," as genius often is. With this, a certain fastidiousness emerges, which goes along with the ability to select, to discriminate; it helps form a strong yet flexible personality.

He shoots up fast. Maynard Keynes was tall, but ungainly; he had thick lips, warm blue eyes surmounted by formidable arched eyebrows. One who knew him at Cambridge described how he gave an effect of awkwardness and clumsiness, with his slouch and his bad teeth and remote suggestion of a gorilla, and then—suddenly—there would be the smile. It formed delicate wrinkles around the eyes, sent the eyebrows higher in their arch and "he would light up—like an electric light." He was a natural leader. His young peers accepted him. He knew how to say things, how to meet social conditions. He regarded himself as a

41

privileged boy, recognizing intuitively the esteem his father and mother showed him without spoiling him. One of his masters refers to his having "perhaps a little intellectual conceit." Then there is a *gamin* side. He can render popular music hall songs, to the great delight of the boys, especially a number called "Three Blue Bottles," which usually receives encores. "I was not a fag who abstained from champagne," he writes his father in 1897 (*aetat* 14). He goes to Chapel. "The Reverend the Provost preached today. He really ought not to be allowed to." He reads Browning, Meredith, medieval Latin; he becomes a book collector; he drives bookstall bargains. "Really the most substantial joys I get are from the perception of logical arguments, and, oh, from reading Darwin's life. How superb it is." The youth writes an essay on the "Responsibilities of Empire." The operative word in his life is "responsibility." He seems to be curious about many subjects. Once he takes an interest, his mind attacks firmly, forcefully and with boundless intellectual vigor. The Boer War comes. Maynard is a pacifist (he is now seventeen); given his role in later wars and war settlements, we note that he discusses logically and clearly the question of participation in school military training. He decides he will not volunteer. He feels that his father's logic has saved him from being "engulfed in this marvellous martial ardour that has seized the school." He sees Queen Victoria and there is no false emotion. "She drove past just as we were going into school and though it was quite cold, she was very little wrapped up." He adds, "Her nose was unfortunately red."

He is authoritative, and he is increasingly impatient with fools. There was "something freezing and terrible about Maynard's style of rudeness," says Harrod, and Maynard admitted this himself, for in his account of his work at the Peace Conference of 1919 he would speak of never having been "in the aggregate so rude to anyone" as he was to a certain French count. Yet when it is a question of diplomacy, he can control his temper and let his mind rule. Harrod remarks on this quality: "He had a heart, without which it is impossible to be a great man. But by reverting to an intellectual interest, he could always terminate his heartache very quickly."

III

Early in 1903, when Maynard had been at King's one term, Lytton Strachey and Leonard Woolf went to call on him. Word of his exceptional presence had reached Trinity. The two were then recently elected members of the Apostles. They felt important. They lived now in certain elegant rooms on Trinity's Great Court. King's, of course, had its unique elegance, its celebrated buttressed chapel, the old college, the Royal Foundation, with its spread of "front" and its lawn reaching to the river. The two from Trinity must have felt, however, that they were slumming, for the newcomer's rooms were tucked away in curious semi-squalor. They passed through a mean court surrounded by a confused jumble of ugly structures in sharp contrast to the magnificence of the college itself. Leonard and Lytton walked down steps, passed through a wretched subterranean passage and reached a set of drab poky rooms called "the Lane" and by later wags "the Drain." Here, up a flight of steps, Maynard lived—although he would soon move into more spacious and elegant quarters with a view of the chapel. Where he was in King's at that moment must have mattered little to him—No. 6 Harvey Road was always within reach; he was almost like a day boy, who, however, had a room of his own in the college. We can imagine the two tall seniors from Trinity knocking at Maynard's door and making small talk with him. If he wondered why they had come, they gave him no satisfaction. They chatted. They were amiable. There was an easy meeting of minds. They politely hoped he would come to tea. They talked with reverence of G. E. Moore. They thought young Keynes would want to meet him. Keynes had read *Principia Ethica*—"a stupendous and entrancing work." Lytton and Leonard agreed. The two visitors left quite as casually as they had come.

Keynes later learned the purpose of their visit, for in February 1903 he was elected to the Apostles. Lytton and Leonard were very "political" in that organization; and their task had been to take the measure of the newcomer, since few first-year men were ever considered. The Apostles was indeed a natural corner of Cambridge for Maynard Keynes, with its little rituals and special vocabulary, its addiction to an ideal of "truth" and ban on pedantry. Virginia Woolf, who had known so many of its members, described it well—"the society of equals, enjoying each other's foibles, criticising each other's characters, and questioning everything with complete freedom." Among minds like G. E. Moore's, Bertrand Russell's, A. N. Whitehead's, Lowes Dickinson's, and others of the recent and new Cambridge generation, Keynes found intellectual peers. Leonard and Lytton both testified that the Apostles was the deepest experience of their youth: on Keynes too the society had a lasting influence. It meant that they had all become, as it were, "insiders"; it brought them into an ideal community, a secret elite. The Society had a mission: "to enlighten the world on things intellectual and spiritual." But it was also a kind of superior fraternity, providing a religion of the mind, an enduring sense of fellowship. They were Apostles in a special sense of that word and G. E. Moore was their Christ; he gave them their religion.

We have already seen the nature of Moore's illuminations: understanding the question before one seeks the answer, awareness of "states of consciousness" and above all "the pleasures of human intercourse and the enjoyment of beautiful objects." Was this not what these young men, in the centuries-old system of English education, had come to prize above all in each other, in their rooms, in their common colleges and halls? Perhaps no country in the world has more refined "the pleasures of human intercourse" than England, unless one looks backward to certain other civilizations, say the Athenians or certain moments among the Romans? We can see in 1903 the cornerstone of Bloomsbury being laid in Moore and the communion of the Apostles: that of a cultivation of the art of friendship, made possible by a certain homogeneity of mind that invites closeness yet safeguards independence—and "social" awareness, and a desire to probe the common enjoyment of the Beautiful, or the kind of pleasure expressed by Maynard when he told his father of the "substantial joy" he found in logic.

No one [wrote Moore in the *Principia*] who has asked himself the question, has ever doubted that

personal affection and the appreciation of what is
beautiful in Art or Nature, are good in themselves;
nor if we consider strictly what things are worth
having *purely for their own sakes,* does it appear
probable that any one will think that anything else
has *nearly* so great value. . . .

Keynes would later say that Moore lived "in a timeless
ecstasy"—and there were vivid memories of Apostolic
weekends and walking tours, of Saturday evenings when in
their rituals they gathered round the little hearthrug on
which the "brother" was supposed to stand while reading
his paper on an assigned subject. No one could shirk his
turn. The subjects were vast or microcosmic. The Apostles
ate sardines on toast and drank coffee and smoked their
pipes in the chiaroscuro of the ancient rooms. Strachey
delivered papers on "Shall We Take the Pledge?" or "Does
Absence Make the Heart Grow Fonder?" or "Will It All
Come Out Right in the End?" Keynes spoke on less
frivolous-sounding subjects—probability, logic, mathematics. In eight years he read twenty papers. He would say
that with the aid of Moore they had repudiated all versions
of the doctrine of original sin. "We accepted Moore's religion and discarded his morals." His later experiences in
Realpolitik made him wonder whether they hadn't assumed
too grossly that the irrational world was as rational as they
were. Leonard demurred. He had always taken a dim view
of society. He argued that the very nature of their discussions showed they knew the world for what it was. But
Maynard maintained that they had been ingenuous uto-
pians with "no respect for traditional wisdom, or the re-
straints of custom." Both Leonard and Keynes had by then
discovered that time itself rubs the *timelessness* off ecstasy:
and the more distant onlooker today, in the light of history,
sees these young meliorists as possessing something they
never seemed to discuss: they were all men—and later
there would be women—endowed with a "work ethic." In
this they were Judeo-Christian. What seemed like intellectual play and high and noble utopian indulgence at the
Apostles resolved itself into years of unremitting toil. That
was the secret they learned at Cambridge; it became the
secret of Bloomsbury, and we can set their later rationali-

zations aside. They learned not to have lazy minds. This gave untold richness to their lives. They were not afraid. They worked as intensely as they made love, heterosexual or homosexual—sometimes even more intensely. And with their endowments and disciplines they could well believe in their superiority. Roy Harrod says that there was a belief that "Apostles were different from ordinary mortals." They decidedly were. The plebeians would never understand what they were talking about.

IV

When Maynard Keynes found himself in a world of dullards, he often took refuge in silence and observation. He looked into faces. He satisfied his own eyes and his senses. He listened. He looked in particular at hands. From his early days he had learned that no hands are alike. They can resemble a claw or a paw; they can be elegant, they can be brutal, they can make one shudder at their brutality. They clasp and unclasp in nervous fidget; fingers drum on a table or the arm of a chair; they can be fussy, reaching, gesturing—a whole nervous system. They *express*, as eyes express, as the straightness or droop of a back expresses, as the way a person sits expresses. Maynard Keynes instinctively learned to read messages in hands. The eminent sitting at the table of the Peace Conference in 1919 little dreamed that the sprawling, loosely put together Englishman with the wispy mustache looked first, and most closely, at their fingers. At fifteen he had described a certain professor: "His hands certainly looked as if he might be descended from an ape." That was boyish observation. Later the observation became more subtle, more piercing. In Paris it was as if Clemenceau knew what Keynes was doing. The great Clemenceau, with his bulk and his walrus mustache, sat on the table, "on his hands," wrote Keynes, "which were never uncovered, grey suède gloves." Keynes returns again and again to Clemenceau's frustrating "grey-gloved hands clasped in front of him!" and then ironically sees him "throned, in his grey gloves." But Woodrow Wilson, with his total "front" of assurance, is pleasantly naked. Maynard judges his hands "capable and fairly strong," yet also—what was it?—they are "wanting in sensitiveness and finesse." Some years later he is in the White House facing Franklin Delano Roosevelt, and the description is but a slight variant: President Roosevelt's hands were "firm and fairly strong, but not clever or with finesse." And Keynes noticed that the nails were "shortish round nails like those at the end of a business man's fingers." They were not a common type, however; Keynes's memory searched promptly, nagged by recollection—he had seen another such pair of hands, and such nails. Where? They talked about a balanced budget, about silver, and public works—and Maynard groped. Suddenly, out of the past, he saw the other hands—they were those of the British Foreign Secretary, Sir Edward Grey, another compromiser, bland and self-assured, who had watched the lights of Europe going out during the summer of 1914. Roosevelt's hands were "much cleverer, much more fertile, sensitive and permeable," and he was also "a more solid and Americanized Sir Edward." But "something all the same which corresponds to those finger nails carried me back to Sir Edward Grey."

Eternal scoffers at selective and "significant detail" would not understand, but to those who know how much men and women express in the smallest things they do, Maynard Keynes's game of private recognitions added a wide margin of certainty—if not infallibility—to his judgments. Giovanni Morelli played this game by looking for the secret detail in every painting—a special use of the brush, a special way of painting fingernails or lace, the distinct expressive telltale stroke, trademarks of "personality." Freud's genius derived from exactly this kind of observation, plus an ability to make use of the secret knowledge. Maynard's biographer quite properly feels a need to tell us of Maynard's own hands. "They were smooth and the fingers long and delicate." He did not wear suède gloves; he had the habit of tucking each hand into the sleeve of the opposite arm, so that the hands were made invisible. Maynard, who could on occasions be quite naked, did not want to display his naked hands. Harrod sees this as suggesting Maynard's "sense of repose"—his way of settling down to see, absorb, learn, ratiocinate. But was this not a completion of the inscrutable part of an otherwise outgoing and sometimes crushing genius?—his hands tucked into his sleeve "like a cat with paws tucked up under her." At such moments Maynard remained a contented mystery to the world.

A First-class Carriage

On a certain November day in 1901 (when the airplane was still a dream of the future) a dark young man, well turned out by his tailor, was reaching into his pocket at King's Cross to see whether he had a few extra shillings for a first-class carriage. Very few were needed, for he was going only as far as Cambridge. His name was Charles Otto Desmond MacCarthy, and he was twenty-four. He felt a bit depressed. Such a mood came on him more often than he knew. He needed company. When he couldn't have the solace of the spoken word, he crawled back into himself. He was a kind of conversational minstrel. He always needed an audience.

Desmond MacCarthy (for he never used the Charles or the Otto) was on his way to Trinity College in Cambridge. He had graduated three years earlier, but on weekends he still liked to return to his college, especially to visit his friend G. E. Moore. He beguiled the philosopher with his jokes; Moore, his pipe in his mouth, his shoulders shaking, laughed with tears in his eyes at Desmond's inventions. Desmond was three or four years older than Lytton, Clive and Leonard and six years older than Maynard Keynes. At King's Cross, that day, alone and melancholy, he bought his first-class ticket. This harmless self-indulgence might relieve his depression.

When he entered the first-class carriage and selected his compartment, he found in it another traveler, a youth with wavy red hair who looked at him out of quick blue eyes. The eyes were filled with amusement. The salient part of him was his costume: his coat, worn to keep out the dank November, was flung open as if he were too hot; his head was framed by a deep astrakhan collar. A third party, looking on these two young men (as in an old novel),

49

would have found both "handsome" and in a blessed state of young manhood. They smiled at the world; the world smiled back—even at Desmond, in spite of his melancholy. He was part Irish, part French, part German: intensely British, he was also "European," cosmopolitan. Certainly he did not have the traditional English reserve. He never waited to be introduced. If you went into a tobacco shop with him to buy a packet of cigarettes, it was almost certain that you would be in the shop for ten minutes. Desmond talked and joked; he wooed and won, and you would be accompanied to the door by everyone in the shop, laughing and talking up to and beyond the threshold. Desmond had a gift of engaging a complete stranger; a word, a phrase, a smile, and they seemed to have always been friends. He radiated charm. His laughter was sociable, contagious. His speech was quiet, grave, or light, always easy; his manners were perfect. The humdrum day lighted up, his melancholy was dissolved—from the moment he had an audience.

It may be imagined then that in very little time the young man in the fur collar—clearly younger than Desmond—was held and transfixed. And then he was quite as outgoing as Desmond, quite as eager for talk. The slightly older magically talking man was on his way to Trinity, his college. Well, Clive Bell said, it was *his* college too. They spoke the familiar language of their world. They had no trouble naming friends and dons. Clive talked well; less suave, more exuberant, as affectionate as a friendly dog, he talked in enthusiastic outbursts to the worldly, polished, modest, gentle, muted, but ever-assertive fellow traveler. They talked of people, books, shooting. Desmond shot too, but he wasn't very good at it. He always managed, he said, to miss the birds. But then he fancied himself a kind of bird—he would later take the pen name of "Affable Hawk." Of course he nearly always missed; shooting birds was a little like shooting at himself. His talk was filled with bird imagery. He used to speak of being "bird-happy." This was his special kind of happiness—hopping from one subject to another, one drawing-room to another, looking this way and that, picking up the crumb—the significant crumb —that suddenly created laughter and warmth.

We can only surmise the train talk of that day. Clive and

Desmond, so alike in their hedonism, so deeply involved with living at a given moment, were yet far apart in their feeling of beauty, in their response to reality. Reality was always surrounded by an exquisite verbal leafiness for Desmond; for Clive it was the real, the concrete, shape, form. They liked one another—and they talked. Desmond felt then, looking at the younger man, that Clive was certainly destined to cut himself an enormous "rich hunk from the cake of life." The slightly older man, who had friends everywhere, had perhaps heard Henry James use that image—that of cutting and flinging big chunks of the sweet cake of life at others. Clive has left us with only one remark that seems to apply to the little journey; he speaks of MacCarthy's having about him on weekend journeys to Cambridge "a faint air of mystery." It suggests that Desmond, who was an Apostle, was probably not communicative about his Cambridge schedule. We must remember that the Apostles were a secret society. When a largely communicative individual betrays even the slightest vagueness, he inevitably generates a sense of mystery.

Desmond had been a member of the Apostles for some time; he had gone to Trinity in 1894 (*aetat* 17) in an afterglow of Eton and had been precociously smooth, gentle, man of the worldly among the Trinitarians. G. M. Trevelyan, the future historian, who preceded him by one year, remembered the young man's arrival in full possession of a flow of conversational feeling that singled him out among his peers. He was kind and gentle. He had none of the crude aggressivity of the young or the cruelty that often creeps into their residual adolescence. He had a catholicity of taste. He had read continental literature. Trevelyan believed this enabled him to appreciate all the more the genius of English letters. He was a product of an era of private libraries and private reading. E. M. Forster also had a memory of him. MacCarthy sat at the back of rooms, in dimness; he was a good listener, very quiet, wholly attentive, speaking only when appropriate, a perfect gentleman but "for all his gentleness he knew exactly what he wanted to say." Many years later, a critic of the new generation, V. S. Pritchett, would describe Desmond as "soft, warm, idling." "Idling" was the illuminating adjective. Desmond himself, in a fantasy a few years before his death—he was reviewing Percy Lubbock's conversation piece about Edith Wharton—projected himself into the world of that *grande dame* of American letters. He fancied himself (out of Henry James) as Lambert Strether to her Maria Gostrey. "I should have enjoyed occasionally taking part," he mused, "in the charms and possible obliquities" say of Madame de Vionnet. "I can imagine myself going to tea, talking, talking, and staying on to supper: a perfect *omelette baveuse*, a cold grouse and a Moselle (the just perceptible violet bouquet of that wine harmonising with the slightly sour flavour of the bird) and then, a triangle of brie and a big yellow pear, both in perfect condition. Yes, I should have been content and most grateful."

It was a lovely thought, a reliving of much of the life Desmond led—an erasure of its less agreeable moments. It breathed the kind of hedonism that existed between Clive and him during the charmed hour's ride in a first-class carriage. But the Christian ethic came barging in at the end of Desmond's fantasy of life with Edith Wharton; Desmond's guilt intruded, for he brings us up short with, "Yet the day would have come when I would have felt as alien in that little *salon* as a tough old, rough old salt at a lecture on Proust. Whether this would have been due to the philosopher in me or the Philistine, I cannot decide but sooner or later I should have failed in sympathy and been cast out." No, it was not the Philistine. It was the Desmond-conscience—a feeling somehow, even while succeeding, that he was failing. That was why he kept on talking. Pritchett's word "idling" comes back—he idled always like a time-deluded Irishman. Clocks might tick and boom the hours; somewhere in Desmond there was a personal and less urgent timepiece. Deadlines, appointments, human insistencies were to be resisted. He clung to the immediate—not to the demanding clocks. The taste of the wine was wonderful; the brie and pear were ripe to perfection. But the feast sometimes left a bitter taste. To keep on talking meant that he would not have to think himself a perfect failure—which of course he wasn't.

The young hedonists in their first-class carriage hit it off as hedonists can, out of their brimming egos. Like the others, they had imbibed the religion of the "Good" and the "true." Clive expansively invited the charming and distinguished stranger to lunch with him in his rooms the next day; Desmond expansively accepted. That evening, eager to match wit with wit and show off his newfound friend, Clive asked Lytton to join the luncheon party. He was a little put out to learn that Lytton had already met Desmond (obviously at the Apostles). What Desmond remembered of the Sunday lunch was the costume of young Clive Bell. The black fur coat, the astrakhan collar gave way to a white hunting stock with a dressing gown thrown nonchalantly over it. Desmond was amused. Sunday was not a hunting day. Clive looked like a young blood in a drawing by Leech "at the delicious moment when he has pulled off his top boots and is about to take his hot shower bath." They must have made a strange picture: the so eminently physical and costumed Clive; the wide-cravated, well-dressed Desmond; and Lytton, whom Desmond saw as long, limp and pale, wearing "a small rather dismal moustache."

They would meet again many times. They would become friends. If they could have had their way, Desmond and Clive would have spent all their lives journeying in a first-class carriage. As it was, they almost did.

II

Desmond had been a quiet, thoughtful little boy, an only son, good at games, dutiful, obedient. His father, Charles Desmond MacCarthy, was a subagent of the Bank of England. Lodged within the mother were the eternal enmities of either side of the Rhine, as her name testified. She had been christened Joanne Wilhelmina Louise von Chevallerie; if we gallicized it, we would have to read it de la Chevallerie. Her way out of the ambiguous Franco-Germanism of her being was to marry an Irishman who lived in England—a different kind of ambiguity. Her concession to the Fatherland was to insert the name of Otto in the paternal name given to her son. We glimpse the family at Windsor. They have brought twelve-year-old Desmond to Eton. He is to take his entrance examination. Boarding the train at Paddington, Desmond noticed another boy, also Eton-bound, and "instantly divined" that the boy was "all I hoped I might become in the new world that lay before me." He fell in love with that boy. But the experience must have been frightening, for he never spoke to the youth during his five years at Eton. He loved from a distance. Only in the last term did he summon up the courage one day to ask this boy what time it was; it would have been a pity to leave Eton without at least hearing his voice.

Shyness? Fear? This timidy with certain individuals, but no trouble at all with strangers in impersonal situations—*this* would be Desmond's secret malaise. The whole complexity of a man afraid to assert himself and finding his escape by roundabout assertion—he would be aloof, shut up in his own magical world of words, with the loneliness of his childhood, yet seeming to be the most social, the most gregarious, the endlessly amusing and spellbinding Desmond.

Mr. and Mrs. MacCarthy spent the night at The White Hart opposite the round bastion of the curfew tower of Windsor Castle. Little Desmond was left at the house in which he would lodge if he passed his exam. One moment he was in his parents' room at the hotel, looking out at the great legendary castle with the gas lamps lit and the dusk deepening into dark, and the next moment the family was in a landau driving down a curving street, over a bridge at which a toll was paid, and into Eton itself. Suddenly he was in his own room with his box, his hamper, his portmanteau; a lot of other boys were around him, watching him unpack and surveying his possessions. The boys filled the little attic room. What was his name? How old was he? Where had he gone to school? Desmond courteously opened his tin of gingerbread and his box of *marrons glacés*, but the boys were glutted with goodies absorbed during the day from other new arrivals. Mr. and Mrs. MacCarthy had been in Rome and had brought back some postcards of the statues in the Vatican. These—especially the fig leaves adorning "some of the worst statuary"—caused excitement and amusement when Desmond produced them. The boys were interested in Desmond's wardrobe. And his nice hairbrushes: his mother had given him these; they had his monogram on them. One of the boys said, "I wonder how these would look outside the window." Anger, as if from nowhere, welled up in the sorely tried Desmond; and suddenly he, who was always so peaceful and quiet, hit the waggish boy, his fist striking the boy's cheek just below the eye. The other boys laughed. Desmond, floored by his own audacity, immediately opened his washstand and started bathing the eye of the boy, who called him "a little devil." Self-assertion was hard. But the boys seemed to respect it. He had stood up for himself. And he had been properly penitent; the hairbrushes were left in the room.

After a convivial supper, little Desmond found himself in his room again. He put on his nightgown. He said his prayers. He prayed that he might be worthy of that nice boy he had seen at Paddington Station; he thought he ought to ask God to help him with his examination the next morning. He believed he was doing this for the sake of his parents, who seemed so much to want him to succeed.

The first exam paper was on the Scriptures. That was written before breakfast. After the interval he wrote other papers. Then he walked along the High Street to the station with his father; his mother had returned to London. His father seemed to be struggling to give advice: he fussed, hesitated, stuttered; nothing came out. He was (we can see) worried about what the other boys would do to his twelve-year-old, his only son, just on the edge of important discoveries about life. Finally he told Desmond to stick to boys of his own age. He must on no account go with boys much older. "It is not," said the elder MacCarthy, "good form. So look out." The matter of sex had resolved itself, Desmond would recognize, into a lesson in "form."

III

To the Bloomsbury Memoir Club of many years later Desmond read this memoir, giving many more details: the exams in arithmetic, algebra, Euclid; his working hard at the elegiacs, "a mixture of Virgilian phrases copied from a Thesaurus," and later the admonitory lecture from the headmaster to the new boys about the evils of sex—with no mention of sex. The imposing Dr. Edmond Warre, with his formidable geniality, his formidable baritone, reminding the young boys, some bewildered, some snickering, that they were "among the fortunate of the nation" and explaining the meaning of responsibility. It is all there in his memories, the fundamental "dynamic" of Desmond—a timidity to put himself forward, a capacity for a flying leap with the clenched combative fist (but used apparently only during that single boyhood moment), the sense of guilt at his boldness (or his thoughts of boldness), his niceties of conscience, and the overpowering need to make himself wanted and liked, a way of making up for deficiencies that perhaps existed only in the mind, but that were no less real to him on that account. "Human life is almost unendurable," he would say. Yet somehow he endured.

In two short stories written by Desmond, his hero is a young boy who commits a transgression (or believes he has committed one) and who agonizes over his inability to face up to this crisis. The particular story of the boy who thinks he has been responsible for the death of a tame bear is very painful to read. Inside the suave man of the world, the Desmond MacCarthy who became a beloved critic of the drama and of letters—a man of probity and certain kinds of energy—there was a hurt conscience-stricken little boy who needed to kneel down and pray for indulgence. Virginia Woolf would describe him as "a wave that never breaks." She said he had "the nicest nature of any of us." But also he seemed to find "pleasure too pleasant, cushions too soft, dallying too seductive." The hurt and conscience-stricken little boy was always trying to comfort himself. This enabled him to comfort others. Words were his comfort. Otherwise, there was a kind of bleak solitude, a deep pool of depression below the bright surface.

Life had hold of him: like many he slipped into it—floundering, not knowing what he wanted to do, save to write, to write some great novel or story, yet feeling that all he wrote wasn't good enough, was "unworthy" of his aspiring self. These seemingly negative forces were transmuted into art—the art of being the ideal critic—because he wrote not for critics but for readers. Lady Ottoline Morrell, whose insights have been less valued than her eccentric-

ities, saw Desmond's innate goodness—he was "full of
human kindliness and generosity." Leonard was enchanted
by Desmond at Cambridge and thought him the blessed
child of all the good fairies—"perhaps the most charming
man I have known," at least in his youth.

Desmond himself expressed his truest nature when he
said, "In order to know yourself, you must let others know
you." A curious utterance, somehow an actor's, a speaker's,
a "communicator's"; there are surely better ways of
knowing one's self than through wearing one's heart on
one's sleeve! And who indeed can take off his mask with
any success, the mask of being, the *persona* that uncon-
trollably performs? Leonard later likened Desmond's eye to
that of "a knowing old dog who understands and appreci-
ates all his master's jokes and can't make as good jokes
himself." This was but to recognize the side of Desmond in
which there existed low self-esteem. The other side was the
brilliant improviser, the perpetual charmer. He could rouse
Henry James—the Master himself—from an afternoon's
lethargy and get him talking excitedly about novel-writing
while munching buns and drinking tea; he could (as E. M.
Forster saw him) perform a *tour de force* one evening
when scheduled to read a paper. Desmond was renowned
for not having papers ready, for defying deadlines. This
evening he arrived at Duncan Grant's studio with his little
attaché case and sat at the back of the room. Asked to
move forward and talk, he said No, he would talk from
where he sat and would prop his paper against the upright
open side of his case. He gave a brilliant paper. It was
easy, smooth, unfaltering, humane, filled with musical
nuances of voice and language, and subtleties of the spirit,
which Desmond's friends knew to be in him at his best.
Then a curious thing happened. In speaking, he made a
gesture; he knocked the attaché case to the floor. There
was no paper in it. The case was empty. Out of this emptiness Desmond had made a work of art. Or rather he *had*
written his paper—and who now can say with what power?
—in the presence of his audience. No one could ever re-
write it. It was like a song sung that might be sung again,
but it would never be quite the same; it existed only in the
minds and hearts of the listeners.

Thoby's Room

A cultivated North American looking at the Cambridge life of Leonard, Lytton, Clive, and Thoby might notice certain things that entered almost imperceptibly into the warp and woof of their experience. The sense of the place: the buildings, the cloisters, King's Chapel, the river, the "backs," the possession of a very private world. Lytton spoke later of "an enchantment lingering in nooks and corners, coming upon one gradually down the narrow streets, and ripening year by year." He spoke of the lawns beside the river, the willows, gardens, crooked lanes, glimpses of cornices and turrets. However, a feminine visitor open to sights and sounds has left us, with the gift of her art, an even greater sense of this masculine seat of the higher learning. The sense, for example, of the gate, as if it were made of lace upon pale green; and the Hall lit up and doors opening and swinging shut with a soft thud; she could hear the clatter of the plates in the dining hall. Or one of the rooms—say Thoby Stephen's—a round table, a photograph of the student's mother, cards from societies with little embossed crescents and coats of arms; notes and pipes—foolscap ruled, with a red margin—perhaps an essay to be written on these sheets, "Does History Consist of the Biographies of Great Men?" And books. Very few French books; a life of the Duke of Wellington; Spinoza; novels by Dickens; a Greek dictionary; the Elizabethans; Spenser's *Faerie Queen*. She notices a pair of shabby slippers "like boats burnt to the water's rim." Photographs of Greek statues and temples. The works of Jane Austen. A volume of Carlyle—a prize for an essay. Books about the Italian painters of the Renaissance. A manual on the diseases of horses; textbooks. The room is empty, just enough air to make the curtain swell. A wicker armchair.

She stands—or imagines she stands—in the Court. The lights are coming on in the rooms and casting gleams on the cobbles, dark patches of grass, lighting an occasional daisy. The young men are now going back to their rooms. Heaven knows what they are doing. One head leans over a window box; one student speaks to another as he hurries past; one can hear stairs being climbed, and "a sort of fullness settled on the court, the hive full of bees, the bees home thick with gold, drowsy, humming, suddenly vocal." Somewhere a waltz answers the "Moonlight Sonata."

She lets her imagination wander into seats of masculinity. One supposes the young men raising their eyes from the books as various sounds reach them. She imagines many young men, some reading magazines or shilling shockers, legs over the arms of their chairs; others eating sweets; still others lying in shallow armchairs, holding their books as if clinging to anchors of safety, reading Keats, long histories —the history of the Holy Roman Empire; and then in other rooms a sofa, chairs, a square table, and one can see two or three or five young men (sometimes just legs visible) and hear talking, talking, talking, bursts of laughter, gestures of arms, movements of bodies; and then as with a camera eye, roofs enclosing buildings, the thick Cambridge night muffling the stroke of the clock.

Cambridge blended in the observant eyes and senses. Virginia Stephen could see rooms, as she said, with "devastating clearness." And out of envy and even anger—for when had England so beautifully planned the education of women?—she would put her sight and sound into a novel, an elegy for her brother Thoby, and call the novel *Jacob's Room*. The room was Cambridge, it was Trinity, the wind lifting unseen leaves—the young man walking through the court, the ring of his footsteps thrown back from the Chapel, the Library, the Hall.

II

Thoby Stephen's father—tall, with a long pointed beard, silent, patriarchal, with that look of benignity and sadness which G. F. Watts caught in a striking portrait—came to Cambridge to spend a weekend with his son. Leslie Stephen —he would soon be Sir Leslie—was on the edge of seventy and no longer the athlete of his earlier years; only the noble, melancholy philosopher and biographer remained. Thoby's friends came to see him with a mixture of awe and anxiety. His walks were legendary: to London in a day and back to Cambridge in time for dinner. He had made a great name for himself as a mountaineer; his book on the "playground" of Europe was widely known. Stephen had always been a man of devastating severities and great silences. Henry James, taking hours-long walks with him around London or in Cornwall, spoke in his letters of their not having exchanged a word—"the silent Stephen, the almost speechless Leslie." But he thought him the most agreeable Englishman he had ever known. He considered him "a purely literary man of the best type, an ideal literary man."

Leslie Stephen had been at Trinity Hall fifty years earlier; he had remained in Cambridge, accepting ordination as required for the particular fellowship he had won. He was shy and distant, and perhaps his taciturnity—certainly not his intelligence and distinction—kept him from being asked to join the Apostles of his time. Then came doubts: the doubts which descended on the mid-century intellectuals in the time of the new science. Leslie Stephen admitted to himself, after a crisis of conscience, that he was a disbeliever. With his customary probity he resigned his holy orders, doffed his bright academic and religious garb to which all deferred, and went down to London to enjoy the anonymity of journalism. He was in spirit a radical; lifting himself out of conformities, he felt free. In this he was "Bloomsbury" before its time. His curiosity and zeal led him far. He went to America, where the North and the South were engaged in their terrible war. Unlike many in England, whose sympathies were with the aristocratic South, he was horrified by slavery. Leslie Stephen believed in emancipation. With his probing mind he also saw the economic realities of the internecine struggle. He went to Washington. Honest Leslie met honest Abe. And Stephen, with that touch of condescension of which the English are fully capable, described the President as "more like a gentleman to look at than I should have given him credit for from his pictures." In Boston—and in the American Cambridge—he met the expansive Lowell, the elder Holmes (the younger was fighting in the war), and the cold, narrow, yet somehow endearing Charles Eliot Norton, whom Englishmen seemed to like. Norton was a friend of Ruskin's, of Carlyle's—indeed, in England he could be more English than the English. Stephen also met young Henry James. All his life Leslie Stephen would have the friendship of Americans.

III

Old Leslie Stephen sat now in Thoby's rooms in the Trinity Great Court. One by one the young tried to talk to him. The man of silence was plunged into a deeper silence still, for his hearing was gone and the young shouted into an enormous ear trumpet. "It is remarkable and humiliating," Leonard Woolf would write in his own old age, "to discover how imbecile a not very imaginative, or even an imaginative, remark can sound when one shouts it down an ear-trumpet into the ear of a bearded old gentleman, six foot three inches tall, sitting very upright in a chair, and looking as if every word you said only added to his already unendurable sorrows."

The experience was "formidable and alarming." The man had immense charm. He liked being back at Cambridge; he liked to meet Thoby's friends. He was pleased by the respect and appreciation of the young. He had once said that "every man ought to be feminine, i.e. to have quick and delicate feelings; but no man ought to be effeminate, i.e. to let his feelings get the better of his intellect and produce a cowardly view of life and the world." Lytton, who saw Leslie Stephen during a summer spent near Southampton, described him with his ear trumpet and tamo'-shanter as "quite deaf and dangerous"—Lytton in that circumstance having to project his squeaky voice, which must have sounded strange indeed at the end of the trumpet. "A nice though wild family," this product of quite a wild family judged the Stephens. He remarked also that there were two sisters, "very pretty."

The two Stephen sisters were more than "pretty." Leonard said, "Their beauty literally took one's breath away." He met them in Thoby's rooms when they came with their father to visit their beloved brother. Both doted on Thoby. Their first Cambridge visit was probably the one described in Virginia's letter to a friend—the sisters had come to Cambridge for the May Week and had gone to the Trinity ball. There Virginia and Vanessa met Clive Bell. Then there was a second visit, in 1901. In Thoby's room, Leonard looked at the sisters, in their white dresses and large hats and general "sweep" and curiosity—a mixture of shyness and curiosity and a show of bravery—as if they were portraits in an art gallery. "Suddenly seeing them, one stopped astonished." It was like coming face to face with a great Rembrandt or Velasquez. He likened them also to the vision of a Greek temple. For the young Jew, out of a matriarchal family, there was the cultivated worship of certain kinds of women; and the Stephen sisters, properly chaperoned by their cousin, the principal of Newnham College, with whom these Victorian young ladies were very properly staying, were exquisite objects of worship. The cousin had come to tea at Thoby's and had brought the sisters; Thoby's young friends were there to meet them as well as the formidable father. Hovering in this social scene was Thoby himself—the Goth—as tall as his father and much bigger, an effect of his classic bulk and masculinity. Before the Stephen sisters, and especially Vanessa, Leonard felt himself in the presence of "astonishing beauty." Lytton, who simply saw them as "pretty," was constitutionally incapable of astonishment at feminine charm. Leonard remembered, "It was almost impossible for a man not to fall in love with them, and I think that I did at once." Their aloofness—or perhaps Leonard's own?—made them seem, in their Victorian dresses, their quickness of speech, their delicate rose-flushed complexions, unattainable, a mirage.

They were like Greek goddesses—"it was rather like falling in love with Rembrandt's picture of his wife, Velasquez's picture of an Infanta, or the lovely temple of Segesta." Years would pass before Leonard would really see this beauty not as art or architecture but as flesh and blood.

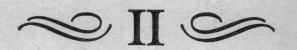

II

A Haunted House

The two young women, wearing their white muslin, with grass-green ribands around their slim waists, their hats bunched with bouquets on the crowns and tied down with black velvet bows at the back—the two young women whose smiles and roseate complexions suggested health and spoke for summer dawns and cloudless skies—lived (as it happened) in a haunted house in fashionable Kensington. Someone less inclined to read art into life might have noticed Vanessa Stephen's silent intensity or the shadowed melancholy of Virginia. Named out of literature, out of Swift, Vanessa was not literary; but she had an eloquent wordless repose and her face wore the light of innocence and candor. When she spoke, her words were accurate and explicit. In contrast, her sister seemed to wear a mask of humility. Spectators had a feeling of distance and surrender. Her body was in waking slumber, her face in eternal dream. So Virginia Stephen appears in all the photographs of the time. Her eyes are veiled. She is lost in fantasy. One moment she carries her head proudly like Vanessa. There should be flashing eyes, an arching of the neck, anger. But instead she lowers her eyes and hangs her head to one side like a wilted or broken flower.

The house in question was No. 22 Hyde Park Gate, a seven-story angular awkward pile of stucco and red brick, situated in a small deadend street. Eight young of two generations lived in it; there were the parents, of course; and six servants. Sixteen in all. By the time of Leslie Stephen's old age and the coming-of-age of his daughters, the rooms of No. 22 were filled with ghosts. They were seldom filled with light—the narrowness of the house, the black-painted woodwork with narrow gold lines, the red-velvet furniture made it seem mortuary and claustrophobic.

Yet these dark period-decorated rooms had once contained the voices of the young. In retrospect the place was "tangled and matted with emotion." We have Virginia's words: "scenes of family life, grotesque, comic and tragic; with the violent emotions of youth, revolt, despair, intoxicating happiness, immense boredom with parties of the famous and the dull, rages, love scenes . . . passionate affection for my father alternating with passionate hatred of him."

We can imagine that haunted house in the dark narrow little street; it is made vivid in eight scribbled and almost illegible pages Virginia Woolf wrote shortly before she died. No. 22 originally had five stories, before two more "of atrocious design" (as Quentin Bell tells us) were added. Virginia's pages begin with her account of the hour at the center of Victorian life—the hour of afternoon tea. From her mention of this ritual, her memories branch out. She seems to walk again on the floors of childhood and adolescence. There are three oddly shaped rooms on each floor, two large and one small. In earlier years the parents located the nursery next to the master bedroom. Later it was moved to the top floors. Two large rooms serve as the day and night nurseries. The day nursery is both playroom and schoolroom. In the night nursery the children are bathed and put to bed and the nurse sleeps with them. Was the window ever open at night? Vanessa wondered in later years. She doubted it. The room is cheerful at bedtime, with a bright coal fire, food, hot water, fuss over the babies, then stillness—only the children whispering stories to one another as they drift off to sleep. Virginia hears the tinkle of her mother's bracelets. Their mother, Julia, arrives carrying a candle to see if all is well. "Like all children," Virginia wrote (it seems almost as if she echoes Marcel Proust), "I lay awake sometimes and longed for her to come. Then she told me to think of all the lovely things I could imagine. Rainbows and bells."

On the floor below are three rooms occupied by the older children, the two Duckworth boys, Gerald and George, and Stella, their sister, children of Julia's first marriage. They are some ten or more years older than the Stephen children. Somewhere in that house there is also Laura Stephen, Leslie's child by his first wife, Thackeray's daughter. Little is said about her; she is mentally retarded.

All in all, a tall somber house with its double room on the ground floor and the dining room sticking out into the back garden, darkened by Virginia creeper. The writing daughter remembered the smells as she climbed the stairs —the smell of candles, a water closet on each landing (three in all, and one bathroom), carpets, dust. Pictures grow less numerous the higher one climbs; and there are crammed cupboards and wardrobes, accumulations of china and glass and family plate. On the floor above the nurseries is the great study of Sir Leslie; every now and again the children can hear the thud of a book dropped on the floor—he drops books all around him as he writes in his rocking chair, with a writing board across its arms. He smokes a short clay pipe. The room has a high ceiling, and its walls are of yellow stained wood. There are books everywhere.

Downstairs again and into the master bedroom on the first floor, which Virginia described as the "sexual centre" of the house, with its windows looking into the street. Four children were begotten in that large bed by Leslie Stephen, who in his widowed state in 1878 married the widowed Julia Jackson Duckworth. There was Vanessa, the oldest, in 1879; then sixteen months later, in 1880, Thoby; after him, fifteen months later, Virginia; and finally after twenty-one months, in 1883, Adrian. Four children in little more than four years. In this bed Julia died in 1895 when she was forty-eight. Nine years later, Leslie, old and honored, also died here with a picture of Julia lying in front of him.

II

"That house of all the deaths, ah me!" exclaimed Henry James, who had known Leslie Stephen since the 1860s. The mother—"beautiful pale tragic Julia." How could he forget her? "She was beautifully beautiful," he wrote, "and her beauty and her nature were all active, applied things, making a great difference for the better for everybody. Merely not to see her any more is to have a pleasure the less in life." And in his elegiac way, the American novelist spoke of Julia as having been "a perfectly precious force for good." One didn't know what to make of the economy of a world, he said, that "could do nothing with her . . . but suppress her." One week the beautiful Julia had been the very center of that house, teaching her daughters in the upper school-room, holding the lives of the large double family together. And then she was gone. Influenza. Probably too many pregnancies. Perhaps the heavy strain of maintaining her beautiful composure. Who can now say? She was described as "a mixture of the Madonna and a woman of the world." Will Rothenstein had said of the daughters, "Beautiful as they were, they were not more beautiful than the mother."

When James spoke of "the house of all the deaths," he was alluding to the swift death of the Stephen girls' half sister, Stella Hills, after Julia, during a pregnancy; the prolonged dying of Sir Leslie, of cancer (and two years after him in Bloomsbury the unexpected death of young Thoby). No. 22 was a house of grief, a house of ghosts. Leslie Stephen was on the edge of breakdown for months. He clung to his children as if still clinging to Julia. He tried to be the absent mother instead of the presiding father. He made his daughters a party to his grief. His friends warned him that perpetual mourning was harmful to the young; they should be allowed to get on with life. The young females felt stifled as their father sat in the old obsolete nursery with his long beard, his gaunt face, his voluble grief, his tears. He was Job in Kensington. Life continued obstinately in the old house in spite of his mourning. Vanessa presided over larder and clothes and servants; the sisters contended with their Duckworth stepbrothers, groping male presences who brought a bewildering eroticism into the dark rooms.

Some years later Virginia would write a little prose poem called "A Haunted House." "Death was the glass," she wrote, "death was between us"—an allusion perhaps to the mirror in the master bedroom in which she had seen the reflection of the dead Julia in the early morning light. Vanessa was fifteen and Virginia thirteen when Julia died. Death changed their lives. In Thoby's rooms at Trinity the young men saw a self-contained and mature Vanessa, a shy birdlike Virginia. What could they know of the stoicism of

the one or the Ophelia-madness of the other? The men—
Thoby and Adrian—had been able to go away, to school,
to university; they escaped from No. 22. The daughters,
like so many other Victorian girls, were cast early in the
role of symbolic wife and mother to the mourning father.
For the women of Bloomsbury, growing up meant confinement to the sepulcher-house; their path into life lay
through a family cemetery.

The Sanity of Art

Vanessa, said Virginia in later years, "has volcanoes underneath her sedate manner." This was true; but the volcanoes rarely erupted. The world saw a quiet, composed Vanessa, a woman of few words. "You have an atmosphere," her sister told her. That atmosphere embodied her heritage of Cambridge integrity and her established role as the oldest child of Leslie and Julia. By the time she was briefly at the Slade School, Will Rothenstein found she had "the quiet courage of opinions." He added, a bit enigmatically, "She spoke with the voice of Gauguin." What are we to make of this? Gauguin's voice in his journals is harsh and edged with life's cruelties. We may judge Vanessa knew how to deliver a snub when she thought it necessary. Years later Kenneth Clark would find that Vanessa exposed "false values and mixed motives." She believed decidedly in nature and freedom; and in many ways she was the "natural" woman. She was also the uncompromising woman. There could be no deviation from her high personal standards. Lady Ottoline Morrell likened her to a Watts painting, and she discerned melancholy in her face. Vanessa had been exposed to the domestic tragedies of the Stephens. Her complications of feeling were channeled into Victorian filial duty, when they were not channeled into her painting. She had become a power in No. 22. She ruled behind the scenes as she would rule later in Gordon Square or at Charleston, simply by her "monolithic" presence. The word had originally been used to describe her brother Thoby. It came to be applied to her. It was a much-used word in Bloomsbury.

What did the word mean when applied to Vanessa? Certainly that she was "all of a piece"—a solid feminine integrity: and the overtones of the word suggest self-sufficiency. There were those who felt that she did not, in reality, care much for people. One can understand this. As Virginia was deeply involved with people in her eternal quest to be loved (seeking in faces and characters some sign or guide to her personal geography), Vanessa, in Hyde Park Gate, from her vantage point, had cut herself off as much as possible from disturbing human elements—parents, siblings, servants, troublesome males. She had elected to stay with the stability and beauty of inarticulate "things"—objects, shapes, colors, the stock-in-trade of the painter. In later life she would wonder why most persons take for granted objects in a kitchen, the plump kettle, the contours of a dish, the gravity of a common pot; for her these common things, dedicated to the daily "functional," had their particular silent beauty. The decoration of houses was much more satisfying than the people who lived in them. Perhaps this is why in a certain number of Vanessa's paintings the faces are left blank. A striking portrait of Virginia shows her body's posture: she is in a folding chair in a garden, wearing a wide-brimmed sun hat. Her hands are in repose. But there is no face under the hat. The picture may simply be unfinished: at the least, we can say that Vanessa seems to leave the faces to the last. This distancing from people and their conversation certainly made Vanessa appear "monolithic." People found her sphinxlike, passive, in touch largely with her physical environment.

Again old Henry James offers testimony. "Vanessa has come to the front and become almost articulate and entirely handsome," he wrote shortly after Julia's death. He was enthusiastic. "How beautiful Vanessa!" She had a "crushed strawberry glow." Four years after the mother died he wrote a novel called *The Awkward Age* about a dead grandmother named Julia and young girls who had to be launched into the world, *jeunes filles en fleur*. Vanessa had come to the front, for there were many things that needed doing, and she responded with all her disciplined responsibility. There was the house. There were the other children. There was the kitchen in the depths of No. 22. There were the servants. There were two overattentive older half brothers. Finally there was old Leslie Stephen, delicate, magnetic, yet often irritable, paternally demanding in his stern rigidities—a walking elegy.

Vanessa stood alone. She was the sort of woman who becomes and remains the keystone of a house. We see many Vanessas in the portraits that remain of her, especially those painted by Duncan Grant. The young face was smooth, with firmly lined brows and liquid gray-green eyes. She had sensuous lips. She rarely used makeup. Somewhere Virginia speaks of "her passionate mouth." Her voice was beautifully modulated; her words were carefully paced. Virginia, so often her historian, likens her to a bowl of golden water which brims but never overflows—or, as we have seen, to the sedate volcano. In another image she has "a queer antique simplicity of surface." To Clive Bell, in one letter, Virginia writes in rhapsody about the name "Vanessa." It contains "all the beauty of the sky, and the melancholy of the sea, and the laughter of the Dolphins in its circumference, first in the mystic Van, spread like a mirror of grey glass to Heaven. Next in the swishing tail of its successive *esses*, and finally in the grave pause and suspension of the ultimate A breathing peace like the respiration of Earth itself." Virginia was making literature out of Vanessa. And in the book she dedicated to her sister, *Night and Day*—in which Vanessa is indeed a scarcedissimulated character—Virginia wrote, "Looking for a phrase, I found none to stand beside your name." *Van-ess-A* was often called (in the family bestowal of animal and fish names) the Dolphin. Virginia's purple passage conveys a sense of her sister's belonging to the earth and the waters.

Virginia's characterizations were a matter of moods. Sometimes Vanessa was "marmoreally chaste"—loaded words suggesting coldness, concreteness, smoothness of surface, virginal severity. Vanessa has "a genius for stating unpleasant truths in her matter of fact voice." The unpleasant truths were simply Vanessa's directness. She was focused: she "concentrates upon one subject, and only one, with a kind of passive ferocity." Vanessa's answer was emphatic: "Virginia, since early youth, has made it her business to create a character for me according to her own wishes and has now so succeeded in imposing it upon the world."

II

In their childhood they were rivals for the love, admiration and companionship of their brother Thoby, who was born between them. When she could not have him to herself, Virginia's energies were employed in trying to take him away from Vanessa. On no ground was their rivalry more intense. This Vanessa set down in words and not in paint, some time after Virginia was dead. At three Vanessa had a baby brother aged one and a half. She mothered him: presided over him; ruled him in the nursery. Then an intruder arrived. The rivalry began when Virginia, emerging from babyhood, spread her little wings beyond the nursery. Thoby, wrote Vanessa, "was the brother both Virginia and I adored . . . he and I had had an intimate friendship before she came on the scene, doing everything together." She added, "Later, though life was more interesting and exciting, it was also less easy." Less easy we clearly see. Vanessa goes on to describe a sister who seems like the prevailing witch-girl of No. 22 Hyde Park Gate, intent on robbing Vanessa of her rights and privileges. "Even then," wrote Vanessa in her old age, "she had the faculty of suddenly being able to create an atmosphere of tense thundery gloom." She explained: "Suddenly the sky was overcast and I in the gloom. It would last for endless ages—so it seemed to a child—and then go. But it was I who had been in the gloom—not the other two—and I suppose, though I cannot ever remember feeling it at the time, that it was simply the result of two little females and a male."

It would be exactly that in later years. In childhood, however, the struggle was sexless, for sex hardly played a role in Virginia's simply wanting to possess what her sister had. In Vanessa's recollections, Virginia appears as a perpetual source of disaster. She stood on her stout little legs and raised her voice in quick and uncompromising challenge. The record resembles the nursery annals of many gifted children in famous families. Virginia's first advantage was unexpected and beyond all control. She had been made the godchild of her father's American friend, the American minister in London, James Russell Lowell, a

bearded, smiling, jesting, magnetic man who liked to play
with words, for he was a poet as well as a diplomat. Vanessa's godparents, on the other hand, were mere dull relatives. Lowell, with his boyish manner, his New England
juvenility—which never left him—would arrive at No. 22
like some foreign prince, with sixpences for Virginia but a
mere threepence for the other children! Then one day he
walked in with a handsome gift for his godchild, a live bird
in a splendid cage. We can understand Vanessa's bitter
words (at sixty): "I suppose the poor man would have
been much surprised had he known what evil passions he
had caused."

The threats to Vanessa's primacy troubled her even if
they left her ultimately unshaken. Thoby could conspire
with Virginia against her, and this was painful. Virginia
would mock her as the "Saint" of Hyde Park Gate. "How
did she know that to label me The Saint was far more
effective, quickly reducing me to the misery of sarcasm
from grownups as well as the nursery world?" Vanessa got
her revenge. She conspired with Thoby to make Virginia
blush. They had discovered their sister's tendency to become
"purple with rage." Vanessa could not remember how they
achieved this; but she watched Virginia's color "mount till
it was the most lively flaming red—and then I suppose
nurses interfered." Virginia's record of these struggles was
that "there were a number of little warfares and sometimes
Nessa and Thoby fought with us and sometimes they were
our friends."

III

They were rivals in ambition, in self-assertion, in love.
Virginia assailed Vanessa with a torrent of mischievous
metaphors; at the same time—for such are the ambiguities
of rivalry—she poured out her deep love, a love sometimes
sisterly, sometimes maternal. Vanessa could dress with flair
—a touch of color in the scarf, a fetching skirt, a properly
placed jewel—and she dazzled the world. Virginia had
problems with her clothes—and with her femininity. No
woman was more feminine, and few more conscious of

androgynous feelings. These got in the way of fashionable clothes, manners, style. Her style was in language and not in dress. The more obvious side of their rivalry has been noted: Virginia's underlining of Vanessa's steadfastness in which she found (from her point of view) a certain prosaic want of imagination. Vanessa's imaginative genius was plastic; it was freest in shape and color. "I am too formal or too feverish," Virginia acknowledged.

Their letters reflect sovereignty—and uncertainty. Virginia tells Vanessa she dreamed that "I was arguing with you and you showed a peculiar bright malice which I sometimes see in you." She marvels how Vanessa is able to see only one thing at a time with such concreteness: "Without any of those reflections that distract me so much and make people call me bad names . . . your simplicity is really that you take in much more than I do, who intensify atoms." Admiration and envy, self-abasement and confidence. Virginia, however, is tugging at the real truth of their difference: Vanessa's eyes did take in a palpable world. Virginia intensified atoms because she was always aware of them. Did she not live, as she said, in a "shower of atoms"?

"I dare say," Virginia wrote on one occasion, "you have cast out so many of the devils that afflict poor creatures like me." Self-disparagement gives way to praise: "I think you are a most remarkable painter. But I maintain you are into the bargain a satirist, a conveyer of impressions about human life, a short story writer of great wit and able to bring off a situation in a way that is ever my envy." Vanessa could have said as much to Virginia. This kind of praise gave way at times to worship: "How I adore you! How astonishingly beautiful you are! No one ever takes the winds of March with beauty as you do."

Vanessa's responses were grateful yet reserved. "I read your letters over and decided . . . that when they are published without their answers people will certainly think that we had a most amourous intercourse. They read more like love letters than anything else. . . . I like love letters. The more passion you put in, the better." And then Vanessa could be concrete—and motherly in her reply. "Are you being sensible or shall I soon have to nurse you through a nervous breakdown?" Of the two artist-sisters, we know that Vanessa possessed the sanity of art, which is one kind of greatness, and Virginia the madness of art, which is another.

IV

Vanessa had imposed herself on the world not with passive strength but with a kind of philosophical belief that if one stood for one's own truths, these would ultimately prevail. She had the voice of the artist when she said (and there was a tone of no nonsense about it), "One ought to go one's way without argument or fuss and without attempting to make the stupid see one's point of view." Vanessa Stephen made the world plastic, with boldness and brightness of color, and a warm sensuousness that belied cold words like imperious, monolithic, sphinxlike. Of course, one could love the voluptuous and be a sphinx, too. Vanessa's husband would say that she had "a will of iron." He knew. She was not interested in worldly things, in the hedonistic champagne-bubbling existence that belonged to Clive and fascinated Virginia. A friend once asked Vanessa what she was thinking about and she answered, "Painting!" Perhaps feeling that this was too laconic, she explained, "I am always thinking of painting."

That was the adult Vanessa, and if the world does not know her as well as her sister, it is perhaps because words make books and books can be carried anywhere; it is more difficult to carry paintings. Vanessa's spatial forms belong to the British art history of our century. She was human enough to want her work to be liked, but she was not nervous about it as her sister was about her novels—that is, about the impact of her writing on the world. Vanessa said once, "I am greedy for compliments and passion." A characteristic juxtaposition—praise and passion and greed! Vanessa was a passionate woman and her "What am I thinking about? Painting. I am always thinking about painting" meant that she painted constantly. As time went on, she painted, as artists must, whenever a moment could be snatched from a house filled with children, a yard filled with chickens and ducklings; she painted in the midst of her household, her long strong fingers, her hands always shaping things, decorating, assembling broken bits of china in the garden to make a dishy mosaic that resembled a Roman floor. "I am in reality the most critical and rational of all the Stephens," said Vanessa. In a certain sense she was. When the painting was done, when all the colors taken in through her eyes had been put on canvas with full intensity, a job had been completed, something was finished. And life had to move on. Occasionally Vanessa exhibited her pictures; but she accumulated more canvases than she could show. They are numerous, some cracked, some victims of weather and crawling insects—the testimony of an abundance that concerned itself with expression rather than preservation. She was like certain writers. Once their book is finished, they cannot read it themselves. Vanessa lived her life for its immediate discoveries and therefore lived profoundly. Lytton, who could admire women in his own queer queenly way, pronounced Vanessa "the most complete human being of us all."

Vanessa had begun to draw at an early age. She possessed considerable skill and won prizes from the first. A sketch of Virginia skating, made at eighteen, a few swift strokes in one of Virginia's letters to Thoby, belongs to the tradition of Thackeray and the *Punch* cartoonists; there is a delightful sense of caricature in it, with Virginia's shawl making her look like a bat and her unsteady feet seeming to suggest that she is about to fall on the ice. Underneath we read the signature as of a professional: *"V. Stephen fecit."* If her father's house had once been filled with writers, there had been painters as well, mostly Academicians, or those whose works were literary in their storytelling and their attachments to historical scenes: Burne-Jones, Watts, Holman Hunt, Val Prinsep, of the old school; or the young Charles Furse, distinct Victorians, only touched by the Pre-Raphaelite Brotherhood or William Morris. Before Vanessa was twenty she was working in a studio. Sir Arthur Cope R.A. taught her drawing. Later she was admitted to the Royal Academy Schools, for which she had to compete. Virginia remarked in a letter to Thoby, "The schools are very empty, so they will let in bad people." As far as we know, Vanessa did very well at the Schools. She learned traditional methods and cultivated the "real," but she was touched very early by the French Impressionists and by Whistler, and her distaste for the Academy was strong. Still later she had John Singer Sargent as her master; like Furse, he had studied in France. He was a sympathetic and encouraging teacher, a large imposing presence. Vanessa liked his voice, his green eyes. He would stare at her canvas and say cautiously, "You've got the right idea." Vanessa began, as is usual, by painting the inanimate; and it was an occasion for rejoicing when she was allowed "a live head to paint."

The stages of Vanessa's professional career can be read in Richard Shone's *Bloomsbury Portraits*. In a few sentences we can say that from 1899 on she was steadily painting, but we do not begin to describe all the pictures she looked at, all the canvases begun and abandoned, all the hours of unremitting work in front of her easel or the quick sketches made on any piece of paper that came to hand. In 1903 she had reached the stage of "nude models three days a week." And in the midst of this there were the care of her father, shared with Virginia; the garden parties; the social world into which her half brothers, enamored of the aristocracy, sought to introduce her. A young woman of Vanessa's class, coming of age a little before Queen Victoria died, was expected to know how to ride and to go to London's great social occasions; and Vanessa in a white satin dress, with an amethyst around her neck, with a blue enamel butterfly (gifts from her snobbish social-climbing half brother) was at eighteen or nineteen an ornament for any dinner table. There were high emotional battles. Vanessa found the parties and dances a bore and said so. As Virginia put it, "Underneath the necklaces and the enamel butterflies was one passionate desire—for paint and turpentine, for turpentine and paint." A vivid essay by Virginia tells of the struggles, evening after evening, with the half brothers—those terrible parties involving meaningless civilities from young men and talk with a lot of condescending dowagers. Domestically we glimpse Vanessa on occasion with a rose in her hair, sitting by the fire: the historian's voice comes in again, "Old Nessa is no genius, though she has all the human gifts, and genius is an accident." With this there is also tribute: "Old Nessa goes ahead, and slashes about her, and manages all the business, and rejects all her friends' pictures, and don't mind a bit. She is said to have a genius for ogranization . . . it would bore me to death." This when Vanessa began to sit on committees and arrange art shows. She was at her studio every day. She began to receive commissions to do portraits.

In 1904 Sir Leslie died. The elderly Victorians and some of the Edwardians had come to see him during his last days; he was peaceful, resigned, ready for the end. With his death came the moment when his two daughters, unlike the sons at Cambridge, had to decide what their "graduation" should be. They could become spinsters; they could marry. But in reality their vocations had been chosen long before. Vanessa was already a painter. Her course in life was set. It seemed to have been set from the day she was born.

The Other Face

In Virginia Woolf's "A Sketch of the Past," written two years before she died, a dream is remembered: *I dreamt I was looking in a glass when a horrible face—the face of an animal—suddenly showed over my shoulder.* Virginia wasn't even sure that it was a dream. It had so much reality that she half believed it had happened. *I have always remembered the other face in the glass, whether it was a dream or a fact, and that it frightened me.*

Who can now say out of what depths of memory and the unconscious, out of what sublimated feeling and perception, this fusion of evil and horror and shame emerged in the mirror's frame like a photograph in the developing fluid. There was her own face—and then *the other face.* Was it the me and the not-me? Was the animal face guilt, self-loathing, madness? The questions are not asked, or answered; but a few lines farther Virginia tells us, "The looking glass shame has lasted all my life." As a grown woman she could not powder her nose in public. It meant taking a mirror out of her bag and looking into it. It also meant risking a glimpse at the face of horror. *Death was the glass! Death was between us!* So she had written in her fantasy of the haunted house.

Virginia Stephen's nature and temperament, and her lapses from sanity, have been laid to her father's temper and emotional aggressions, her mother's sudden death when Virginia was still a young girl, and to boyish sexual treatment by one of her half brothers, to which she was exposed while a child. She herself spoke of "violent moments of being." And certainly aggression, death, confusion of infantile sexual feeling, in a child and woman of particularly intricate perceptions, can damage an entire life and sometimes lead to madness. But we must not simplify. Between the lines of "A Sketch of the Past" we obtain some glimpses into the tragic—and also heroic—story of Virginia Stephen's struggle long before she became Virginia Woolf. What were the violent moments? Three are juxtaposed for us in her sketch of Cornwall summers and the mirror in the Talland House hall into which she could look only on tiptoe as a child. On the shelf beside the mirror one day Gerald Duckworth, then sixteen, placed Virginia (she was probably five or six), "his hand going under my clothes; going firmly and steadily lower and lower." She stiffened and wriggled. She was helpless, with the inarticulate anger of a child; she felt frustration and "dumbness," and the mounting anger was apparently unexpressed. There had been an earlier and forgotten episode which someone told her, of her "being thrown naked by father into the sea." Leslie Stephen, we may judge, would have failed to make this into a moment of fun—it was not in his nature; there must have been surprise here, too, and the same kind of helplessness. And then there was the moment when she wrestled on the lawn with her older brother, Thoby, and he pommeled her. She wanted to hit him with her fist; but "why hurt another person?" So she told herself. She suffered the violation in silence. Within, we may judge, she was a childish vessel of wrath. "I have remembered it all my life."

Her "private parts" explored by the older boy; thrown into the sea naked by her strong, bearded father; pommeled by her beloved sibling—clearly the males of Virginia Stephen's world treated her too much as if she were an object. What chance could there be for relation with men when the girl-child discovered so intensely her body's vulnerability? So Virginia carried with her into her growing years a powerful anger and with it shame and guilt, for in the Victorian years little girls were not supposed to have such feelings or be involved in such doings.

The definitive blight of Virginia Stephen occurred when to this emotional confusion was added a kind of perpetual mourning and melancholy. She was thirteen when her mother died. The doctors said that Julia had influenza—and all of Virginia's later breakdowns were ushered in by bouts of this illness. There was no preparation for death—

only a sudden summons early one morning. Leslie Stephen's grief was uncontrollable, and George Duckworth, the oldest half brother, then in his mid-twenties, assumed the father's role. "Led by George with towels wrapped round us and given each a drop of brandy in warm milk to drink, we were taken into the bedroom. I think candles were burning; and I think the sun was coming in. At any rate I remember the long looking glass; with the drawers on either side; and the washstand; and the great bed on which my mother lay." She noticed that one nurse was sobbing "and a desire to laugh came over me, and I said to myself as I have often done at moments of crisis since, 'I feel nothing whatever.' Then I stooped and kissed my mother's face. It was still warm. She had only died a moment before."

With feeling banished, Virginia Stephen could simply look at what was happening in detached sadness and silence. Someone else, shaken and grieving over the death, would be filled with too much emotion to observe. Virginia's account is both touching and intimate, as if she had coldly taken notes of the little tragic and ironic facts and physical sensations of long ago. At thirteen—that age of the *jeune fille en fleur* when all the senses tremulously listen and feel the world—Virginia heard and sensed and touched and saw. And recorded and remembered. But she could not mourn.

The death cast a permanent pall over No. 22, more terrible perhaps for Virginia, given her nature and experience. Vanessa, then fifteen, was better prepared for life's shocks. Virginia's mercury of emotion, the stimulated nature of her sensibility, the rush of pain, hurt, rage, the sense of loss, of termination, as of the world coming to an end—all this could not be expressed and released as it might have been in other circumstances. Somewhere within Virginia another door slammed, and she immediately turned the key so that she might not *feel*. The process is carefully described in her novel *Mrs. Dalloway*. Septimus Smith can think, read, calculate; he can see with the clarity and the sharpness of immediacy. "He could add up his bill; his brain was perfect; it must be the fault of the world then—that he could not feel." Those who *can* feel find it difficult to understand this kind of "dissociation." By shutting out feeling, one also shuts out pain. And that is why Virginia was able, in all her later recollections, to give us so much detail, shorn of all affect. "We were made to act parts that we did not feel; to fumble for words that we did not know."

Had Virginia been able to grieve with the rest of the family, there would not have been the formation of a kind of pool or reservoir of melancholy within her which was never fully released. It was a dead weight: she describes it in *Mrs. Dalloway* when she says, "This late age of the world's experience had bred in them all, a well of tears." Virginia Stephen left the room of death carrying her well of tears with her and returned to the nursery. She looked out of the window. She saw Dr. Seton walking up the street, his head bent and his hands clasped behind his back. Her memory had photographic sharpness. Pigeons floated and settled. She felt calm and sad. "It was a beautiful spring morning and very still. That brings back the feeling that everything had come to an end."

Thus we may see the *tristimania* of Virginia's life. Dissociation of grief enabled her to watch the pigeons, defensively mock the weeping nurse (she thought the nurse was pretending), see the depressed movement of the doctor, who had just lost his patient. Ever after, all terminations were death. This was why she was often on the verge of a breakdown when she finished a book; it represented a termination. Her own poignant mourning was shut away—and shut away also was the terrible unexpressed rage of a thirteen-year-old who experiences death in the manner of childhood, as an abandonment by the mother—the rage of being deprived, deserted, of being snatched from the warm-bodied Julia. Such rage is transformed into the eerie wailing and chanting and funereal self-immolation among primitives often described by travelers in remote lands. In the little girl perched at the window of Hyde Park Gate, in the early morning of May 1895, the rage was transformed into controlled calm. There was only a general stillness, a sad quiet, the wheeling pigeons. She could not mourn. She could not experience mourning.

On the next evening, the evening before the funeral, her half sister Stella took Virginia back to the chamber of death. There stood the looking glass, in which she had seen

Death reflected the day before; and on the bed the same still figure, now no longer on her side, but on her back, like some knight's lady in a tomb. There was only the "hollow stern, immeasurably distant silence." Virginia kissed Julia again. It was like kissing cold iron. "Whenever I touch cold iron the feeling comes back to me—the feeling of my mother's face, iron cold and granulated." Step by step Virginia dispassionately takes us through these terrible moments. People crept in and out. Rooms were shut. Flowers were piled in the hall. For years the scent of certain flowers would bring the memories back to her. Everything seemed —as we might expect in someone to whom this death was "external"—a series of scenes, "melodramatic, histrionic and unreal." There was an unreality in the sisters' going in a cab to meet Thoby at the station when he came up from Clifton for the funeral. As Virginia had noticed the mirror by her mother's bed, so now the great glassed-in arched roof at Paddington merged with the shrouded Kensington room. The glass refracted the sun in a magnificent blaze of light "as if a burning glass had been laid over what was shaded and dormant." The train steamed into the station. Thoby embraced his sisters, amid tears. For Virginia Stephen this was "melodrama." ("Death was the glass! Death was between us!") The long looking glass of the dressing table in the bedroom, the burning glass at Paddington came to stand for death, melting together with the mirror of violation in the hall at St. Ives.

We know that the emotional coalescence of the emotions, confined within, ultimately kaleidoscoped in Virginia not as mourning, but as mental disorder. There were moments when Virginia Stephen identified herself with her dead mother to the extent of wanting death for herself. She was ill for many weeks. Then came the death of her second "mother"—Julia's daughter Stella—two years later. Virginia, now fifteen, still could not assimilate the idea of loss. She wrote that "just behind the surface lay the other death. Even if I were not fully conscious of what my mother's death meant, I had for two years unconsciously been absorbing it." The second blow of death struck "on my tremulous, creased self sitting with my wings still stuck together in the broken chrysalis." The image of herself as a barely hatched butterfly arrested in the spread of her wings by two deaths merged later into the image of a dying moth. She had watched the moth on her windowsill in Hyde Park Gate. One moment it seemed alive. Then she realized that she had witnessed its last flight. Its wings were folded, never to unfold again. The image of the diaphanous butterflies, on the edge of birth and on the edge of death, became one and the same. "Oh yes," she made the dying moth say as it lay on her windowsill, "death is stronger than I am." And yet Virginia would spend her life trying to be stronger than death—trying also in life to repair the damage to her selfhood, her womanhood, that made it impossible for her to be on terms of full comfort with any man.

II

The damage to Virginia's selfhood seems by her own evidence to have been done in her childhood. There was, however, strong reinforcement of it in her years of late adolescence. It came this time from George Duckworth, the adult half brother, whom she pictures with a certain fierceness and directness that hardly dissimulates the hatred and disgust she felt for him, until she swings to pity, telling herself that he was "a stupid good natured young man of profuse, voluble affections." Her pen is at its most bitter-ironic when she draws him as a sexually repressed Victorian, given to tears, embraces and kisses sought from reluctant troubled sisters. Under the name of "unselfishness" he committed acts which others would have called "tyrannical"—"profoundly believing in the purity of his love, he behaved little better than a brute." He tried to get Virginia to attend parties. In one terrible scene he mocks a certain green dress in which she tried to meet his demands that she turn herself into a pretty social object. She remembered standing in front of George's Chippendale mirror seeking to make herself tidy and presentable. He made her feel, she recalled, as if she were a tramp or a gypsy. She felt shame at the parties, where she was a wallflower. She was ashamed of her clothes. She was made to feel "queer." George remained chaste until his marriage, Virginia said, but she and Vanessa paid the price for his sublimated desires. He seems to have gone as far as he could with his half sisters. "He acted in public the role of a good brother. He acted with success. How could we resist his wishes—how could we cherish other desires?" She describes him as having "the curls of a God, and the ears of a faun," but, she adds, he had "unmistakably the eyes of a pig."

This adult brother "lavished caresses, endearments, enquiries, and embraces as if, after forty years in the Australian bush, he had at last returned to the home of his youth and found an aged mother still alive to welcome him." Virginia repeated that he was "abnormally stupid." He could pass no examinations. He refused argument. He would always say, "Kiss me, kiss me, you beloved"—kisses were a substitute for all argument. "His passions increased and his desires became more vehement," so that Virginia said she felt like "an unfortunate minnow shut up in the same tank with an unwieldy and turbulent whale."

The supreme scene is given us by Virginia, apparently with some exaggeration, as a scene of seduction. She had gone with George to one of those interminable parties in which her self-esteem suffered terribly. She describes the Holman Hunts in her brightest style. "The ladies were intense and untidy; the gentlemen had fine foreheads and short evening trousers in some cases revealing a pair of bright red Pre-Raphaelite socks. George stepped among them like a Prince in disguise. I soon attached myself to a little covey of Kensington ladies. . . ." They found the painter Holman Hunt in a long dressing gown, holding forth on the ideas that had prompted his painting *The Light of the World*. He was sipping cocoa and stroking his flowing beard. The tone of the assembly was "bright and high-minded." "At last—at last—the evening was over," wrote Virginia. When they returned to Hyde Park Gate, she went to her room, took off her satin dress, unfastened the corsage of carnations, and began to think of her Greek lessons.

"Many different things were whirling round in my mind—diamonds and countesses, copulations, the dialogues of Plato." She thought how pleasant it would be to fall asleep and forget them all. She was almost asleep when the door creaked. "Don't be frightened," George whispered. "And don't turn on the light, oh beloved. Beloved—" and he "flung himself on my bed and took me in his arms." To which Virginia added, "Yes, the old ladies of Kensington and Belgravia never knew that George Duckworth was not only father and mother, brother and sister to those poor Stephen girls; he was their lover also."

III

One important source of Virginia Stephen's will to live—in the face of her will to die—came from her father. The world has accepted Virginia's own belief, written one day into her diary, that if Leslie Stephen had lived into extreme old age, "his life would have entirely ended mine. What would have happened? No writing, no books;—inconceivable." This was but a statement of her confusion of feeling. Along with her haunted sense of her dead mother and her desire for death was her identification with the two life-giving forces in the Stephen household: her intense rivalry with her sister, which gave meaning to her life; and her wish to possess the life force of her mountain-climbing and writing father. These forces of competition and emulation fed Virginia's will to live against the destructive death forces nourished within. Vanessa remembered how in childhood Virginia pinned her down one day in the bathroom. Whom did she love most, mother or father? Vanessa had no wish to make a choice. She finally and most uncomfortably said that, as much as she loved her father, she loved her mother more. Virginia then thoughtfully replied that her love belonged to her father. The preference was stronger than she ever allowed. After Stella's death, Virginia assumed much of the care of Leslie Stephen; Vanessa was occupied with running the house. And however much Virginia found Leslie a difficult, crotchety, irritable, demanding old man, she gave proof again and again of a deep attachment. They lived in an "odd fumbling fellowship," she said; its roots lay in their common love of books and reading. She had always been given the run of the great study. "Read what you like," her father said to her when she was fifteen. She read in this big room lined with books. There stood the father's rocking chair, upholstered in American cloth, where Leslie stretched his legs and lay almost recumbent, rocking the chair like a cradle as he wrote. On the writing board he had a curious Chinese inkstand and an inkwell at one side. The Watts portrait of Sir Leslie Stephen, in its finely chiseled sadness and severity, hung over the fireplace. Some of his rusty alpenstocks stood by the side; some old trophy, a silver cup, on the mantelpiece. Through three long windows Virginia saw the roofs of Kensington. Her father remarked casually one day that he had just seen an eagle on St. Mary Abbots—an eagle in London! Probably a refugee from the zoo. She remembered his making a special trip to the London Library to bring Hakluyt's voyages. She was enraptured by the large yellow pages. "I used to read it and dream of those obscure adventures, and no doubt practiced their style in my copybook." Leslie Stephen made his children critical. He asked them to say *why* they liked this or that storybook. The literary roots among the Stephens were strong; out of these grew the atmosphere of Virginia's prose—out of her total saturation in English literature.

Perhaps most touching, as we seek the life-giving affinities between father and daughter, was Leslie's gift to Virginia on her twenty-first birthday, just a month before he died. "Father gave me a ring—really a beautiful one, which I love—the first ring I have ever had." Leslie said that she was "a very good daughter." It was as if there were a marriage and also a laying on of hands, a literary succession. The father, who had been Thackeray's son-in-law and editor of the *Cornhill*, the man who had fashioned a great national institution, the *Dictionary of National Biography*, who had been visited by Tennyson and Browning and Henry James, performed a marriage between Virginia and the world of letters. He had been eccentric, troublesome, severe; he embodied certain forms of masculinity Virginia detested. She could blame him for her mother's hard life, and yet she wrote when he was dead, "I am happy about that ring." At moments she felt guilty. "I can't bear to think of his loneliness . . . the dreadful thing is that I never did enough for him all these years. He was so lonely, often, and I never helped him as I might have done." And then she said the opposite of what she wrote years later in her diary: "If he had only lived we could have been so happy." She helped Leslie Stephen's biographer, Frederic Maitland, prepare his book. And many years later, when she was writing *To the Lighthouse,* she recognized that she was more like her father than her mother and "therefore more critical." She added in a mood of recognition, "He was an adorable man, and somehow tremendous."

We have tangible evidence of Virginia Stephen's identification with her father. She began to smoke a pipe a few weeks after his death. Few Victorian daughters dared to take such liberties. "I find it very soothing." Having written this, she exclaimed to her friend Violet Dickinson, "Oh my Violet! I do want father so!" In her later affectionate essay on Leslie Stephen, she recalls "his taking his hat and stick, calling for his dog and his daughter" and striding off into Kensington Gardens. Now that he was dead, Virginia took to striding in solitude, shouting the odes of Pindar into the air, which caresses her "like a stern but affectionate parent."

In the end Leslie's sternness counted less than his affection. And what counted most was the image of the father writing in his rocking chair, with his pipe in his mouth, dropping books around him with a thud. Her breakdown was not long in coming after Leslie Stephen's death—the same troubling symptoms of dissociation and depression which had followed Julia's death. Violet Dickinson suggested a trip to Italy, and the sisters had their first experience of Florence and Venice. Vanessa was delighted; there was much to see, and she discovered the old schools of painting. But Quentin Bell tells us "there was practically nothing that the elder sister did not like and very little to please the younger."

They returned by way of Paris at the end of April 1904. When they reached London, Virginia completely broke down. Her usual symptoms: a swing from euphoria to silence; refusal to take food; apathy. Violet Dickinson took her into her country home. Virginia threw herself from a window. Fortunately, it was a low one. She clearly did not want to die. After that she was in the hands of the doctors. She always hated doctors. They prescribed in those days of primitive psychiatry quiet, bed rest, nourishing food. Medicine was little aware then of the nature of depression except for its classic symptoms. "All that summer she was mad," the family historian tells us.

Twenty years later, sketching *Mrs. Dalloway* in her diary, Virginia wrote, "Mrs. Dalloway has branched into a book; and I adumbrate here a study of insanity and suicide." She added, "The world seen by the sane and the insane side by side." In the novel she invented an insane male and a dissociated female. In life, however, the two were not "side by side." They lived within the one: they were the two faces of Virginia, the frightening face of anger, shame, guilt, death; the benign face of literary experience, the heritage of Sir Leslie Stephen. In some such complex way the madness of Virginia was metamorphosed into the asperities and sanities of her art.

46 Gordon Square

During the weeks before Leslie Stephen's death, Gerald Duckworth, his younger stepson, made a welcome suggestion to his half sisters. With Leslie dead, he said, it would be sensible for the Duckworths and Stephens to go their separate ways. They were, after all, of different generations. Perhaps the Stephens would wish to "take a small house —possibly in Bloomsbury." Vanessa and Virginia, with memories of the satyrlike performances of the Duckworth boys—their prying hands and caressing kisses—thought this a splendid idea. The two generations had stumbled over each other for too long in the narrow passages of No. 22.

One day in December 1903 the two sisters went from Kensington to unfamiliar Bloomsbury to search into the mysteries beyond Tottenham Court Road and in the winter squares—Gordon, Brunswick, Tavistock, Bedford. December was certainly not an ideal month. The Bloomsbury trees were leafless; the buildings were naked. The British Museum seemed more austere and domineering than ever. Henry James, Leslie's friend had described Bloomsbury as "an antiquated ex-fashionable region." For him it had smelled strongly of the eighteenth century. For the Stephen sisters on that December day it probably reeked too much of the nineteenth. "We have been tramping Bloomsbury this afternoon," wrote Virginia to her loyal friend Violet. They had stared at dingy houses. There were many to be had. "But Lord, how dreary! It seems far away, and so cold and gloomy. Really, we shall never get a house we like so well as this, but it is better to go."

Virginia must have felt homeless and orphaned. She clung to the familiar haunted house. Much as she wanted freedom, the possibility of change gave rise to anxiety.

Vanessa, we gather, had no misgivings. Her decorator's eye saw possibilities even in dingy houses. Thoby, due to come down from Cambridge and planning to study law, could join the household. Adrian, the youngest, now up at Trinity, would have a *pied-à-terre* in London. The time to escape from the past had come. As Virginia put it, Vanessa had looked at a map of London and had seen the distance between Kensington and Bloomsbury. There was nothing like putting distance between past and present.

II

Sir Leslie died two months after their house hunt, and Virginia had her breakdown that spring. Vanessa continued the search alone and came upon a commodious mid-Victorian house at 46 Gordon Square. It fronted the old square, its large windows opened on trees and lawn; it was filled with light and air. Its four stories of solid brick and basement scullery provided the equivalent of four apartments for the two sisters and two brothers. They had inherited modest incomes; they could be practical about their future. Each sister would have a bedroom and sitting room of her own. The rooms were tall and clean and "rather frigid"; that is, heated only by coal fires in old-fashioned open fireplaces. There was a narrow outside ironwork balcony on the first floor, with tall full-length windows opening into it.

Vanessa bought the lease during the summer of 1904 while Virginia was in the country recovering at Violet Dickinson's. With a house to decorate, she was definite and unhesitating. The walls had to be painted white, the best background for showing works of art. Then she began the difficult task of sweeping out the clutter of the decades at Hyde Park Gate. The father's library, literary relics going back to the Thackeray connection, and certain pictures were moved to Gordon Square. Vanessa burned and sorted, sold and gave away. There were more than enough fine china and silver and splendid pieces of old furniture to fill the house. George Duckworth, who had first announced, to the consternation of Vanessa, that he too would move to Bloomsbury, suddenly became engaged and conveniently married an aristocratic lady. Gerald took a bachelor flat in Berkeley Street. The Stephens were left to create their new home alone. They were free, for the first time, of all responsibilities to the older generation. They were responsible only to themselves and to one another. And when, that autumn, Virginia came briefly to London—the doctors still watched her closely—she found a Bloomsbury that wasn't the least bit dingy or dreary. In October 1904 Gordon Square seemed to her "the most beautiful, the most exciting, the most romantic place in the world." She stood in the uncarpeted drawing room and looked out at the tall trees, not yet leafless, in the watery autumn sun. All she had been able to see in the Kensington house from her room was old Mrs. Redgrave washing her neck across the way! The changing Turneresque London light, often crepuscular, sometimes bright, came into the rooms and touched Vanessa's tints and textures. Some of Watts's pictures had been hung, Dutch cabinets were placed in strategic positions, the blue china was properly displayed. To be sure, there was traffic in Gordon Square after the muffled silence of the little Kensington street. More important than street sounds, which Virginia's ear picked up one by one and in chorus, was the fact that each sister had privacy. On evenings when the weather permitted, they could sit on the ledgelike balcony. With the lamps lit and the lights reflected in the umbrageous green, Gordon Square looked "romantic." No more red plush. No more black paint. No more Morris wallpapers. The influence of Vanessa's masters was evident. She drew then on Sargent's colors and arrangements, he who painted always from chiaroscuro into brightness; and she used her own sure sense of textiles (Sargent would be disliked later and discarded). There would be an Augustus John phase. Now there were white and green chintzes. The general whiteness brightened their daily lives even when the fogs and rains settled in. Virginia remembered, "We were full of experiments and reforms. Everything was going to be new; everything was going to be different. Everything was on trial." In the drawing room visitors noted curtains, both blue and white; a pianola; an early Victorian table; basket chairs. No. 46 Gordon Square very quickly became the center, the heart, of the Bloomsbury of our story.

III

For the first time since the days of their childhood and youth, Vanessa and Virginia Stephen had Thoby to themselves in their newly decorated house. He was a solid male presence. Lytton said that Thoby was "hewn out of the living rock." His character was "as splendid as his appearance, and as wonderfully complete." Leonard, half a century later, said that Thoby "had greater personal charm than anyone I have ever known." Thoby was loved alike by the Cambridge intellectuals and the hedonists. He shared with Clive Bell a delight in the out-of-doors—hunting, birdwatching, riding, walking, fishing. Lytton, for obvious reasons, adored him: his masculinity overwhelmed. Thoby shared with Leonard a lively interest in politics, in philosophy—always with that poise and detachment out of which large figures are made. He shared with Vanessa a delight in form and color and was himself an excellent draftsman. Virginia, in vision, pictured him as the all-around Englishman, the future Mr. Justice Stephen, or an important government official, "with several books to his credit, I suppose, some on law; one or two on birds . . . some essays on literature and history; public matters; some attack on abuses." In short, the professional English gentleman who is also an admirable amateur and is wholly at peace with the world. In these fantasies Virginia told herself, trying to see the truth, that Thoby would be "more a figure than a success." She believed that he was not clever but "gifted"; he mastered things rather than felt them as she did. She remembered him as a clumsy little boy, very fat, bursting through a Norfolk jacket, but others described him as "Napoleonic" when he was a child. He was determined and resolute. He could have "very thorough and formidable rages." He had delighted Virginia when he came home from his first school (Evelyn's) and told her about the Trojan War; later they argued over Shakespeare; and then they got into the habit of walking upstairs and down in Hyde Park Gate on each return from school (Clifton and still later Cambridge) as he described his school friends in "a blend of mastery and sensibility." He took pride in both his sisters. And Sir Leslie had taken great pride in him. Thoby had, Virginia wrote militantly, "the burden, the glory of being a man." He was gentle and amusing and agreeable—and impartial. When he was at home in the evening, they talked, they played games, they read, they sketched. He had a touch of the Stephen artistry and a sense of the comic, even the ribald and gothic. He sketched murderers escaping and criminals being hanged; and then in irreverent moments he drew for his sisters "the back view of God Almighty." On occasion Vanessa would read aloud, in her beautiful voice, "the silliest novel we can find, at which we all roar with laughter." What made their life seem Arcadian was that for the first time they were peers and together. In Hyde Park Gate there had been three or four generations, each representing different phases of Victorian life. Now they were close enough to have similar tastes; and they had come out of the same world, and were all, as Virginia noted, "of the same age."

IV

Vanessa's and Virginia's experience of men, as we have seen, had been limited to the Duckworths and to one or two others, such as Stella's young widowed husband. Vanessa, to be sure, from the moment she began to frequent studios, had expanded her horizon, although Thoby still remained for her the supreme and attaching figure. There had been a brief romance with the widowed brother-in-law, but it had been defeated by family pressure. Virginia, a creature of the library, immersed in her studies at home, had moved largely in the world of women. She had not been able to link herself in any intellectual or emotional way to her half brothers; and at the parties to which she had been taken by them, she had been gauche and brooding. In casual conversation her tongue was too sharp, and she had no confidence in her clothes or her manners. She too found herself most comfortable with Thoby, and in her posthumous memories we can see how much she valued the way in which he accepted her when he was home from school. He never treated her as a superfluous younger sister. In a long passage written years later, Virginia tried to analyze her relation with her older brother. She felt that they had been brought together in particular by the family tragedies. The relation "was more serious than it would have been without those deaths. The unspoken thought was there, in him, in me."

> A shell-less little creature, I think he thought me; so sequestered, in the room at Hyde Park Gate, compared with himself; a very simple eager recipient of his school stories; without any experience of my own with which to cap his; but all the same not passive; rather, on the contrary, bubbling, inquisitive, restless, carrying on my own contradicting, at any rate questioning.

They argued about books. He swept away many of her remarks with his masculine force. A competition of wits, and Thoby, with his pipe in his mouth, sitting before his self-doubting sister with the look of "one equipped, unperturbed, knowing his place, relishing his inheritance and his part in life, aware of his competence." Sex, of course, was never discussed. Only much later did Virginia learn from Clive that Thoby considered Lytton's sodomies merely an amiable absurdity.

Virginia's letters to Thoby are those of a younger sister grateful for brotherly consideration. She is full of girlish worship, elaborately and ironically deferential to "my lord," "melord," "milord"; but she also stands up for her opinions and her distinctive literary tastes. "I have to delve from books, painfully and all alone, what you get every evening sitting over your fire and smoking your pipe with Strachey, etc. No wonder my knowledge is but scant." She adds, "Still I try my best with Shakespeare." Virginia remembered how she had suddenly one day seen Thoby dressed up in a new suit, and how beautiful he appeared. She fell in love with her brother on that day. He lounged on cushions, "monolithic, in giant repose." So she painted his memory in *The Waves*, using Lytton's word. And always he was a figure who could command, with his curious air of detachment. "He is conventional; he is a hero." Yes, little boys had trooped after him, Virginia fancifully said. If he blew his nose, they blew their noses; but they couldn't quite do it with his style. His style was grandiose—aloof, judicial, conventional. In Gordon Square, Virginia had tremors of fear lest Vanessa should marry or Thoby become engaged. "I only wish we could always go on like this," she wrote.

V

It will be recalled that from the first Vanessa had claimed Thoby as her own and that Virginia constantly sought to take him from her. Thoby, far from feeling caught in the middle, sided diplomatically now with one and now with the other. He felt, in this situation, endowed with the love of both his sisters; and this gave him large confidence and easy power: he lit up a room when he entered it. His "primitive" or Apollonian physical mass—it depended on how one saw him—brought comfort to everyone. A family picture taken when Julia was still alive shows Thoby in profile in the back row to which the older children are relegated. He is making a funny remark to the smiling and jubilant Vanessa, whose entire posture expresses enchantment. She has her arm locked in his and holds his hand. Virginia, on Thoby's right, looks away from them. Vanessa always clung to Thoby. Virginia either flirted with him or engaged him in literary conversation.

By the time they had settled into Gordon Square, the sisters no longer tugged in different directions when Thoby was in the room. He was now the man of the household, and we may see that in some invisible way he played Leslie to Vanessa's Julia, while Virginia played the perpetual younger sister who sought both to charm and woo from her mother-sister this delightful father-brother. Some such interpersonal and "incestuous" equation existed, stabilized by their newfound freedoms. This is not to say that Virginia's rivalry with Vanessa had diminished. She oscillated between abasement and respect. She could always fall back on mockery. There was envy: "Nature has done so much more for her than for me." Lucky Vanessa, unlucky Virginia! Or she would say, "Vanessa's character remains very hard and calculated to outlast the sphinx," but also, "We are so much dry or green wood thrown on her flame." Envy melts into adoration: Vanessa is "the richest and ripest creature under the sun." Worthless Virginia! Virginia sometimes had dreams in which Vanessa received fatal injuries under the wheels of an omnibus. From this kind of psychic obliteration, she swung to direct and amusing competition. Vanessa painted while standing at an easel. "I daresay painters are more concentrated, but less amiable and loveable in their marmoreal chastity than we are," Virginia would write. But she wasn't going to be outdone by her sister, erect in front of her canvases. She got herself a stand-up desk for her writing.

Had the Stephens not found so fine a house which freed each of them and enabled them to lead their own lives, there might have been at this time a more serious and more bitter side to the sisterly rivalry. But what Gordon Square did for the freedom-seeking Vanessa and the fragile self-doubting Virginia was to separate them sufficiently into privacy. They could be together when they wished; they had the means of escape. Vanessa had her painting and Virginia her writing. The latter was now a regular book reviewer for the *Times Literary Supplement* and nourished thoughts of writing fiction. During her recent illness, Virginia had displayed a marked hostility to Vanessa, a violence of the spirit which Vanessa understood. But Gordon Square fostered the benign rather than the morbid in her. And a new world was opening up. For Thoby brought into Gordon Square all his Cambridge friends.

Clive in Paris

Clive Bell took his bachelor's degree in June 1902 and, unlike some of his fellow graduates, showed no desire to cling to Cambridge. The world beckoned. He received a second in his Tripos, but he had never had large scholarly ambitions; and he was pleasantly surprised when Trinity offered him a studentship in history. He was twenty-one; his goals were not defined. He liked company, sport, food, women. The studentship was in a way a consolation, for he had been passed over for the Apostles. Trinity was showing him that his intelligence and ability were valued. He decided to write a dissertation on British foreign policy at the Congress of Verona; he would always like large subjects. The Congress of Verona in 1822 would have suited Lytton Strachey's historical style admirably; the confrontations between Metternich and Wellington, the foundering of the post-Napoleonic Holy Alliance—here was a drama and an action ready-made for the kind of historical ironies and condescensions Strachey would ultimately practice. For Clive Bell, it was simply a thesis subject. In the autumn of 1902 he began work in the Public Record Office. He had rooms in London; he could go up to Cambridge as necessary. He had not been cast idle into the world—not that he would ever consider himself an idler. He seemed to enjoy burrowing in old documents, even if he did not have the fixity of purpose needed to be a professional historian.

In this way he passed an agreeable year in and around London, interrupted during the summer of 1903 by his father, who asked Clive to accompany him to the Canadian Northwest for some larger game than might be found in the British Isles. Clive went, as he said, "most unwillingly," crossing an ocean and a continent to discharge his filial duty. He was back in London in November of 1903.

Now it occurred to him that what he really needed for his thesis was the French *Archives* rather than the British Public Record Office. The Vicomte de Chateaubriand had been more active than the Duke of Wellington at Verona. Clive accordingly left sooty London for drizzly Paris in January 1904. He did not know the French capital. His French was "abominable." It seemed to him logical to find a good bourgeois *pension* and learn the language. Having the means, he lodged himself in a particularly fine middle-class establishment behind the Trocadéro, in the rue Bouquet-de-Longchamp, a goodly distance from the heart of the Parisian pleasures known to all tourists. The Bois de Boulogne was at hand. But he might as well have been in the big family house in Wiltshire; and indeed his description of the smart widow who kept the pension and her apparent lover, a retired French colonial officer, suggests that the couple for a brief spell served as parental figures to the young inexperienced exile. When one considers the later *bon viveur*, it seems curious that it did not occur to Clive that Paris had a nightlife and countless distractions for an active young male adult. He lingered in the archi-respectable neighborhood of the Avenue Victor Hugo learning polite French table talk. On one evening he and the French ex-officer put on tails and white tie and went to see Sarah Bernhardt in a mediocre play. Clive got himself accepted at the Government *Archives* as a historical re-searcher, but he was losing interest in the Congress of Verona. There was one way of dissipating the dullness of the life into which he had fallen: "I went daily to the Louvre."

II

The Paris in which Clive settled in conformity with his bourgeois breeding was a city of horses, top hats, wide comfortable cafés, ladies with sweeping costumes—we can see them in the paintings of the time, in Manet, Toulouse-Lautrec, Renoir and in the works of other painters not of France—Sickert, for example. Clive rode to the Louvre every day from the altitude of the Avenue Victor Hugo in a horse omnibus across a wintry Paris. The streets were filled with fiacres; their drivers wore shiny "toppers." The day of the motor was only beginning. Simply to ride through the Parisian thoroughfares, in the January drizzle, or when the winter sun bathed them in hard cold light, was pleasure enough for a relaxed young Cambridge graduate who was in no hurry to get anywhere. In the Louvre, Clive for the first time systematically learned the history of painting. In other galleries he sought out the pictures that interested him most—the works of the Impressionists. He had read, while still at Cambridge, Camille Mauclair's pioneer work on this recent art movement and had even bought some Toulouse-Lautrec reproductions. He now bought a Renoir engraving for five francs.

At the end of his picture-haunted days, he recognized that he had exchanged his familiar Cambridge and winter London for a dull *pension*, which, in spite of the ministrations of Madame B. and its middle-class comfort, was intolerably dull. He wanted companionship. He missed friendly talk. He wanted someone to whom he could describe his new discoveries in the world of art. After eight weeks he remembered that he had a letter of introduction to a Cambridge graduate named Gerald Kelly, who was now living in some studio and trying to paint. One day in late February or early March, Clive took the omnibus to the then out-of-the-way part of the city called Montparnasse that had branched off from the *Quartier Latin*. It was at the opposite end of Paris from Montmartre. He had no trouble finding Kelly's studio in the rue Campagne Première. It was located picturesquely among a warren of studios beside a stable yard. He knocked at the door. A young man only a few years his senior opened it. The studio was large and filled with canvases. Kelly received Clive with undisguised pleasure. Cambridge was a ready bond between them; and Clive soon realized that the painter was as starved as he was for good talk about books, ideas, philosophy. The painter was a man of wit and culture, better educated than many of the artists with whom he associated. And Clive could easily hold his own in all kinds of company.

The new friends promptly went for a drink at the Café de Versailles near the rue de Rennes, and later to dinner at the Chat Blanc in the rue d'Odessa near the Gare Montparnasse. The *patron* of the Chat Blanc was a retired horse dealer, and Clive knew a great deal about horses. Downstairs there was a general public room; upstairs there was a narrow room with three tables reserved for particularly congenial artistic spirits. Clive met artists and writers and their mistresses. The room was filled with smoke and the smells of fine French cooking. He felt himself suddenly transported to all the things in life he valued. His new acquaintances seemed free, liberal spirits. The English painters were fluent in French; the conversations were bilingual; and Kelly soon discovered that this young man, who talked seriously of his work in the French *Archives*, cared "passionately" for pictures, especially for those of the Impressionists. Moreover, he seemed to know something about them. Kelly introduced Clive to two older men, both painters: Roderick O'Conor, a big-mustached and very Irish artist, and James Wilson Morrice, a little man with a pointed beard, who came from Montreal and painted small Impressionist canvases. They were—the two young men from Cambridge and the two middle-aged men from Britain's outposts—provincials or former provincials. Under the common banner of art they now lived their lives of freedom in cosmopolitan Paris.

Clive returned to Montparnasse the next day, and the next; he ate at the Chat Blanc and drank the excellent brandy of the Café de Versailles. After a visit to the Closerie des Lilas near the Bal Bullier, and much more talk, Kelly told Clive that the Trocadéro and the Avenue Victor Hugo were hardly the place for someone like himself. Clive agreed. He made his excuses to Madame B. at the *pension;* he bade farewell to the colonial captain. He rented a room just down the way from Kelly's studio, in the Hôtel du Haute Loire at the angle of the Boulevard Raspail and the Boulevard du Montparnasse. Raspail at that time ended at Montparnasse. It had not yet been cut through to the rue de Rennes. Clive's chamber was commodious and had a small alcove, where he could read and write. Aside from the washbowl in his room, a toilet, and the chamber pot under the bed, there were no conveniences. The hotel had no bath, but Clive had no trouble doing as the Parisians did. He walked daily to a nearby *Établissement de Bains* located between the small Café du

Dôme right beside his hotel and the Closerie des Lilas. Bathed, red-cheeked, his hair combed, with all his ardor and enthusiasm, Clive could saunter forth at his ease into his new world.

This was his first real break with his middle-class past. He flirted with shopgirls, models, barmaids. He had men of art—and the fraternity of art—around him. He dined at the Chat Blanc at least five nights a week from that early spring until Christmas. It never lost its attraction for him. The restaurant had been one of the hangouts of the young Somerset Maugham shortly before, and it is described in some of Maugham's early works. Another Englishman usually came to dine once a week, a Staffordshire provincial, bulky and with buck teeth. He lived in a small apartment filled with gimcracks. "We rather liked him," Clive said of Arnold Bennett; but he never truly cared for this industrious man with showy manners who made himself into a writer by sheer tenacity and who a half dozen years later would use his French saturation in a famous novel, *The Old Wives' Tale*. Bennett on his side recognized and accepted Clive's young patronizing air. When Jack Pollock, son of the famous jurist, came to Paris for a holiday, Clive took him to meet Bennett. The latter recorded in his direct and honest manner, "They neither of them thought that they had anything to learn. They were tolerant, from their heights, toward the pathetic spectacle of humanity. Always Bell was the least priggish and convinced. But I liked them both." Bennett would come to know Bloomsbury. And Bloomsbury would make him, through Virginia Woolf, the target of "the old" and the symbol of bourgeois fiction in a famous manifesto entitled "Mr. Bennett and Mrs. Brown."

III

In later years Kelly would become Sir Gerald Kelly and gain renown as a highly efficient president of the Royal Academy. He was never, to Clive's eye, an important painter, although certain of his works received praise. In Paris, however, in their early days, he could offer the new doctrine of art to Clive Bell, and Arnold Bennett's journal suggests his manner of talk. "We paint like governesses,"

Kelly said in one of his outbursts. Painters, he said, were afraid of making mistakes, afraid of vulgarity and "they never use their eyes in search of material." They monotonously painted the same subjects. The new "visuality" was at the center of Kelly's art-talk, and Clive liked all that he heard.

Kelly's middle-aged companions, O'Conor and Morrice, proved to be Clive's principal mentors. O'Conor had a strong infusion of Irish aggressivity; he railed against Whistler and Sargent; he had known Charles Conder and Puvis de Chavannes and, more important, had painted at Pont-Aven with Gauguin and had had many talks with him. Like Morrice—and like Clive—he came from a sufficiently affluent family (his father was a landlord) to be able to live with ease in Paris. He liked books and was an excellent hunter of rarities on the quays; he had a fine collection of Bonnards, Rouaults, Gauguins. He had photographs of paintings by Cézanne. Something about Clive —his naturalness, his eagerness, his desire to learn— appealed to O'Conor, and they lunched for some weeks almost every day at a restaurant called Le Petit Lavenne. In his studio in the rue du Cherche-Midi near St.-Germain-des-Prés, O'Conor would play his violin to himself, paint, and talk freely to Clive. He was misanthropic and tended to be a solitary; yet to the young man he offered his keen eye for the new ways in which painters looked at subjects —and the new subjects they were finding.

O'Conor was a good resource, but "from Morrice I learned to enjoy Paris." Clive was a willing pupil. Morrice very early had convinced his Scottish father in Montreal that a career in art could be both profitable and congenial; he proved it to his parent in due course. His pictures were in demand and sold at high prices. Matisse would call him "the artist with the delicate eye." Morrice took the young Bell to the galleries and systematically showed him how an artist, an Impressionist, looked at the world. There was nothing of the academician in the Canadian. He was sensual and sensory; he painted brilliantly with his senses. He was not a draftsman. He simply applied color to canvas; and his scenes, whether in France or in Canada, had a magical quality of light and air, contrived out of small easy brush strokes with scintillating pigments. Clive characterized him much later as "first-rate—almost." That Morrice was a man of character we may judge by the way Arnold Bennett and Somerset Maugham both put him into their novels. He was a little bald Scot with sharp, wild eyes, and he had been abroad since the early 1890s. He had known Toulouse-Lautrec and Conder, Harpignies, Monet, Whistler, Bonnard, Vuillard, and later would be a friend of Matisse. His most serious failing was his love of absinthe, and he also drank whiskey to excess. He took Clive to cabarets and *cafés chantant;* they drank Pernod at the Café de la Paix; they delighted in the *cèrises au cognac* at the Concert Rouge. He revealed to Clive beauty on billboards and in shop windows; in itinerant musicians singing sentimental romances; in smart frocks and race meetings, and arias by Gounod; in penny steamers and sunsets and military uniforms. They often went to the Opéra Comique and the Comédie Française. Like O'Conor, Morrice had his musical instrument; he would play his melancholy flute in his studio "when he could keep his breath" and went often to concerts.

Donald Buchanan, his biographer, has described how the Canadian lived in a continual present. He could take delight in anything that met his eye. Arnold Bennett testifies to this in his journals. Morrice would say that he had seen an old woman when he got up that morning, and she was the finest he had ever seen. She was magnificent. He had to do a sketch of her. Then there was the neighborhood *marchand de quatre saisons*. His cry was beautiful. "I began to enjoy myself almost immediately I got out of bed. It is a privilege to be alive." Morrice knew Parisian out-of-the-way corners and always found something interesting in them. Clive visited his large studio on the Quai des Grands Augustins. From his windows Morrice had a splendid view of the Pont Henri Quatre and the towers of Notre Dame. He painted the busy quayside life of the Seine: pedestrians, boats, men browsing at the bookstalls, the sun on the buildings of the Île de la Cité. When he was absorbed in his painting, he would order up a plate lunch from La Pérouse, the gourmet restaurant nearby. In the studio and at the Chat Blanc, Clive met Morrice's mistress of many years, the plump Léa Cadoret. Morrice often disappeared; he would be off to Canada, to the south of France, to Tunis.

Sooner or later he would come back to his Léa. The Canadian used to tell how one day the Seine had washed over the quays, and for several days he had climbed into his studio on the first floor by means of a tall ladder. Remembering this companion of his first-found freedom, Clive said of him that he enjoyed beauty, the simple scenes and happenings of life, as some enjoy wine.

IV

What did Clive Bell learn during his year in Paris? We know that he did not try to paint. From the first he simply used his eyes, and they looked on paintings old and new—he saturated himself with the art in the Louvre and the art in the studios. He discovered earlier than most critics—that is, in the English-speaking world—the lessons of the Impressionists. Morrice gave him the play of his own sensibility in relation to what they saw and, in the galleries, in relation to the paintings of his contemporaries. O'Conor was more scholarly, more documented: he painted in the manner of Cézanne before many knew who Cézanne was. If O'Conor gave Clive theory out of Gauguin, Morrice gave Clive a sense of his sheer delight in shape and color. The Canadian was full of the poetry of things, of the poetry of painting. The young Cambridge graduate had led a comparatively rural life until now; he found himself in an expanding world of palettes and canvases; at the Luxembourg he saw the Caillebotte Collection, that great and permanent gathering in of Impressionist art made by a painter who had been an Impressionist himself. Clive was exposed to the first generation of Cézanne's disciples and to the work of the Fauves shortly before that name was bestowed on them. He looked closely at the "Douanier" Rousseau, much admired by O'Conor.

In his later writings we get occasional echoes of the doctrine he absorbed during his evenings at the Chat Blanc. The artists had been in danger of losing "the very stuff of which visual art is made—the direct emotional reaction to the visible universe." This had been the lesson of Morrice. And he described how the new school of this time had been determined to free artists from "utilitarian vision and the disastrous science of representation." This had in it something of O'Conor. For the rest Clive's later knowledge and expertise came from studies quite as serious as those of his peers at Cambridge. His art passion remained for them a jest: for in their memories there remained Clive, the young man of the hunt, arriving with gun and rod at the university. Sixty years later, Leonard Woolf wrote in his autobiography, "I never heard Clive talk about pictures at Cambridge." One suspects that Clive didn't talk about pictures because he did not have a receptive audience. Leonard and Lytton, as Leonard admitted, "set little or no store by pictures and painting." In his trivializing manner, Lytton waxed sarcastic when he got news of Bell in Paris. Clive, he wrote, was haunting the Latin Quarter, "where he discusses painting and vice with American artists and French models." But what Lytton in his flippancy overlooked was that Clive discussed art not with models but with finished artists. In his own recollections, Clive saw himself as a young rebel who had "a peculiar feeling for art" and an intelligence which could not be molded to the life of middle-class England. As he put it, "English civilization is so smug and hypocritical, so grossly philistine, and at bottom so brutal, that every first-rate Englishman necessarily becomes an outlaw." He later retouched this passaage in one of his essays and incorporated it into his book *Civilization*. One wonders indeed whether he would have written it had he not recognized that the world opened up to him by Paris in 1904 made him a kind of "outlaw" in his other world—the middle-class conformity of Wiltshire. All his life he would be *à cheval* between the two worlds, as he was now, between the pleasures of life and the constant craving of his intellect for serious employment.

Vanessa and Virginia Stephen, homeward bound from Italy in the spring of their father's death, looked up their brother Thoby's Cambridge friend when they reached Paris. They found him in Montparnasse. Clive was delighted to see them, and he did them all the honors of his newfound world. He seems to have taken them to his various haunts, including the Chat Blanc. Virginia met Roderick O'Conor, who later told Clive she was the only woman who had ever frightened him. "She put the fear of God in me," he said. One understands why. Virginia was on the edge of one of her worst breakdowns. We know that the sisters met Gerald Kelly, for Virginia wrote in one letter, "We stayed talking of Art, Sculpture and Music till 11:30. This was in the common café, while we smoked half a dozen cigarettes apiece. Kelly is an enthusiast." For Virginia it was "a real Bohemian party." Vanessa would always feel at home in Bohemia, and she relished the art talk and the Café de Versailles. For the first time she may have discovered a closer bond with the young and cocky Bell, whom she had met at Cambridge. He shared her passion for paintings.

Leonard in Ceylon

Leonard Woolf experienced a "gentle melancholy" when his undergraduate years ended. He felt himself in a "twilight experience." Most of his friends (save Strachey) had gone down, and life seemed solitary. He was not afraid of solitude, however, and he spent the long vacation in Cambridge reading for his Civil Service examinations. The summer was hot; it seemed to pass very slowly. Unlike his friends Clive, Thoby, or even Lytton, the end of Woolf's university years meant a return to old insecurities and anxieties. If, in Cambridge, he was received and welcomed for himself, he remained in those early Edwardian years a member of his race for whom opportunities were limited. Medicine? business? the rabbinate? These were unthinkable, although he had originally believed he might follow his father and become a barrister. This required more money than was available to him. He had earned a first in his classical Tripos, but his tutors were not wholly satisfied. In the second part, he took Greek philosophy and received a second. Then, unwisely, he read for his Civil Service exams at Cambridge instead of going to London to "cram" scientifically, as candidates usually did. The result was "a considerable shock." Accustomed to passing with honors and receiving prizes, Leonard Woolf perhaps did not realize how much he was in conflict about where to turn and how much the university retained a hold on him. He "resisted" the examinations and did poorly. He was not placed high enough to qualify for a good domestic position. He didn't want the Post Office or the Internal Revenue. But with characteristic decision, driven by a sense of desperation, he did not waste emotions in regret. "I applied for Ceylon," he wrote, "and I was high enough up on the list to get what I asked for."

When the news of his appointment as a Cadet in Britain's senior Crown Colony arrived, he was dismayed. Life had suddenly taken matters out of his own hands. "I was simply overwhelmed by circumstances," he wrote to G. E. Moore. It was like going into exile. He took his medical examination (and was complimented on having the only pair of clean feet that the medical officer had seen that morning). He took riding lessons. He bought himself tropical outfits at the Army and Navy Stores. He went to farewell dinners with his Cambridge friends. Desmond gave him the Oxford miniature Shakespeare and four volumes of Milton, so that he would carry into remote parts the immortal utterances of the English tongue. On his side he bought seventy handsome volumes of Voltaire in an eighteenth-century edition, in Baskerville. Thoby Stephen invited him to dine in Gordon Square, and Leonard had a renewed glimpse of the two graces, Vanessa and Virginia. Then his world suddenly became unreal; his Cambridge years came tumbling down about him. In October 1904, with his boxes of books and his wirehaired terrier Charles, he boarded a steamer at Tilbury Docks. He watched as it slid through the oily waters of the river toward the misty sea. The whole of his past life in Brighton, London, Cambridge vanished. He was making a complete break with his past.

II

He would later call this trip into the unknown "the voyage out," taking the title from his wife's first novel. "Out" remained a mystery for three weeks. Then it resolved itself into the Grand Oriental Hotel in Colombo, on the west coast of Ceylon, a city swarming with humans and flies, flitting rickshas, creaking bullock carts. He would remember the smell of dung, oil, fruits, spices, beasts, men. While his friend Lytton Strachey was writing in Cambridge about the East India Company's history on the Indian mainland, Leonard was a participant in the later history of British colonial rule on the large island of Ceylon. It had been settled long ago by Indian tribes and had seen Dutch and Portuguese colonial entrepreneurs. The island was half the size of England; it consisted of flat arid plains, fertile mountainous areas and fearsome silent jungles; there were great tropical downpours, long rainless periods, and a people struggling with old feudalisms and primitive superstitions. They often lived on subsistence farming. Leonard Woolf spent a few days of indoctrination at the Colombo headquarters and was assigned to northern Ceylon, to Jaffna, the flat desert area. As he walked out of the colonial headquarters, the hot sun struck his face as if it were a burning hand.

He went through a period of deep melancholy as he accustomed himself to the life of a young white sahib. His thin, spare twenty-four years, dressed in slightly oversize tropical suits, and his solid education, stood him in good stead among the Kiplingesque colonial officers. In Jaffna, which was a biggish town, he shared a bungalow with a fellow functionary and found himself accepted because he had all the gentlemanly appurtenances. He could play a good game of tennis; he had a decent hand at bridge; he got by tolerably well in a game of golf. They were impressed by his sporty green flannel collars. The work in the *kachcheri*, or general offices, was drudgery. Bit by bit Leonard felt as if a curious kind of greatness were being thrust upon him. He had the respect of everyone. He was sufficiently eccentric, with his dog, his Voltaires, his general sincere and serious manner, and he was unafraid of work. He aroused friendly interest. In fact he might have been accused of having too much zeal. To be a young white sahib was something not dreamed of in Putney; but to find himself also in his way a figure of ever-increasing authority, with the natives showing him deference, was something for which he had not been prepared.

His half-dozen years of continuous service took him from the dry and hot areas of Jaffna, which was Tamil and Hindu, to the mountain villages of Kandy, which was Buddhist; and finally to the jungles of Hambantota. He served thus in the north, the center and the south of the island. His early sense of righteousness and justice, his high seriousness, which was his inheritance, guided him at every step. He tried to deal justly with the natives, but he was stern and harsh. If he was not sure of himself, he could be sure of the law. As he acquired authority, he showed equal severity to his subordinates. He was always severe with himself.

He rose rapidly from Cadet to Office Assistant and finally to Assistant Government Agent at Hambantota, the youngest colonial officer to serve in that capacity. By the time he attained this position, he had mastered Tamil and Sinhalese so that he was in ready communication with the natives. If his father had been a highly trained barrister, Leonard now sat as a magistrate and district judge with minimal training for these duties. In Kandy there were mornings when he had to rise early and at the jail read the warrant of execution to the condemned; and then, facing the criminal or victim in the cool morning air, and looking at the beautiful distant hills, he would give the signal to the hangman for the "drop." He did this with great coolness. His facade was that of the implacable "ruler." But he shuddered inwardly, for he did not believe in capital punishment, especially applied to the crimes of impulse and passion which were mostly the case here. More painful still was the task of presiding at floggings. This brutality seemed to him greater than the hangings. He was always vigilant against manipulations and frauds. He checked the weight of the salt collections, an important government-controlled resource, and when he found cheating he suspended the workers, sometimes for six months, sometimes for a year. "The only check possible is by unexpected visits like this and short shrift to those responsible if the figures point to inaccuracy." So he recorded in the official diary at Hambantota.

He was less happy with the role imposed on him to investigate each case of cattle disease during a serious outbreak of rinderpest. The natives tended to leave their animals untethered. This spread the disease with great rapidity. Coercive measures had to be taken to enforce isolation of the healthy cattle. Leonard himself often shot the diseased animals. The natives only understood that they were being deprived of their beasts of burden. "I was part of the white man's machine, which they did not understand. I stood to them in the relation of God to his victims: I was issuing from on high orders to their village which seemed to them arbitrary." He invariably parted from the natives feeling guilty and dejected. He had "no more desire to be

God than one of his victims." But it was his job to play God, and sometimes this could be delightful. Once in Kandy he had to ride high into the hills and arrived at a village in a thunderstorm. Despite the weather, the villagers waited for him and brought him into the town with tom-toms and dancers. And then he had to stand in the rain like a prince or a king while each member of the crowd prostrated himself, touching the ground with his forehead. The young sahib, in his oversize suit and sun helmet, who looked as if he had scarcely left the playing fields of England, was once more made aware that he was "ruler of a subject people."

He did not conceal from himself the sense of pleasure this power gave him in spite of what his intellect told him about imperialism. He felt all the temptations of power and position; and he recognized that he was often "too severe and too opinionated." Some of his methods, he told himself, were "too ruthless"; they smacked too much of the "strong man." He was not impervious "to the flattery of being a top-dog liked by the under-dogs." But what saved him from outright arrogance and despotic acts was his long-learned air of humility, his other-worldly demeanor. He brought human sympathy to the endless hours he spent dealing with the castes and classes and individuals in their perpetual comings and goings in the *kachcheri*, transacting with them the most trivial or the most important business, helping them make decisions, "listening to their requests, their lies, their fears, their sorrows, their difficulties and disasters." What were these? we might ask. Leonard could enumerate them: a native needed a cart license or wanted to buy a piece of Crown Land, or he sought protection against a dishonest headman or contrived the ruin of a neighbor. Often Leonard found himself contemptuous of or irritated by these people; and he wondered how he—a European intellectual—could settle the ways of life of a primitive people driven by primary necessities. Leonard accepted the primitive nature and sordid lives of the people, which he could hardly romanticize or sentimentalize. He liked their earthiness, their strange mixture of direct-ness and deviousness, of cunning and stupidity, of cruelty and kindness. They lived so close to the jungle (except in the Europeanized towns) that they retained "something of the litheness and beauty of jungle animals." The Sinhalese he found had supple and subtle minds. And then Leonard was attuned to their melancholy and their fatalism, which he found "beautiful and sympathetic." He could say in later years that few things had given him more pleasure, once he had learned Sinhalese, than to sit under a tree in a village and discuss with the villagers their interminable disputes and grievances. This feeling Leonard passionately documented in *The Village in the Jungle*, the novel he wrote when he returned to the heart of the empire.

III

As time passed he became absorbed in the multiple experiences of the life of the people and the responsibilities of the administration. There were periods when his days were routine and monotonous. On such days he kept up some of his correspondence, particularly with Lytton Strachey, distilling the essence of his work for the amusement of Cambridge and London. He wrote: "In Kandy I worked about ten hours a day and played in tennis tournaments and went to intolerably dull dinners and duller dances and played bridge and drank and became the bosom friend of the planters. So as a reward a month ago they sent me here as Assistant Government Agent." He told how he was on his own in about 1,000 square miles of territory with 100,000 people, "and I am supposed to be very 'young' to have got it." He then described the Residency in which he lived. He was almost the only European in the area. The house, probably built during the Dutch period, had walls of astonishing thickness. There was an enormously broad veranda and vast high rooms. Day and night he could hear the sea "thundering away almost at the gates of the compound, which is vast with nothing in it but sand and three stunted trees and is surrounded by a wall which the wind, which blows here unceasingly, has blown into ruins." Thus Leonard to Lytton when he had attained his highest post. And he also wrote: "One changes inside too. . . . I have no connection with yesterday: I do not recognize it nor myself of it. I am of and in today moulded and marked by innumerable things which have never touched you and when

I come back and find you all the same, someone will say quite truly 'Really they seem to be interested in none of these things.'" He was right. How could one convey the complexity of Leonard's experiences? Lytton characteristically translated such a letter into the terse communication that Woolf was "absolute lord there of a million blacks." What Lytton did not report were the hours of despondency Leonard experienced, hours during which at rare moments he was on the verge of suicide. In 1906, "I took out my gun the other night, made my will, and prepared to shoot myself." But like Tolstoy he could put the gun aside after a while. He saw no future: "I shall live and die in these appalling countries now."

Of Leonard Woolf's relations with women during his years in Ceylon we know little. There were certain young European women who eyed him as a prospective husband, but he tended to be aloof, a natural solitary: and these women were not sufficiently lovable. There were others with whom he spent agreeable hours in the limited social circles of Jaffna and Kandy. He felt himself distant from them; he did not flirt easily. He breaks his reticence in his memoirs only once to describe how, riding on horseback down a street in Jaffna, he could see over the veranda blinds, and on one evening, "thinking of nothing in particular, riding slowly, relaxed, a little melancholy," he exchanged smiles with a native girl and a few minutes later was shouted at by a little boy who ran after him, "Sah! Sah! That young girl ask she come to your bungalow tonight." Woolf dropped his caution sufficiently to say yes "and she came and spent the night." This was fairly early in his stay in Ceylon. From his other remarks one judges that this was his first experience of a woman, and he later found out (as he might have judged by her signal) that she was well known in the town for her promiscuities. Leonard Woolf, who was a man of deep passion, successfully sublimated his sexual drives in his work, yet periodically he allowed himself a casual adventure such as this one.

In one of his *Tales of the East*, written years later, a group of whites in a colony like Ceylon discuss sex and one character says, "A boy kisses a girl in the moonlight and you call it love and poetry and romance. But you know as well as I do it isn't. It's just a flicker of the body, it will be cold dead, this time next year." For Leonard, this was what sex was during this period of his exile. He did not fall in love; he simply allowed himself an occasional "flicker of the body." His description of a children's brothel in this story, to which a hitherto frigid English visitor is conducted, is authentic enough; and we may be sure that whatever Leonard's participation in the free Eastern sexual life of the towns, he returned to his sense of reality. The "flicker" was not "the real, the mysterious thing" which goes by the name of love. The rest of his brief tale is very much like a Graham Greene novel in which the inhibited traveling Englishman finds himself attached to a young native girl and lives with her until he realizes that beyond the language of the body, there can be no communication. In Ceylon, carnal love sufficed for Leonard Woolf. As he wrote to Lytton, "I am beginning to think it is always degrad[ing] being in love: after all ninety-nine one hundredths of it is always the desire to copulate."

IV

If one searches the record of Leonard Woolf's Ceylonese years, one finds that the jungle represented the essence of his experience. His life in Ceylon itself had a closed-in jungle quality. It was chaos, violence, nature in full command; and as a constructive order-seeking man he had to make his peace with it, use it, and recognize its supremacy. He claimed that in Ceylon, the jungle aiding, he acquired a taste for solitude, "not for the permanent solitude of the hermit, or even for long periods of it, but for interludes of complete isolation. Even today, when evening falls and the door is shut in the street or in the village, and all life except my own and my dog's and my cat's is for the moment excluded, and for the moment there is cessation of the incessant fret and interruption of other people and outside existence, I enjoy the wordless and soundless meditation and the savour of one's own unhurried existence, and psychologically I am almost back in the empty silent Residencies of Mannar and Hambantota or camping in the thick uninhabited jungles." This was the more stoical side of Leonard.

Qualified acceptance of isolation led to his sympathy for Buddhism, which he explored when he learned Sinhalese. If one had to have a religion, he felt, Buddhism was superior to all others. He learned his Sinhalese from a Buddhist priest. Buddhism was for him more a philosophy than a religion, a metaphysic which eliminated God and gods, "a code of conduct civilized, austere, springing ultimately from a profound pessimism." It was also "a civilized and a humane dream of considerable beauty: and it eliminated most of the crude theological nonsense" which encrusted other religions. He liked the way in which Buddhists, when they withdrew into isolation, did so not for penance but simply to throw off worldliness. These feelings did not prevent Leonard from seeing the corruptions of Buddhism and of its priesthood whenever he encountered them.

Leonard Woolf's ability to face isolation stood him in good stead in his jungle experiences. In spite of his love of animals, he became a hunter in the later stages of his Ceylon life to supplement his own meager fare and in this way perhaps for the first time understood what hunting meant in the life of Clive Bell or Thoby Stephen: the use of his eyes in the thick impersonal wood and the presence of a predatory world—of life preying on life—in an endless struggle for existence. For Leonard the jungle became a person: it was himself versus this person, himself versus Ceylon—a battle of wits and endurance, of brain over instinct. The jungle was a cruel and dangerous place. Leonard avowed himself a coward; he knew he was afraid of it, yet he could not keep away from it. The challenge— the love-hate—was too strong. For the jungle was the symbolic embodiment of the world as Leonard knew it. "I liked the complete solitude and silence and every now and again the noises which break the jungle's silence and which as one learns its ways, tells one of the comings and goings around one."

On one occasion he heard a most unnatural horrible noise, a kind of sound as of a struggle and anguish. He thought it might be a roaring bear, but what he found in swampy water was a crocodile, which he shot to put it out of its agony. He then discovered that it was toothless with age and had swallowed a tortoise on which it had been choking to death. Virginia Woolf would absorb this bit of

Leonard's history in *Between the Acts* and describe a snake choking on a frog that had to be put out of its misery. On another occasion Leonard recorded in the official diaries (and later in his memoirs) the spectacle of two great elephants locked in terrible combat, their collisions creating unearthly reverberations. But aside from the violence, Leonard found many moments of surprising beauty in the jungle—five or six dazzling peacocks suddenly in a clearing, or a superb sambar deer with its antlers silhouetted against the sky. Once, when he set out to shoot a preying leopard, he encountered the animal staring straight into his eyes, eyes ferocious and beautiful: he was for a moment carried away and he did not think of shooting. As a lover of animals he was never tired of seeing them in their freedom and danger. Jungle, and jungle life, were ugly and beautiful, horrible and cruel.

He lost his way twice. Both experiences were terrifying. On one occasion he was saved by the sounds of his pony in the distance, which gave him his direction. His second experience occurred at twilight. There had been rain; an overcast sky deprived him of his bearings. He had not marked his trail. He had to face an entire night's wait for the sunrise. The jungle was soaking wet. He lit a fire with his last match and spent half the night gathering wood to keep the protective flames high enough. Under this protection he stayed up until about three. Then, taking direction from some stars that had appeared, he started out; but he was soon in a thickness of wood and thorns and could go no further. Nor could he turn back. He was too far from his fire, which he could no longer see; and in this blackness he decided there was nothing to do but curl up and go to sleep. Sleep finally overcame fright. He was awakened by the sun and in an hour had found his way out.

This experience perhaps contained within it the very essence of Leonard Woolf's long adventure in the world of colony and Empire far from the securities of civilization. He was living in a land of fevers, ringworm, dysentery, a merciless climate. His jungle adventures showed his tenacity and the ultimate courage that surmounted despair, fear and suicidal loneliness. In *The Village in the Jungle* he would describe the life of the natives, ever prey to terror, personifying it in terms of spirits and devils, the devil from the bush. "All jungles are evil," wrote Leonard Woolf. In life man was driven to conquer this evil, knowing all the while that it is unconquerable, that it resides in the depths of the primitive Self. That was the supreme life force, and the existential center of Leonard Woolf's philosophy.

Lytton in Cambridge

Lytton Strachey lingered in Cambridge for more than two years after his friends moved out into the world. Clive had gone to Paris and then settled in London. Leonard was beyond the seas. Thoby was reading law and living with his sisters in Gordon Square. Lytton alone, of the comrades who had enjoyed three years of irresponsible happiness amid cloisters "consecrated to poetry and common sense," had not budged. He did not want to budge. And yet his doom had been brought home to him in 1902 when he received a second in his historical Tripos. An honorable grade, but inadequate to one who aspired to the heights of academe. "I am restless, intolerably restless, and Cambridge is the only place I never wanted to leave though I suffer there more than anywhere else," he wrote. He had expected to go on to triumphs of the pen and the mind—and a Fellowship at Trinity—so that he might devote his life to new generations of young males. He would also continue in the role he was establishing for himself among the Apostles, as of some plumaged Eminence arranging the fates of the Elect. Instead, there loomed for him only the grayness of Lancaster Gate, life among some of his siblings, under the presiding mother. He had no vision of a career other than Cambridge. "We are the mysterious priests of a new and amazing civilization," he said. His hopes of becoming a High Priest were now gone.

Still, he had won a Chancellor's Medal for an ode; he had always displayed a bright mind, and he consoled himself that he might try again: perhaps he would make a show of brilliance that would override his failure; he might dazzle the examiners and still win the place he cherished. He stayed on in his old rooms, plunging himself more than ever into the cloistered yet for him passionate life of Cambridge and (as we have seen) its "sad atmosphere of paradox and pederasty." An enchanting sadness! He found a new lease on life, after his intimates had left, in his friendship with Maynard Keynes (three years younger), who had a keen mind, a vigilant attacking imagination. This was, however, a troubled friendship. It seemed to veer from love to betrayal. Lytton felt that Keynes had "a curious typewriter-intellect," yet he could be "so oddly and unexpectedly emotional." With Woolf gone, Keynes seemed to combine for Lytton both the qualities of a younger brother and a father-confessor. Lytton confided his loves to Keynes, not realizing how ruthless the future economist could be—that is, intellectually and actively ruthless. The political Lytton, a politician of gossip and character, was not an adept in the schools of the practical and "functional." He would feel himself deceived by Keynes, who on his side simply reached out for whatever he wanted with less romanticism—and much more realism—than did Strachey. Lytton could dissolve in tears and slide into depression when one of his beloved boys was out of sorts or met with some slight accident. How could he know that Keynes had already won the love of this very boy from under his very nose? Tears of empathy often had to become tears of frustration. Yet power admires power. Lytton and Maynard could separate in hurt and resolve their quarrels in guarded affection.

Lytton floundered; Keynes moved with directness and calm reason. "I find Economics increasingly satisfactory, and I think I am rather good at it. I want to manage a railway or organize a Trust. . . . It is so easy and fascinating to master the principles of these things." This must have seemed disconcerting to Lytton, who was struggling for mastery not of principles but of human nature. His friends (so Desmond MacCarthy said) were for him "diagrams of the human species." His tastes were classical. He did not care how railways were managed or trusts organized. Keynes, he wrote, "doesn't seem to be in anything aesthetic, though his taste is good." In any gambit, Keynes with his probing mind and his natural enthusiasm—whether in art or economics—could outplay Lytton. All Lytton could do was to complain that his ambiguous confidant was "lascivious without lust . . . an Apostle without tears." And then Keynes inspired so little pity. "It's only when he's shattered by a crisis that I seem to be able to care for him." There could be no true basis for conciliation: Keynes's mind was sharp and organized; Lytton's was literary and inclined to wallow in the mazes of love. They had one thing in common: they were reformers disguised as rebels. They would have liked to reform the Establishment. But they also loved all that ministered to the life they were leading; therefore, they really loved the sustaining Establishment. Keynes's way of rebellion lay in dreams of reorganization. Lytton's was to laugh at the past and to chide the present from a high seat of historical wisdom and orderly thought.

II

Lytton knew that Cambridge could never be all "bed and boys," however much he pretended it might. In 1903, when he was wavering about his career, he decided to apply for a Civil Service job in the Education Department. His old mentor Walter Raleigh gave him an extravagant letter praising the very things that were shaky in Lytton—tact, judgment and his temper, which Raleigh said was "reasonable and gentle." These qualitites did not somehow describe the loosely hung Lytton (with his thin arms and legs and high voice), whose wit was aggressive and whose sallies could be insulting. A more tactful tutor at Cambridge emphasized his wide culture, his literary gifts, the vein of originality in his writing. The Civil Service was not convinced. Lytton failed again.

What to do? Lytton decided to risk everything. A surge of confidence made him believe that his talents could outweigh his unhappy scholastic record. He would write a book-length dissertation on the Strachey family hero, Warren Hastings. The Stracheys, after all, were rooted in India. Sir Henry Strachey, born in 1736, had been secretary to Clive of India and had written a compelling narrative on the mutiny of the officers in Bengal. There had also been an Edward Strachey who had known India intimately; and Lytton's father, the retired general, had served there with distinction. His uncle, Sir John, had in 1892 published a work on Warren Hastings and the Rohilla War. Lytton had written an earlier essay on Hastings. He had seen him as a "superman" in his devotion to the public welfare. The essay had been praised, but it did not win the prize he sought. Here was "one of the most enthralling and stupendous interludes in English history," and it had been left untouched by English historians. Macaulay had damned Hastings with Olympian hyperbole; James Mill had simply not looked into all the documents. Lytton was a sufficiently alert researcher, and assiduous reader, to know that he had abundant material: nine volumes of minutes of the impeachment proceedings, secret papers in the Indian Office, Hastings's own private and public correspondence in the British Museum. He would refute Mill. He would boldly correct Macaulay. He would vindicate Hastings. Most of all, he would vindicate Lytton Strachey.

It is possible to glimpse a few of the unconscious promptings that led Lytton Strachey into the labyrinths of his hero, upon whom Edmund Burke and others had visited the crimes of the East India Company, in the late eighteenth century, during seven years of proceedings in the House of Lords. Hastings had finally won an acquittal, and Lytton hoped he too would win an acquittal from the opprobrium of his second-class standing at Cambridge. It is an old psychological truth that historians write histories because in some way they read themselves into historic happenings, and the lives of history's villains and heroes. Indeed, the major struggle of a historian is to disengage himself from his subject and view the past with dispassion. Lytton could hardly undertake the entire history of Warren Hastings. He would focus on the one side-drama that he felt had never been sufficiently recorded. This was the time when, in the kingdom of Oudh, Hastings sought money from one of the leaders and two matriarchs —the Begums, grandmother and mother of the Grand Vizier. In Indian history, Lytton Strachey found those figures that would always fascinate him and be the subject of his ironies: the fallible British leader, military, political or religious, and the powerful matriarch—Florence Nightingale, Victoria, or Queen Elizabeth. And human vanity, human folly. He would be the wise historian who interprets, justifies, vindicates, and explains. As Bertrand Russell once said, Lytton "liked to appear lordly in his attitude towards human affairs."

He filled four hundred foolscap pages with his saga of "Warren Hastings, Chet Sing and the Begums of Oudh." It was a story of Hastings's need for money to keep the East India Company's army equipped and in control of a rebellious India and of his demand for support from the kingdom of Oudh. There followed the insurrection of the Vizier, Chet Sing, with the complicity of the two Begums, who sat upon the State treasury with maternal and matriarchal power. The details of that absorbing historical incident need not be rehearsed here. Suffice it to say that Lytton worked with a certain passion and involvement. He quoted large extracts from documents which earlier historians had passed over. At the beginning he could tell Maynard, "You don't know how superb one feels—writing a real book, with real chapters." Within the pages of the dissertation, the dynamic of his own struggle for power, recognition, defiance was lived out. Cambridge was his India; the Begums sat on the State treasury as Lady Strachey omnipotently presided over Lancaster Gate. Warren Hastings's impeachers were the dons for whom Lytton was reliving a brilliant chapter in colonial administration. And, to sustain his romantic mind, there were treacherous eunuchs belonging to the Begum, who had to be punished: it was a kind of Oriental sexuality, corruption, opulence that appealed to his own love of the exotic. He struggled alternately between obsessive work and a profound resistance. Completion would confront him with judgment. To Keynes and to Woolf he spoke of his nervousness and his periodic physical symptoms. What he aimed at was a high literary style. He said in his ultimate preface that Macaulay's view of Hastings would inevitably prevail "until there arrives a greater master of the art of writing who will choose to invest the facts of Indian history with the glamour of literature, and make the truth more attractive than even history itself." The time would come when Lytton Strachey would invest historical figures with such glamour. But his examiners at Cambridge were dispassionate and factual; they read with critical eyes. The verdict came soon enough. He had failed once again.

III

His examiners, in their critique, gave Lytton an extraordinary lesson in the writing of history, which he badly needed. What they told him applied particularly to biography. Lytton had quoted his documents too abundantly to prove his case; he had not recognized that often in quotation there could be material irrelevant to the argument being pursued. If he had aspired to literary writing, he had, in other words, blocked his "story line" with indigestible documentary extracts. Subordinate matter intruded at every turn. We can read in this verdict the supreme lesson of Cambridge that would light up Lytton's work in later years. Here was an emphasis upon that summary, brevity, relevance which he made his own in his ultimate works. He himself would, in his own vigorous rhetoric, echo his examiners and give their criticisms universality in the manifesto to *Eminent Victorians*. In 1905, however, he faced defeat; it had been heaped upon him. Only time—several years—would reveal to him the uses of adversity.

Lytton was finally forced to accept the reality. His adopted Cambridge-Mother had cast him out. "My misery is complete." And the prodigal son was received again by his own mother, the mother of Lancaster Gate. Foreign parts did not beckon. The Civil Service seemed closed—or at any rate he had not tried, after his single attempt. He described himself as "dejected, uncouth, unsuccessful," and he bowed to the inevitable—a bed-sitting room in the family house "with a folding bed, and all my books ranged in two bookshelves." He added to Leonard Woolf in far-off Ceylon, "It's pretty dreary, and when I'm to do any work, heaven alone knows." He was desperately homesick—"but for what home?" "Home" was Cambridge, and however much he congratulated himself in later years that his had been a fortunate fall, the truth was that academe would have suited him perfectly. His journey into exile now was the journey of Adam and of Dante. He had had his Paradise. Lancaster Gate was Purgatory. "After Cambridge, blank, blank, blank," he wrote to Leonard Woolf.

Bloomsbury: First Phase

They were dispersed—the "originals" of Trinity—the general's son who had been ducked in the fountain; the serious young Jew from Putney; the young sportsman from Wiltshire; their aristocratic Kensington friend. The fledgling years had blown away with the Cambridge dawns. Poetry was dethroned. The demanding world spoke only of careers. The late nights in the May term, the walks through the Cloisters of Neville's Court in Trinity to the "backs," the ghostly willows, the soaring song of innumerable nightingales were now memories. They had been students and chanted the poetry of transitory things, the sentimental-melancholy-romantic of the "Hymn to Proserpine."

> Thou hast conquered, O pale Galilean; the world
>   has grown gray from thy breath;
> We have drunken of things Lethean, and fed on the
>   fullness of death.

Cambridge, the willows, the nightingales . . . *the glass of the years is brittle,* Swinburne sang; *the world is not sweet in the end.* London, after the sweet years, the untried years, seemed gray and brittle. Leonard was in the Ceylon jungles; Clive, after Paris, was agreeably living in elegant rooms in the Temple; Lytton's world—Swinburne had also said it—was *a sea without shore.* Even Maynard, youngest of the Apostles, child of "organization" and order, was being asked which of his multiple passions counted for a lifework. He too now debated the second Tripos versus the Civil Service. And monolithic Thoby, "the Goth," who of all his fellows had truly fed—and bitterly—*on the fullness of death,* longed for his friends and, living in Gordon Square with his comely sisters, mused on the evanescent years. He would (he decided) build a little Cambridge—why not?—in Bloomsbury. On Thursday evenings, he announced, he would be at home at No. 46. They would turn back the calendar; repeat old stories; read poetry; laugh with the old laughter—and not only the four we have mentioned, but Saxon Sydney-Turner, mathematician-musician, now a clerk (how dismal!) in the Estates Duty Office; or Desmond MacCarthy, the older Apostle, now a critic, said to be deeply in love with a young girl who had grown up at Eton. Thoby summoned his friends; they would shore up the still-fresh memories from the middle distance of their twenties.

Thoby planned his Thursdays at first quite automatically as an all-male reunion. That was the way it had been in Cambridge. He probably gave no thought to the female figures in the Gordon Square landscape. Vanessa was positive about this in later years. She and Virginia were "not included in the arrangement." It was only later that the very serious young men recognized that the little Cambridge-in-Bloomsbury not only had a new setting, but was destined to be "co-educational." The pipe-smoking young men, carrying their Cantabrigian importance in mien and stance, came into No. 46 expecting a drawing room that would melt into Thoby's or Lytton's Cambridge rooms, and in it they found not only Thoby but his sisters. There the young women were. There was nothing more to be said about it. The coalescence of Bloomsbury and Cambridge began in a strange, awkward silence and a period of "adjustment." We must remind ourselves that the awkward conjunction of the sexes was very real to the Victorians and the Edwardians. And also, as Virginia put it, "It never struck me that the abstractness, the simplicity which had been so great a relief after Hyde Park Gate were largely due to the fact that the majority of young men who came there were not attracted by young women."

II

The shy young women had, for the most part, been accustomed to chaperons and a hothouse social life in Kensington. Their Duckworth half brothers had unsuccessfully sought to draw them into the parties and balls of Mayfair. These had proved a bore, and Vanessa and Virginia, as we have seen, had resisted them. Behind Virginia's dream-like eyes, and in her wilted-flower look, there resided a tiger cat, with a quick verbal pounce. The animal growled inwardly as the Cambridge young arrived—"hesitatingly, self-effacingly," and, said Virginia, "folded themselves up quietly in the corners of sofas." No conversational openings seemed good enough. They were silent. They puffed at their pipes. Saxon Sydney-Turner took his pipe out of his mouth as if to speak—and put it back into his mouth without having spoken. This tergiversation put Virginia in a rage. "Oh women are my line and not these inanimate creatures!" she exploded to Violet. She was forgetting that men were (for some of them) *their* line quite as much as women were hers.

It was Saxon who will go down in history as the "in-augurating" guest of Bloomsbury. On the first Thursday he was the sole visitor. He sat in silence most of the evening (we are told), although we must remind ourselves that Virginia tended to sketch these memories as caricature. After the silent inhibited evening, she asked Thoby why he had always considered Saxon a kind of "genius." Thoby answered: "If you mean wit, then no, he is not witty! but he is truthful, and if he is silent it is because he is careful to speak the truth." Truth was then a major Cambridge preoccupation. Virginia thanked God that she had been educated at home. But she protested the discrimination. It seemed that at Cambridge "the standard of what was worth saying had risen so high that it was better not to break it unworthily." They had sat all evening and looked at the floor. Vanessa took a less militant view. "The young men were perhaps not clear enough in their own heads"; but they didn't mind "trying to get them clearer by discussion with young women who might possibly see things from a different angle." Virginia, less aware of the needs of the young men, winced at the Cantabrigian condescensions. "How I hate intellect!" And, describing some dons, she saw only "brains floating like so many sea anemones, nor have they shape or colour. They are bloodless." Clive, however, livened up the proceedings as attendance at the Thursday evenings grew. He had a way of suggesting subjects. He possessed social generosity and heterosexuality. Desmond MacCarthy could take over all the conversation when he was in the room; he was a walking monologue. Lytton Strachey was unpredictable. He could fall into devastating silences. But also, Vanessa said, "he might place some remark in his high voice which was incredibly amusing—or shattering!" Then again he might not. It depended on how he felt.

The first phase of Bloomsbury, with women acting as a dam to the free flow of male talk, tended to be abstract and philosophical. Saxon told nothing but the truth; and then beside the Truth there were "the Good" and "the Beautiful" —and G. E. Moore's exploration of all three in the *Principia*. Vanessa uttered the word "beautiful." She was talking about some pictures. One of the very serious young men lifted his head—slowly—and with a deliberate and thoughtful voice said, "It depends what you mean by beauty." The pictures were forgotten. Virginia spoke of "atmosphere" in literature. What did she mean? They sat in a circle. At the end of the questions and abstractions, Saxon finally removed his pipe. This time he spoke. He was a summarizer. Virginia said, "The marvellous edifice was complete, one could stumble off to bed feeling that something important had happened." And Virginia added, "It had been proved that beauty was—or beauty was not—for I have never been quite sure which—part of a picture."

Virginia was mischievous; she mocked; her sarcasm was encased in Elizabethan fancy. Outside her letters, we can read her description of a Thursday "at home" in the disguises of fiction. In *Night and Day* she has a meeting of "a society for the free discussion of everything. . . . They were all young and some of them seemed to make a protest by their hair and dress, and something sombre and truculent in the expression of their faces." The talk was confined to groups; it was spasmodic, "and muttered in undertones as if the speakers were suspicious of their fellow-guests." A paper is delivered full of quotations—"the supreme pearls of literature." There is a discussion. A speaker tries "as with an ill-balanced axe . . . to hew out his conception of art a little more clearly." Vanessa wrote: "We seemed to be a company of the young, all free, all beginning life in new surroundings, without elders to whom we had to account in any way for our doings or behavior, and this was not then common in a mixed company of our class."

Old family friends heard that Thoby and his sisters were having informal "mixed" gatherings in their own home. Was it true, they asked, that the young women "really sat up talking to young men till all hours of the night"? What did they talk about? It would have been hard to explain to these disapproving elders that the talk was all about "the Good" and "the Beautiful," the Truth and the philosophy of G. E. Moore—with long intervals of meditation in between. They got echoes of the disapproval. "Deplorable! Deplorable!" Henry James said to the good Fanny Prothero, his neighbor in Rye, who lived in Bedford Square when she was in town. Remembering how Vanessa and Virginia had seemed like vestal virgins attending their old father, James added: "How could Vanessa and Virginia have picked up such friends? How could Leslie's daughters have taken up with young men like that?" When he met some of the young men, he wasn't happy. For the vocal Clive, in particular, he developed an active antipathy. He spoke of the unpleasant "little image." "Tell Virginia—tell her—how sorry I am that the inevitabilities of life should have made it possible even for a moment that I would allow any child of her father's to swim out of my ken." There was no way of bridging the generation gap.

III

Two pages of manuscript which survived among Virginia's papers reveal her early resentments. She refused to take the university young as seriously as they took themselves. These pages seem to have been planned as a review of a chapbook of verse assembled by Clive Bell. It contained stanzas by the Cambridge friends—Lytton, Leonard, Clive himself. With elegant classicism they invoked one of the ancient Graces and called the book *Euphrosyne*. Virginia's unpublished review is a long chuckle, a series of as yet unskilled sarcasms. The verses (she remarked) dealt with "Love & Death & Cats, & Duchesses, as other poets have sung before, and may, unless the race is extinct, sing yet again." These young men, said Virginia, used words like "supreme" or "astounding" for English writers one loved (but they damned them if someone else loved them). They were rather a melancholy company. They had no tolerance for anyone outside their group. They had had the privileges of Oxbridge denied womankind, and they behaved as though during their college years "some awful communication had been made to them." They were burdened "with a secret too dreadful to impart." Virginia referred to "S.T., and G.L.S., and C.B., and W.L."; and there were, she added, others too, "if I chose to continue the dismal catalogue." Without expanding the catalog, we can expand the initials—Sidney-Turner, Giles Lytton Strachey, Clive Bell and Walter Lamb, a Cambridge don, later secretary of the Royal Academy. Virginia rejoiced that women had been spared "the omniscience, the early satiety, the melancholy self-satisfaction" induced in the males by the privileges of Oxbridge. In one denunciatory sentence Virginia Stephen said that the young men expressed "for the most part a serene and universal ignorance; which does not disqualify them, however, to pronounce the opinions of others absurd."

Time and propinquity thawed Virginia out. By early spring 1905, we find her writing in her diary, "Sydney-Turner and Strachey came after dinner and we talked till twelve." Three days later, "Home and found Bell and we talked about the nature of good till almost one." In May, "Our evening: gay Bell, D. MacCarthy." To Violet she wrote, "We have our Thursday evenings—and talk a great deal about style." Long afterward she wrote: "These Thursday evening parties, were, as far as I am concerned, the germ from which sprang all that has since come to be called—in newspapers, in novels, in Germany, in France—even, I daresay, in Turkey and Timbuktu—by the name of Bloomsbury. They deserve to be recorded and described. Yet how difficult—how impossible. Talk—even the talk which had such tremendous results upon the lives and characters of the two Miss Stephens—even talk of this interest and importance is as elusive as smoke. It flies up the chimney and is gone."

Which is why Bloomsbury has come down to us confusedly, a series of telescoped evenings and fragmentary phrases. Its development was quite distinct. The first phase of 1905–6 was a "getting-acquainted" phase. Everything was tentative; freedom of talk between young men and young women of their class could come only gradually. What particularly distinguished the first from the latter was that the bright young men were still abstract, still dewy-minded, still close to the *Principia*. The word "sex" was never mentioned.

IV

The Thursday evenings were well established by the summer of 1905, when the four Stephens decided they would go to Cornwall. This was a nostalgic return to the summers of their childhood and youth. They took ample quarters and invited their friends, including some of the Thursday regulars. By this time Virginia's fears that there would develop a Jane Austen atmosphere—that Thoby might be snatched by some female, or that Vanessa might be wooed by a predatory male—began to take on reality. From the first, Clive had liked Vanessa: they shared a great interest in modern art. Vanessa was under the impression that Clive considered her "rather stupid and illiterate," so much did she respect his intelligence and undervalue her own. Clive had more frequent access to Gordon Square than most of the others did. He was, after all, a close friend of Thoby's. He was charming and clever and ranging in his aesthetic interests. Vanessa liked him. There were increasing signs that sooner or later he would be an earnest and ardent suitor.

The Stephens settled into the familiar landscape and even stole over to Talland House, where so much of their family life had been spent—the summer villa Virginia would place at the center of *To the Lighthouse*. "We have had visitors for the last four weeks," wrote Virginia. The latest were Saxon Sydney-Turner and his economist friend Ralph Hawtrey. "They sit silent, absolutely silent, all the time; occasionally they escape to a corner and chuckle over a Latin joke. Perhaps they are falling in love with Nessa; who knows? It would be a silent and very learned process." There was nothing silent or learned, however, when Clive Bell came to visit. "We seem to live in a perpetual love-

the fullness of time she would be the founder of Bloomsbury's "Memoir Club," perhaps the most important club of the many Bloomsbury created for its own diversion. Desmond, handsome, filled with the poetry of love and literature, married Molly on 10 July 1906. The MacCarthys settled first on a farm in Suffolk and later lived in Chelsea. There were times when Desmond said, "My happiness is more than I can bear." He used to rub his eyes quite suddenly with both hands, "rather like a fly that seems to be vigorously washing its face," said Molly. He would not always be happy; but through joy and tribulation he never lost his gifted talk in the drawing rooms of London. He and Molly reared a family, and the years passed in a dream of the great novel Desmond would write—the novel of the future, as it were. While he waited for leisure and inspiration, there were the pleasantest of London firesides—and not least the pleasantness and fascination of Bloomsbury itself.

Thoby

Late in the autumn of 1906 the four Stephens took a long-planned trip to the Continent. Thoby and Adrian left earlier and rode on horseback through Montenegro and then into Greece. Here they met their sisters, who had come out with Violet Dickinson. They toured the cherished sites of their Greek studies. One may read Virginia's impressions of this tour in *Jacob's Room*. Vanessa was ill during a great part of the journey, and Violet Dickinson nursed her in Athens. She was said to have "appendicitis," a diagnosis of that time which probably meant a bad and continuing gastrointestinal upset. She improved sufficiently for the young women to go to Constantinople while their brothers returned to London. But in Turkey, Vanessa became ill again, and the three women abandoned all their plans for further travel.

Back in Gordon Square, they discovered Thoby in bed with a high fever. Vanessa soon began to improve, but Violet Dickinson came down with typhoid at her home. Virginia and Adrian alone seemed untouched by the trip. Virginia took command of Gordon Square and its two invalids. Nurses were brought in; distinguished doctors were called. One of Virginia's letters to Violet speaks of "drains and boilers, carbolic and bedpans. . . . I discuss enemas at afternoon tea with Clive." Clive came daily out of concern for his love, Vanessa, and his friend Thoby.

From the first, in the case of Thoby, the doctors made a ghastly mistake. His temperature continued to be high, and he was miserably ill. They treated him for malaria. It was one of the nurses who ventured the opinion that Thoby had typhoid fever; and the doctors had grimly to acquiesce. By the end of the third week they spoke of "some perforation" and thought of surgery. But it was too late. The massive, monolithic, handsome and beloved brother of Vanessa and Virginia sank into death on 20 November 1906, with the same simplicity as he had lived. "Thoby was splendid to the end," Virginia later said, "and his life was perfect." When Lytton heard the news, he wrote to Maynard Keynes, "I am stunned. The loss is too great, and seems to have taken what is best from life." To Vanessa, recovering from her illness, and to Virginia, it seemed as if the blight of Hyde Park Gate had descended on Gordon Square. Everyone had predicted that "the Goth" would live to be eighty—and have a splendid career. The last thing the sisters could believe was that in civilized London their brother should die of the illness from which Violet Dickinson was now comfortably recovering. He had picked up his typhoid somewhere in Montenegro or in Greece—a terrible price to pay for a holiday. Julia, Stella, Leslie—and now Thoby! Once again—and for the fourth time—the surviving Stephens were face to face with profound personal grief. Between Vanessa and Virginia, their brother Thoby had stood like some Greek god. Now there was a horrible emptiness.

Two days after Thoby's death, Clive came to see Vanessa. Love and death melted together. Vanessa reached out to Clive to fill the void. She told him that she would marry him.

On the other side of the world, Leonard Woolf woke up one day with a bad headache. At breakfast, in his bungalow, facing a thick rice pancake called a "hopper," on which sat a greasy fried egg, he "felt as if my last moment had come." His fellow officer, who lived with him, took his temperature. It was extremely high. There was no hospital in Jaffna, nor was there a doctor. The officer rode to a mission six miles away and brought back the American doctor who was in charge. In that climate, Leonard might have had malaria, but the doctor was very definite that it was typhoid. He took him to the mission and lodged him in a shack at the rear of the hospital. Ceylonese caste systems had to be observed; the Tamil nurses had never touched white patients. The doctor told Leonard that if he would be quiet and eat practically nothing, his temperature would gradually go down, and on the twenty-first day would be normal again. Leonard took his own temperature readings daily. The nurse came, but always kept her distance. Three weeks passed in a state of haze and dream. Then Leonard's temperature was normal again.

In primitive Ceylon, Leonard survived his typhoid. In civilized London, his friend Thoby died of it.

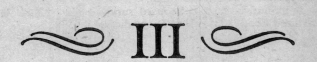

Resurrections

Vanessa Stephen's sudden change of heart toward Clive Bell, whom she had twice refused, spoke much more for reason than for love. She was experiencing a profound confusion of feeling. Life without Thoby seemed intolerable. She had taken him under her wing when they were children; he had been close to her in maturity. Clive could hardly replace Thoby, but he might be his surrogate. He would help to make life tolerable again. Some months earlier Vanessa had said she could be happy living "with anyone whom I didn't dislike, if I could paint and lead the kind of life I like." There was a strong fund of egotism in Vanessa, and she could definitely say that she didn't "dislike" Clive. He had been an ardent suitor. He was amusing, gracious, loyal. He had been her brother's friend. And then he valued Vanessa as artist; he had a love of painting. If she told herself that love had to be edged with compromise, her practical nature told her also that Clive Bell in Gordon Square would help to lift the pall of terror, her sense of loneliness and despair. An alliance with him would free her to go on with her life and her career. Out of depths of feeling understood neither by herself nor by Clive, the two came together.

Vanessa's decision washed like a great wave over Virginia. Thoby had stood between the sisters. For Virginia he was an object of rivalry and competition. Vanessa had seemed in full possession. He represented courtship and young manhood—and it was Virginia who most often courted him. He was Vanessa's ideal younger brother, but he was Virginia's handsome and attaching elder brother. And when Clive, in a manner of speaking, stepped into Thoby's shoes, Virginia—like her sister—experienced him not only as Clive, but also as Thoby. He might become Vanessa's husband, but this could not change the family constellation. He belonged to Virginia as well. Out of very old patterns rooted deeply in childhood, there evolved Virginia's bewildering and prolonged flirtation with Clive in the ensuing years. Before the marriage, Virginia's first reaction spoke for a classical sisterly situation. Clive would take Vanessa away from her. He was, however, also Thoby—resurrected—whom she had to take away from her sister. "Clive is a new part of her, which I must learn to accept." That was one of her many ambiguous remarks. Then there had to be, given Virginia's nature, feelings of hostility. Clive wasn't good enough for Vanessa. "When I think of father and Thoby and then see that funny little creature twitching his pink skin and jerking out his little spasms of laughter, I wonder what odd freak there is in Nessa's eyesight." Clive was "slight," said Virginia; he was "acid." Then again she acknowledged that he was kind, gentle, considerate—even "interesting" and "clever." As Virginia made her way through this maze of feeling—"I shall never see her alone any more"—she at the same time experienced a powerful and active jealousy. Quentin Bell has pointed to an interesting slip of the pen Virginia made in a letter to her friend Violet Dickinson. She begins by saying that Vanessa and Clive are inseparable; this prevents her from getting to know Clive better. Then her pen traces an unconscious wish, for she writes, "It will really be some time before I can separate him from her." Virginia's confused relation with Clive would inevitably be a source of great pain to Vanessa; in the end it would be a source of pain to Virginia too. Years later she would write to Gwen Raverat that her "affair with Clive and Nessa" had "turned more of a knife in me than anything else has ever done."

II

In a novel Virginia wrote thirty years later, *The Waves*, there is a character named Percival who resembles Thoby. He dies young. In writing of the grief of those who know him, Virginia sets down the words "to let the light of the world flood back—to say this has not happened." She was recording belatedly what she seems to have tried to tell herself in the days following Thoby's death—*this has not happened*. The form this fantasy took was odd and painful. Her friend Violet was recovering from her bout of typhoid. Virginia, apparently in terror that she might lose her, as she had just lost Thoby, invented an elaborate story of her brother's continuing recovery. Her daily bulletins to Violet make grim reading. Thoby has left his bed; he is eating solids; Clive is reading to him. The epistolary resurrection was maintained for a month. Then Violet read in the press an allusion to the recently dead son of Sir Leslie Stephen. To her protest against the fictions practiced on her, Virginia offered the only excuse she had: she had lied to keep shock and suffering from her. But Violet, eighteen years older, needed no such defense. Virginia had been keeping shock and suffering from herself.

An onlooker at Gordon Square might have properly asked why Virginia did not at this moment have her usual breakdown. She had already had two after deaths in her family. Certainly we can recover in *The Waves* the old dissociation of death, when she relived Thoby-Percival's extinction years later. She resorts in her familiar way to circumstantial detail. "My past is cut from me. . . . Women shuffle . . . with shopping bags. People keep on passing. . . . The butcher delivers meat next door; two old men stumble along the pavement; sparrows alight . . . but you exist somewhere. Something of you remains. . . . Here are gardens; and Venus among her flowers; here are saints and blue madonnas. . . . I remember his beauty. 'Look, where he comes,' I said." These are the thoughts of one character in *The Waves*. In the book she returns also to an old fantasy. Percival "would have done justice for fifty years, and sat in Court and ridden alone at the head of troops and denounced some monstrous tyranny." In *Jacob's Room* and *The Waves* Virginia would write out elegies for Thoby unspoken at the time of his death.

What seems to have saved her from her usual spiral downward into depression and apathy was her sister's impending marriage and the decision that the newlyweds would take over No. 46. Virginia and Adrian would have to look for another house. Such immediacies set her into the party of life rather than of death. There was the prompt visit in Wiltshire, as soon as possible, to meet Clive's parents. And then Virginia looked on and wished it were she who was marrying—yes, even "funny" Clive. On their way back from Wiltshire, they stop for a day in Bath. Virginia's jealous pen tells us how Clive and Vanessa "swung along the streets arm in arm; she had a gauze streamer, red as blood flying over her shoulder, a purple scarf, a shooting cap, tweed skirt and great brown boots. Then her hair swept across her forehead, and she was tawny and jubilant and lusty as a young God. I never saw her look better."

They were "the most honest" couple she ever had seen. "A little more imagination and they would be less scrupulous—but on the whole, I doubt that man or woman are made much better in the world." As for Clive, he had "a very sweet and sincere nature, and capable brains and great artistic sensibility of every kind. What you miss is inspiration." Virginia could supply that. All her life she would swing from praise of Clive to mockery. She led him a merry dance out of her hesitations and fantasies. In the phantasmagoria of her inner world, Virginia loved Vanessa. She wanted total possession of her. To possess Vanessa would also mean possessing Clive. To possess Clive, by the same token, would mean having Vanessa. Thus the circular dance of Virginia's buried incestuous feelings. One has to read her letters remembering that we read not of Clive but of Clive-Thoby. The language of her psyche was old. What was new was the *persona* of her sister's husband.

A few days before the marriage Henry James came to see Vanessa. "I suppose she knows what she is about," he wrote his friend Mrs. Clifford. Vanessa had seemed "very happy and eager and almost boisterously in love." Mrs. Clifford sent her a Florentine tea set; James brought her an old silver box "for hairpins." James added, "She and Clive are to keep the Bloomsbury house, and Virginia and Adrian to forage for some flat somewhere—Virginia having, by the way, grown elegantly and charmingly and almost 'smartly' handsome." James liked being with them; but he found it also "strange and terrible"; he was only too conscious in his old age of "the hungry *futurity* of youth." 'All I could mainly see was the *ghosts,* even Thoby and

Stella, let alone dear old Leslie and beautiful, pale, tragic Julia—on whom these young backs were, and quite naturally, so gaily turned." James would never approve of Clive.

The gaiety was Vanessa's and Clive's. Virginia was burdened with the permanent elegies of her being. The two sisters and husband-brother-in-law spent the last evening before the marriage—"our last night," Virginia called it—hearing Beethoven's *Fidelio,* with its musical flights of love, rapture and anguish. Clive and Vanessa were married at the St. Pancras Register Office and left for Manorbier in Pembrokeshire, Wales, to spend a honeymoon. Virginia felt "numb and dumb"—her usual reactions to any terminal event—but this termination was tempered by the establishing of her own household with Adrian. For the moment she could genuinely say, "I don't much realize what has happened." She had lost a brother. Her sister was distanced from her. Yet she also possessed them. "I feel elderly and prosaic," she announced, and she confessed to "a passing melancholy." She also said, "I wish everyone didn't tell me to marry."

III

Virginia found a temporary substitute for Thoby—and an ambiguous one—in her brother Adrian. He was twenty-three and just down from Cambridge. She spoke of him as "a poor little boy," and she would make a home for him, she promised, on "remarkable lines." Adrian was the forlorn last child of Julia, twenty-one months younger than Virginia. He had been called "the dwarf" of the family; by the time he was eighteen he had defied the name at an angular six feet five. Henry James, seeing Adrian and Virginia together at Rye during the summer of 1907, described the former as "interminably long and dumb," marching beside Virginia "like a giraffe beside an ostrich—save that Virginia is facially most fair."

Adrian had been a deeply troubled child. He had to make his way against brilliant siblings; he felt himself always an outsider. He was loose-bodied, frustrated, aggressive. Admitted to the bar, in emulation perhaps of Thoby, he decided later to study medicine. This took him distinctly outside the orbit of art and literature. He finally became a psychiatrist. He did not figure as intimately in Virginia's life as Thoby had; there would be troubling friction between the two during their housekeeping days together and legendary battles in which they threw butter at one another. In early 1907, with Virginia setting up house away from Vanessa, they lived, however, under the truce of common grief and in the euphoria of home-building.

Virginia went house-hunting promptly. She looked beyond the old Bloomsbury squares to the other side of Tottenham Court Road. This had once been a delightful part of London. It was now giving way to offices, small shops, lodgings. In Fitzroy Square, No. 29, on the southwest corner, she found a substantial residential house; the buildings nearby were taken up with commerce. No. 29 had been Bernard Shaw's home during the 1890s; he had lived there with his mother. "The Square remains," Virginia Woolf would write years later, "one of the few Bloomsbury squares that are still untouched and dignified, with its classical pillars, its frieze and the great urn in the middle, though the roar of Tottenham Court Road sounds not far away." No. 29 had a view of two fine Adam facades. It had the same kind of spacious privacy for the brother and sister that they enjoyed in Gordon Square. The ground floor became Adrian's study. Behind it was the dining room. The entire first floor was a large drawing room, pleasantly proportioned, with long windows looking on the square. Here Virginia hung red brocade curtains, laid down a green carpet, and gave prominent place to the Watts portrait of her father. An old-fashioned pianola was set into the back part of the room, one of those instruments which bellowed both classics and popular music. Adrian often expelled his rages at its heavy-breathing automatic keyboard. Above the drawing room were Virginia's rooms. They were piled with books and papers. She still used the upright desk at which she emulated Vanessa. Double windows were put in on this floor to shut out the brouhaha of Tottenham Court Road. The place had neither the decorative touches of Gordon Square nor the particular color gifts of Vanessa; however, it became very much the kind of home Virginia Stephen needed. With her cook, her maid, and her legendary dog Hans, Virginia was at last mistress of her own establishment. Years later she would remember with feeling how she wrote her first novel "in comparative splendour—a maid, carpets, fires." Adrian on his side, emulating Thoby, announced that he would have his special night for entertaining his Cambridge friends. No. 29 Fitzroy Square became an extension of the nascent Bloomsbury.

In April of 1907, while the painters and plumbers were at their work and the landlord was installing a bath in No. 29, Virginia accompanied the newlyweds on a trip to Paris. She put up at the Hôtel Rastadt in the rue Danou while Vanessa and Clive stayed in another hotel. Virginia reported that her sister "sings to herself as she walks, and buys strange plumes and draperies . . . but as we decided at lunch, she looks best undressed. We talk a great deal about Beauty and Art, and meet various old bachelors who have known Whistler, and play the violin and can't paint." This sounded as if they were seeing Clive's Irish friend, the painter Roderick O'Conor.

One day they encountered the dark and languid-looking Duncan Grant, who was painting on the Left Bank. "What a quartet," Duncan reported to his cousin Lytton Strachey. "I seem to like them all so, so much." He had met Clive and Thoby some years before in Lytton's Cambridge rooms (he was now only twenty-two), and he had also met Vanessa in Bloomsbury. "As for Virginia," wrote Duncan, "I think she's probably extremely witty and amazingly beautiful." As it happened, he would, on his return to London, find two rooms in Fitzroy Square to use as his studio.

The Education of Duncan Grant

D. H. Lawrence saw Duncan Grant as "a dark-skinned taciturn Hamlet of a fellow"; this was the way he put him into *Lady Chatterley's Lover*, naming him Duncan Forbes. Duncan did have a bronzed sultry Hamletesque look. But to his friends he was certainly not a Hamlet and the opposite of taciturn. He was "shy, vague and elusive" to Lady Ottoline. He was "wonderfully nice—and nice-looking" to his cousin Lytton (who was in love with him). David Garnett speaks of him as having inherited his mother's beauty and adds that he was "the most original man I have ever known."

In what way was Duncan Grant "original"? Garnett explained, "He is a genius who can only do things in his own way." Uncorrupted by formal education, Duncan was free of "received ideas." He learned to think for himself. Clive Bell and Maynard Keynes used to tease him because he didn't know the multiplication tables. He had his own way of handling figures; he found new ways for handling his art. He was that strange person in Bloomsbury, a "natural," yet he wasn't a primitive. He liked quiet experiments in painting and in living. He disliked fuss. He was reticent. He was comfortable sexually, having none of the bourgeois feelings that sex is immoral. Since Bloomsbury specialized in conversation, he was a listener. "How bad pure conversation is for the morale," he said. He lived by his well-controlled and disciplined feelings. He was a soft, passive man, but also lively and inventive, and certainly not a passive painter. During his penniless bohemian days, he knew when to turn up in Bloomsbury houses to get a hot meal. He seemed then a graceful figure of comedy. He wore hand-me-down clothes from various friends; his jackets were paint-stained, his too-large waistcoats were wrapped around him; he was always hitching up his over-size trousers. Yet he carried poverty lightly; he took the world as it came, and with a great sense of fun. There was something loose and relaxed about him. He liked practical jokes, good food, laughter. A rather short, solid and sturdy man, he had a single most striking feature in his face: his veiled blue-gray eyes. He was observant—always attentive. David Garnett tells us that "he would notice a woman brushing her hair in front of a second-floor window, or a cat stealing fish on a basement table while the cook's back was turned." Roger Fry goes beyond observation: "He can look at every face in the street and never miss one that has something in it, and all the time be seeing the whole effect and all with such a curious imaginative intensity." Those wide, pale eyes which saw everything and stood out against his dark skin were dramatized by his full lips. Lytton found them "lascivious." But then Lytton entertained lascivious thoughts about his cousin from the moment they met, as we shall see.

II

His full name was Duncan James Corrowr Grant. He was born in 1885 in Scotland. Six years younger than Vanessa, three years younger than Virginia, he was closest in age to Maynard, who was two years older. Lady Ottoline, who sat to him early for a portrait, said that Duncan had "the rare secret of eternal youth." She was prophetic. Duncan out-lived all Bloomsbury and witnessed its apotheosis. At ninety (in 1973) he was still painting at Charleston and going up to London for art shows and cocktail parties. Lunching with him at a table decorated long before by Vanessa was a lively experience. Two bottles of wine were placed on either side of his plate. He filled his glass with either hand; his androgyny was not the only two-sided part of his nature. His longevity was of a piece with his equanimity. He tended to have few quarrels with the world —his longest quarrel was when it tried to send him to the front lines as a soldier during the First World War. He wanted to be left alone: he wasn't one for killing his fel-lowmen. So long as he had his paint, his canvas, his turpentine, he was happy. If one offered a blank wall for a mural, that was all to the good. He might in these respects have been Vanessa's twin.

Duncan Grant's father, Lady Strachey's youngest brother, had, like General Strachey, gone out to India. But he had more of a touch of the artist than one usually expects in career soldiers. The Major liked good food; he was an amateur botanist; he improvised drawing-room songs. He married a beautiful though poor Scotswoman who painted and played the piano. Duncan's childhood exposed him to the finer elements of civilization. He witnessed the life of the British in India and experienced contrasts of light and color, vivid pageantry, and the subcontinent's poverty and Imperial dignity. There was also a shuttling between England and India during his father's furloughs.

His earliest memories were of temples, palaces, bazaars, processions, the magic and squalor of a Kiplingesque India. Duncan remembered sitting as a boy on a fence in the Himalayas; he recalled the comfortable bulk of Burmese elephants. At Valletta, in Malta, "the houses and churches seemed to tumble over each other down to the waterfront." Then there was the contrast, after long sea voyages, of Scotland. A different palette altogether, grays and greens and purples. Duncan drew pictures in his boyhood letters—sketches of Oriental palaces, Scottish scenes, eighteenth-century characters. His interest from the first was in faces, anatomy, clothes, decor, and, like Vanessa, in the ordinary things of life: a kitchen stool, an egg, a piece of fabric. At school he studied languages but was helpless in mathematics. He warmed up to his art lessons, and his masters indulged his talent. He went to Hillbrow Preparatory School, Rugby, with James Strachey and Rupert Brooke. He entered St. Paul's in 1899 when Leonard Woolf was leaving. He had no classical studies, so he was put to studying science and history—but he won a prize for painting. Then, while his parents returned to India, he went to live with his Strachey relatives and became a day boy at St. Paul's.

In this way Duncan fell into fortunate circumstances—into the hothouse of words and children and playacting that was Lancaster Gate. Lady Strachey, his strong-minded aunt, gave him free reign in this crowded, stimulated family. He could paint; he participated in family theatricals; there was music. There were boy-cousins and girl-cousins. Within this circle he found an early mentor. The French painter Simon Bussy had married Lytton's sister Dorothy. Duncan listened attentively to Bussy's advice; it was as if he listened to an oracle. A painter painted every day, even when he didn't want to, even if what emerged was a mess and had to be thrown away; art was a regularity, not a waiting for inspiration; artists learned by knowing what had been done in the past; they had to copy old masters—in this way they worked out of knowledge, not out of ignorance. A painter had to have, above all, regular hours at his task, very much like the workaday world. This was the doctrine of Simon Bussy.

Duncan's father felt that a military career would assure a stable future, but his son was as ill-suited to soldiering as was his cousin Lytton. Lady Strachey urged her brother to give Duncan the freedom of his talent. So Duncan was sent to the Westminster School of Art in 1902. He passed three undistinguished years. In 1904 his mother took him to Florence. He copied Piero della Francesca, an exciting experience, and the Masaccios in the Carmine. Italian art, the spell of Italy, took hold of him: a world of color, decoration, murals, artifacts—a world filled with objects created by the use of one's hands.

III

A singular thing happened to Duncan Grant one morning when he was eighteen. He was staying with his parents at Streatley-on-Thames and painting a landscape. He heard a voice. It was clear: it had a tone of command. He remembered every word. "You must go out into the world to learn all that there is to know and to be seen in the world of painting . . . and there are other things going on at this very moment about which you know nothing." Duncan listened. He agreed. In effect, he seems to have felt that easy and pleasant though his world was—his world of painting and Strachey connections—he needed more education in the life of art. The mysterious voice was a summoning of the self to a vocation; it was direct and explicit. No fanciful dancing of minuets with the Muses. To paint, one had really to work at it. To learn, to be in the immediate world, to hearken to the experiences of his peers—it was as if he had redreamed the lesson of Simon Bussy.

A kindly aunt in due course gave Duncan enough money to go to Paris for a few months. Bussy suggested that he work with Jacques-Émile Blanche in the Blanche studio, La Palette. The French painter strolled through the place in the usual way twice a week offering criticism. Blanche moved in a high social world. He was a "society" artist. He knew Marcel Proust, whose portrait he painted. His literary models included George Moore, that inveterate Irish model of so many French painters; Thomas Hardy; Henry James. It is difficult to imagine that Duncan Grant could have learned much from such a *mondain*, but he did. In La Palette, Duncan found students from many parts of Europe; and he acquired strong discipline. "I work in the dark," he would say to Will Rothenstein. But he worked; he never stopped working. After his mornings in the studio he spent his afternoons copying classic paintings in the Louvre. In the evenings he would go to the library of the École des Beaux Arts to study anatomy and drawing.

During the spring of 1907, when Duncan met the Stephen sisters and Clive in Paris, he had taken a studio in the rue Delambre in Montparnasse. In his period he met the future Vorticist and litterateur Wyndham Lewis, later a vehement critic of Bloomsbury. Duncan's dislike was instant. Easygoing and tolerant himself, he could not stomach the perpetual belligerence of Lewis. "My gorge simply rises whenever I see him," Duncan wrote. Wyndham Lewis had similar feelings about Duncan—"a little fairy-like individual who would have received no attention in any country except England." He was wrong. The French painters Duncan met paid attention. In his memoirs Blanche says that the professional painters of Bloomsbury, "the charming Duncan Grant, and Vanessa Bell, are among the most distinguished in England. I am reminded by their decorative work of Rowlandson and of our own neo-impressionists." Later Duncan designed sets and costumes for a French play, for the director and leader of the *théâtre nouveau*, Jacques Copeau, and for his American production of *Pelléas and Mélisande*. However, there would be a long apprenticeship before Duncan Grant would attain celebrity: an inconsequential term at the Slade, after Paris; rejection by the Royal Academy Schools; unremitting toil for a number of years in his own studio at 22 Fitzroy Square.

IV

Duncan Grant's initiations into love were quite as precocious and charming as his initiations into art. An early wooer, as we know, was his cousin Lytton Strachey. It seemed an unexpected stroke of fortune to him to discover Duncan, a clean-limbed, liquid-eyed youth, living in his own home. The record of Lytton's homoerotic passion is found in his letters not only to his love but to his Cambridge companions, including Maynard Keynes, who, on Leonard's departure for Ceylon, became for a while Lytton's confidant. "I have a sort of adoration," he wrote to Keynes. And to Clive, "I have fallen in love hopelessly and ultimately."

As it turned out, the "hopeless" was more accurate than the "ultimate." Duncan Grant was fond of his cousin, but he found Lytton's hysterical proclamations of love more than he could bear. Lytton was too possessive, too oppressive. Duncan was unaccustomed to his kind of operatic style; and so he distanced himself. "Duncan tortures me," complained Lytton. And then it all became a Restoration comedy, because Duncan met Maynard Keynes in Paris and they became lovers even while Lytton still confided in Keynes and extolled Duncan's virtues. "He's a *genius*—a colossal portent of fire and glory," wrote Lytton. This was exactly the sort of language that embarrassed Duncan. Then came the denouement. Lytton was crushed, but after a spell he put on a bold face. In the triangle Maynard had upstaged him, but they had been friends too long "to stop being friends now." He wrote to Maynard, "If you were here now I should probably kiss you, except that Duncan would be jealous, which would never do!" He added: "There are some things that I shall try not to think of." To

Duncan he wrote that, though he liked Maynard, "I cannot think of him as you do, or else, I suppose I should be in love with him too! . . . I don't take your affair as seriously as you do. . . ." In the circumstances he didn't see why he should cease "liking both of you as much as I always have." But he took the affair very seriously, for he signed this letter *Adieu.*

From this time on, and for many years, Duncan Grant and Maynard Keynes—the economist who was an artist in his field, and the painter who knew the economy of art— shared homes and traveled together. The man of reason and intellectual power and the man of visual emotions accepted each other without claiming possession as Lytton had done. They respected each other's attainments. May-nard had a logical mind but a very flexible one, and Dun-can was nothing if not flexible in his sense of form and color. He was "disarmingly logical" as well. Maynard found many of his artistic aspirations expressed by Dun-can, who helped him form an art collection; and Duncan could identify easily and comfortably with Maynard's spir-itual suppleness. Both had a great sense of "fun." Their friendship would endure beyond Duncan's love for Va-nessa, beyond Keynes's marriage to a Russian ballerina. They were both at ease with themselves and with one an-other. In this sense they were much more perceptive of human relations than was Lytton, whose life was a series of dependencies and entanglements. Even when they shared rooms they lived and worked independently. Usually it was Duncan who occupied the rooms, and Maynard, fixed as he now was at Cambridge, who came and went. They knew instinctively how to harmonize their private lives. Keynes had begun to speculate in the market with enormous success. He helped Duncan during moments of hardship. They traveled—to Orkney, where Duncan painted Maynard's portrait, now in King's College; to Paris and Versailles; to Greece and Turkey. Duncan painted on the Acropolis and was deeply influenced by Byzantine art. They journeyed to the site of Troy. Duncan decorated Keynes's rooms at Cambridge with an androgynous series of panels alternating men and women of splendid physique and stature (Vanessa painted the women).

In 1911, after they had journeyed to Sicily, Tunis, and Florence, they took rooms in Fitzroy Square and became the neighbors of Virginia and Adrian. Duncan was soon a close friend of Adrian's. As Maynard Keynes's biographer puts it, "Sharing houses, sometimes here, sometimes there, Maynard became a member of the Bloomsbury family. He lived as a bachelor in college for part of the time, but Bloomsbury was in a real sense his home, providing the feminine interest and the human interest which were the background of his daily work." And Richard Shone, commenting on this enduring intimacy, observed that for the genius of economics, Duncan's "natural process of thought was unclouded by dogma and disarmingly logical in its personal way." On these grounds of logic and love the two exemplified one of the finest harmonies of Bloomsbury.

Phase Two: Fitzroy Square

In Fitzroy Square, Virginia and Adrian Stephen now began to create their separate worlds. Given the style and worldliness of Gordon Square, it was inevitable that these should at first be satellite worlds. Virginia emulated—and envied. Vanessa, she said, surrounded herself with "all the wits and poets" and presided like a goddess. "When Nessa is bumbling about the world and making each thorn blossom, what room is there for me?"

Virginia needed a great deal of room. She set about finding it, in spite of her self-pity and envy. Fitzroy Square, on the down-at-heel side of Tottenham Court Road, gradually became a part of the original Bloomsbury of Gordon Square. Indeed, Bloomsbury now had separate houses and separate hostesses. To avoid competition, Thursday evenings were held alternately at each house. A new play-reading club was formed, a sort of revival of the old Trinity College Midnight Society. The Friday Club, Vanessa's special art club, remained active. And Adrian began to bring his contemporaries into Bloomsbury. Virginia soon had neighbors, as we have seen. Fitzroy Square and Fitzroy Street—sometimes alluded to as Fitzrovia—harbored entire cells of both prosperous and impecunious painters. Duncan worked at No. 22. Roger Fry would locate his Omega Workshops at No. 33. Walter Sickert and other non-Bloomsbury painters displayed their works at numbers 8 and 19 Fitzroy Street. Augustus John painted in Whistler's old studio in the same street.

So Bloomsbury—still not known by that name—entered this second and wider phase. The first phase had had a quality of delayed adolescence about it: a mixture of homosexuals with young virgins on the neutral ground of "the Beautiful" and "the Good." By the time of Fitzroy

Square the boy-girl and boy-boy complexities seem to have gradually dissolved. There was greater candor. One day Lytton used the word "semen." Someone else used the word "bugger." The *lingua franca* of the new century began to fall from feminine as well as masculine lips. Virginia liked the word "copulation," but she wasn't above using "fuck." In this late Edwardian London the Victorian-bred young threw away verbal reticence and cut themselves free from hypocrisy. "I knew there were buggers in Plato's Greece," Virginia wrote. "But it never occurred to me that there were buggers even now in the Stephen sitting-room in Gordon Square." By the time the buggers reached Fitzroy Square, Virginia had made the mental adjustment. "Sex permeated our conversation. The word bugger was never far from our lips. We discussed copulation with the same excitement and openness that we had discussed the nature of the Good." Clive's complaint was that Virginia discussed copulation but went no further. They listened with "rapt interest in the love affairs of the buggers." Vanessa did so sympathetically but with great curiosity; Virginia did so "frivolously, laughingly." While she accepted buggers as persons, she did not at first approve of homosexuality, because there was something "unreal" to her in boy-boy love. In her virginal mind there always had to be a boy and a girl to make a good love story. In the condition of virginity, Leonard's later verdict was, "They simply don't know what desire is."

Virginia Stephen still bristled at academics, whether *homo* or *hetero*. "I detest pale scholars and their questionings about life, and the message of the classics, and the bearing of Greek thought upon modern problems." She received the young Cambridge men in their pallor and erudition with hostesslike dignity but unconcealed asperity. Duncan Grant remembered the Fitzroy Square days—Virginia presiding, he said, with an "inner fierceness." Outwardly she was shy; and she was clearly at ease when older Victorian women were present and mingled incongruously with the new generation. In the big drawing room with its respiratory pianola, amid the hilarities and aggressions of these social occasions, Virginia continued her struggle to find herself, like her heroine in the novel she was now writing, *The Voyage Out*. The voyage was Virginia's. "This shyness and fierceness," said Duncan, "was a necessary self-defence in her war with the world."

Virginia was waging the war from her personal citadel. The young men continued to bring to her parties "the old ideal of truth and free-speaking." She, as a woman, could supply her belief in art and feeling, as against intellectual aridity. Maynard brought relaxation and good spirits. So did Lytton. He possessed a cultivated rudeness, divided between hostile silence or brief cutting remarks. Gerald Brenan, who had observation later of both sisters, wrote in his diary: "Wherever Virginia goes she undoes a knot, like a Lapland witch, and lets out a war; an old practiced war, whose tactics have been polished up by many previous encounters. If it is not the Older Generation versus the Younger, it is Writers versus Painters or even Men versus Women." These well-worn topics "produce the most brilliant and fantastic conversation that one can hear anywhere in England."

II

"Brilliant and fantastic conversation" has a way of not getting itself recorded. When it is recorded by accident or design, it sounds strangely discontinuous and fragmented. It needs cigarette smoke, gestures, colors, a ballet of body postures, smiles natural and artificial, the nuances of verbal warmth or venom. Accounts of Bloomsbury parties across the years (and we have more accounts of the later years than of the nascent periods of Gordon and Fitzroy) sound like intellectual parties anywhere. We must take it on trust that they were remarkable. Certainly there were remarkable persons present; and in her second novel, *Night and Day*, Virginia gave us glimpses into remembered occasions. We can also read some emanation of them in *The Voyage Out*, in which a young man who bears a striking resemblance to Lytton Strachey cross-examines the virginal heroine:

"About books now. What have you read? Just Shakespeare and the Bible?"

"I haven't read many classics," Rachel stated. She was slightly annoyed by his jaunty and rather unnatural manner, while his masculine acquirements induced her to take a very modest view of her own power.

"D'you mean to tell me you've reached the age of twenty-four without reading Gibbon?" he demanded.

"Yes, I have," she answered.

"*Mon dieu!*" he exclaimed, throwing out his hands. "You must begin tomorrow. I shall send you my copy. What I want to know is—" he looked at her critically. "You see, the problem is, can one really talk to you? Have you got a mind, or are you like the rest of your sex? You seem to me absurdly young compared with women of your age."

Rachel looks at him but says nothing. Virginia learned very quickly, however, to say a great deal. She could spin her fantasies in endless invention, piling the grotesque upon the ridiculous. On occasion we see her at her worst, displaying the "fierceness" of which Duncan Grant spoke.

Such a record is to be found in Adrian Stephen's diary; it is a minute account of an evening in Fitzroy Square. The people drift in slowly—Duncan, Clive, Vanessa, and then an apparently harmless and well-dressed Miss Cole, otherwise unidentified, who settles herself in a long wicker chair. Her *chic* affects Virginia, who always had trouble dressing properly. Virginia's clothes were often linked by safety pins, and she is known to have lost her "drawers" at the opera and in Oxford Street. "Of course," says Miss Virginia to Miss Cole, "you are always dressed so exquisitely. You look so original, so like a sea shell. There is something so refined about your coming in among our muddy boots and pipe smoke, dressed in your exquisite creations." We do not know whether Miss Cole liked being original like a seashell. Clive, falling in with Virginia's chaff, offers masculine flattery; and when Miss Cole refuses to accept his undulant phrases, he wants to know why she dislikes him. Other women enjoy nice things said about them! "I think Miss Cole has a very strong character," Virginia remorselessly pursues. Miss Cole, the diary tells us, left after an hour. We wonder why she did not leave sooner. Then (Adrian's record continues) Virginia makes a great many statements with tremendous intensity and snaps at those who laugh. Someone tries to refute what she said. Virginia does a turnabout and says that the refutation "has put her point exactly." Small wonder that Osbert Sitwell years later spoke of "the Bloomsbury Junta."

This suggests the "tone" of one kind of Bloomsbury party. Most often chronology is scrambled; we never know in which period social history is being made. There was a famous party when Vanessa, heated with dancing, began to shed her clothes until she was "topless," a striptease which may have given rise to a Logan Pearsall Smith *canard* that Maynard and Vanessa made love on the drawing-room sofa. There was a later party—after the war—in which Duncan, who could be artfully lyrical, imitated Nijinsky beside the winged feet of the ballerina Lydia Lopokova. What is clear is that the transitions from Gordon to Fitzroy Square and later to Brunswick Square show how friendship and propinquity, love and marriage, and the various minuets and sarabands of personal relations loosened the hard intellectuality of early Bloomsbury. Lady Ottoline's memories of Fitzroy Square are of the same year as Adrian's diary. They are, however, much more accepting and adoring. She sheds a haze of glamour over all the young people. Long-legged men, she writes, were in long basket chairs smoking pipes and talking inaudibly of "thrilling and exciting" subjects. In the midst Virginia's "bell-like voice" was audible and it was "swinging, swinging, and resonant, awaking and scattering dull thought, and giving warning that a light would be thrown into the darkness, the rays of which would light up her own lovely face and our stagnant prosy minds." The great lady of Bedford Square felt humble and enjoyed remembering Virginia "with her little circle of companions"—Adrian and Vanessa, Lytton, Duncan, Roger and Clive, "that happy, flattering, good-tempered Autolycus holding out gay leaves for us to admire." Did Lady Ottoline know that Autolycus was the son of Hermes and the master thief of antiquity? They seemed "a delightful company," but Miss Cole might not have described them in this way.

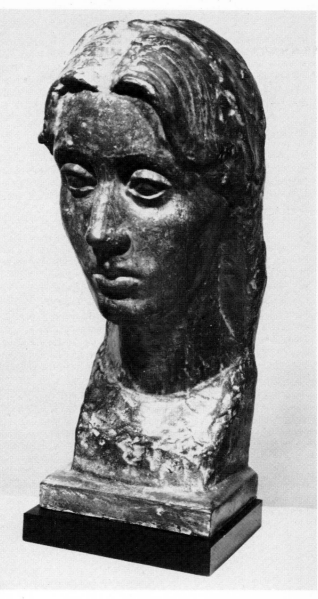

Vanessa Bell by Marcel Gimond

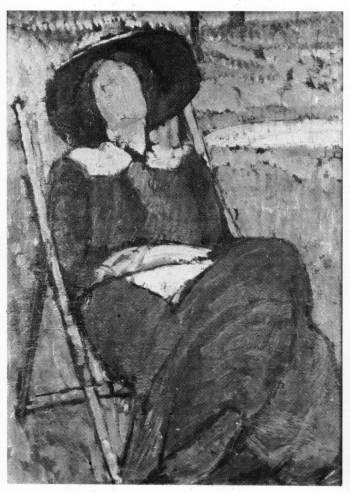

Virginia Woolf by Vanessa Bell

Opposite page top: *Virginia Woolf, unfinished portrait by Vanessa Bell* Opposite bottom: *Lytton Strachey by Simon Bussy*

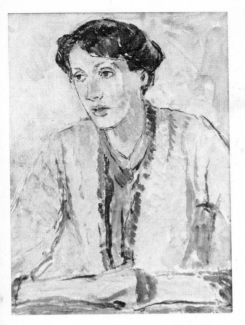

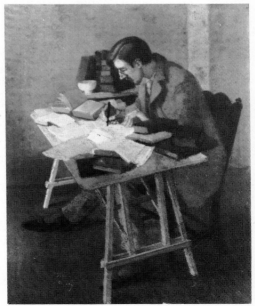

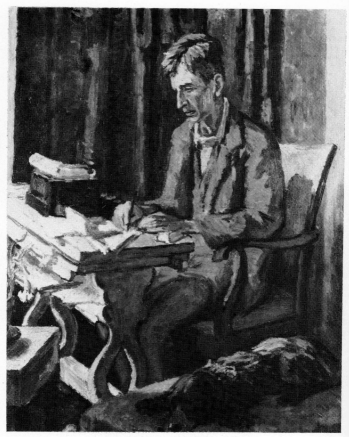

Leonard Woolf by Vanessa Bell

Opposite page top: *Roger Fry
Self-Portrait* Opposite page bottom: *Clive Bell by Roger Fry*

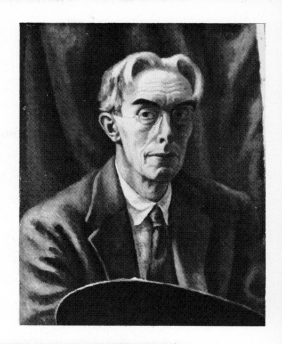

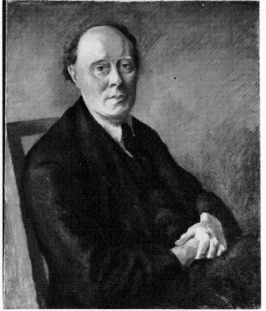

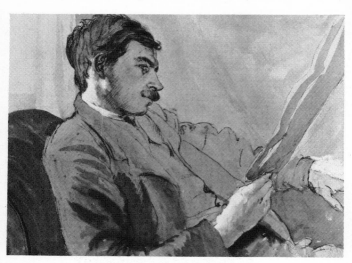

Maynard Keynes by Gwen Raverat

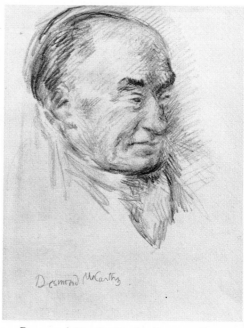

Desmond MacCarthy by Duncan Grant

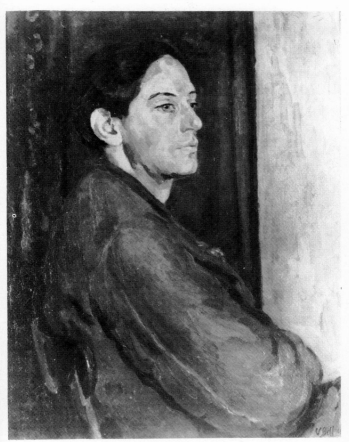

Duncan Grant by Vanessa Bell

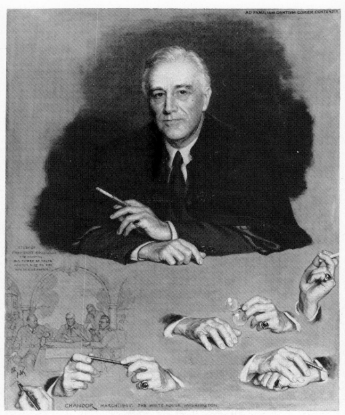

The Hands of FDR by Douglas Chandor,
from his portrait of President Roosevelt, 1945

III

Virginia's flirtation with Clive Bell began after Vanessa's first confinement. The painter gave birth to a son, named Julian after Thoby, whose full name had been Julian Thoby Stephen. The name also recalled his grandmother Julia. Virginia, having envied Vanessa her marriage, now envied her state of motherhood. But she was also made vividly aware of the responsibilities of bearing children. "A child is the very devil," she wrote. As for pampered Clive, he may have felt an unconscious rivalry between himself and little Julian, who took Vanessa away from him. She could no longer give Clive her undivided attention. This often happens, as we know. Also, he was too self-indulgent to readily accept the sounds and smells of infancy in Gordon Square. Vanessa stayed home with the baby and her painting. Clive and Virginia were thrown together. "Clive and I went for some long walks," she wrote during one of ther visits to Cornwall, "but I felt we were deserters; but then I am quite useless as a nurse, and Clive will not even hold it." The "it" was the helpless Julian.

The "deserters" found pleasure in one another's company. Clive was an amiable companion; and Virginia had known no young men with whom she could be so intimate —except her brother Thoby. In this way the relationship revived old family emotions. For Clive it was an adventure with a woman whose mental agility delighted him quite as much as did Vanessa's more silent beauty. The correspondence between Virginia and Clive shows how they drifted through "dangerous" moments. Clive would doubtless have taken advantage of these, given his pose of libertine and tendency to be a perpetual young-man-about-town. Virginia held back, not so much through virtue as simply her fear of men. A letter of 1908 accuses Clive of tormenting her by describing her as "vivid and strange and bewildering." It mentions that "though we did not kiss . . . I think we 'achieved the heights' as you put it." It is difficult to believe that in this relationship those heights were sexual. They were rather the enchantment Virginia always felt when she was admired. And Clive's love was (given Clive) the superficial-romantic of a "man of the world." Virginia responded to him without giving herself. In alluding to the absent kiss, she adds, she had been "willing and offered once" but felt restricted by "the sight of your daily life"— that is, his life with Vanessa. In the next letter she says, "Nessa has all that I should like to have and you, beside your own charm and exquisite fine sweetnesses (which I always appreciate somehow), have her." She sees herself as an "erratic external force" to Vanessa's marriage, "capable of shocks, but without any lodging in your lives." Another letter to Clive tells him "how very much attached to you I am, and how much pleasure you give me." They enjoyed their walks. They enjoyed the banter of love and their teetering on the edge of intimacies from which Virginia had no difficulty in drawing back. The tone of the flirtation is sisterly—incestuous without the incest.

Sending a book to Virginia during this period, Clive sings in verse. Later he published and dedicated these verses to Virginia. In the crabbed lines, more gallant than poetic, he speaks of his "dear and fairest friend." He offers memories. Did Virginia recall the sunlight and the firelight too? The pregnant hours, the gay delights? The pain, the tears maybe, the ravished heights? "The golden moments my cold lines commend?" The verse is full of hints and suggestions, but we do not know what to make of "ravished heights." "The pain, the tears maybe" seems to allude to their quarrels. "There were scenes," Quentin Bell tells us. Virginia became jealous every time Clive kissed Vanessa in her presence. Clive on his side felt "delighted, thwarted and enraged by her coquetry." In September 1908 and in April 1909 Virginia went with her sister and husband to Tuscany. The second time, in Florence, the three grated considerably on each other's nerves. Vanessa pronounced Virginia "tiresome," and the latter beat a retreat to London. At one point Lytton hinted to Virginia that she was causing her sister pain and told her that Vanessa was watching Clive "more carefully even than usual." Vanessa was understandably disturbed. Some of the Clive-Virginia badinage and quarrel seems to have been inserted by her in *Night and Day*. Katharine, the Vanessa character, agrees to marry a man she does not love, and another lover describes him as "that little pink-cheeked dancing master . . . that gibbering ass with the face of a monkey on an organ, that posing, vain fantastical fop with his tragedies and his comedies, his innumerable spites and pettiness." Both Leonard's and Virginia's negative feelings about Clive are incorporated into their fictions between 1914 and 1919. Virginia wrote to Clive, "It would be comfortable to reach a simple state in which we would feel easy." She added, "The main point of all this is that we are very fond of each other." Finally, "I expect we shall make out a compromise in time."

In later years Virginia would mock Clive quite as much as she would her other friends. She would call him "an absurd little cockatoo" and often likened him to some form of parrot or peacock. To her friend Vita Sackville-West she confided more than a decade later, "I love him, and always shall, but not in the go-to-bed or sofa way." She admitted to having written passionate letters to him. He considered them not passionate enough. Both little understood that Virginia was distanced by a double taboo: her difficulties with men and the invisible incestuous feelings embodied in this relation. What—in their egotism—neither took sufficiently into account was the alienation Vanessa would feel, her sense of betrayal both by husband and by sister.

IV

The mixed mordancy and charm which Virginia displayed during the Fitzroy Square years were the correlatives of her confused spirit. She was writing a novel about a virgin —herself. First she titled it *Melymbrosia* and later *The Voyage Out*. She worked at it for half a dozen years, writing and rewriting it. She seems to have returned to the unexpected death of her half sister Stella; but the book contains the emotion of all the deaths she had experienced. With blind courage and much pain she was seeking to unburden herself of her melancholy and mourning. Incorporated into her story is her flirtation with Clive or his Thoby-attractiveness. We also see her fascination with Lytton and her desire to be a great novelist; and there is discussion of all the questions she would tug at during ensuing years, the mystery of people, feminism, suicide— "the things people don't say"—and her own desire for a marriage like Vanessa's. With her unresolved androgynous feelings and her love-scorn for the male, she wanted to discover and understand the men around her. She would dismiss her novel as a "harlequinade." It was the harlequinade of her life—the tragedy of "beginning things and having to end them." The old fear of mirrors occurs when the heroine sees her face in a wineglass and finds that it is "not the face she wanted, and in all probability never would be." Virginia's "voyage out" is her journey from Hyde Park Gate to Gordon Square to Fitzroy Square, and also the inward voyage of a creature questioning her two worlds—the abysses of madness and the mystery of genius. She names the ship on which the voyage is made the *Euphrosyne*, the title of the early Cambridge anthology she had mocked, and we remind ourselves that the Greek word for madness is *aphrosine*. So the ship is Bloomsbury afloat, and Virginia afloat on her madness. Rachel Vinrace in the novel is condemned by her author to die rather than to live; she moves in a series of perceptions and dissociations until she is carried off like Thoby by a fever. However, the description of Rachel's death comes closer to accounts of Virginia's lapses into insanity. Rachel dying feels "completely cut off, unable to communicate with the rest of the world, isolated alone with her body." This cuts very close to Virginia's withdrawals when she sank into one of her breakdowns.

In *The Voyage Out* we can see how a writer diffuses personal life experience among different characters. Terence Hewet is Virginia when he talks of his ambition to write novels and his desire to find words that will render human silences. He is also a version of Clive Bell (Heward was a Bell family name). Terence Hewet's love for Rachel follows the curve of Clive's flirtation during which Virginia discovered for the first time those tremulous feelings of unrealized love she now describes. She was writing a strange mythical novel. Bloomsbury is floated to a South American shore, where it is divided between a hotel and a villa—Gordon Square and Fitzroy Square. In its luminous and often painful pages we read a tale of innocence and waste, anguish and ignorance, and the world of talk in which Virginia moved and which Leonard would so sharply criticize. "Talk was the medicine she trusted to, talk about everything, talk that was free, unguarded, and as candid as a habit of talking with men made natural in her own case."

Virginia confided the early pages of her novel to Clive. She needed male sanction. She dreamed, when she began writing the book, that she had shown it to her father, and he snorted and dropped it on a table, "and I was very melancholy, and read it this morning and thought it very bad." She could not accept Clive's praise. He was supposed to disapprove, like her father. She thought he was up to his usual gallantries and flatteries. But he recognized, with his strong critical sense, that Virginia had the ability to show "the thrilling real beneath a dull apparent." He told her the prose was "feverish." He chided her for making the women subtle, sensitive, tactful, gracious, delicately perceptive; and the men obtuse, vulgar, blind, florid, rude, tactless, emphatic, indelicate, vain, tyrannical, and stupid. Here again Clive seems to have served functions Thoby—and later Leonard—exercised for Virginia. In the end she acknowledged, "You were the first person who ever thought I'd write well."

V

The story of the Fitzroy Square years has one footnote. In the annals of the Bloomsbury friends are recorded many leg-pulling and practical jokes, a residue of school days. The story is told of Duncan Grant's dressing as an old lady with a German name and hoodwinking Lady Strachey by paying an afternoon call, leaving her mystified without identifying himself. Leonard Woolf tells how his mother, bored during a rainy summer in the country, dressed herself in a black dress and black hat with a thick black veil and called on her husband to ask for advice. He spoke to her as "my good woman" without knowing she was his wife. But the best known escapade was the *"Dreadnought Hoax"* hatched in Fitzroy Square by a friend of Adrian's. Adrian himself years later wrote an account of that event in which the navy briefly believed it had received a visit from an Eastern potentate. Virginia was roped into the prank and dressed up as one of the retinue of the Emperor of Abyssinia, as did Duncan. Adrian took the role of the official translator. A telegram sent to the navy as from the Foreign Office aroused no suspicion. A photograph of the masquerade party suggests characters in a school play, and one wonders how the navy was deceived; but it was. The party traveled from Paddington to Weymouth. The navy had everything ready. Adrian used a mixture of something like Swahili heavily larded with Greek and Latin words out of Homer and Virgil, and phrases like "Bunga-bunga." Virginia made gruff noises, to sound masculine. They were taken through the important ship by officers, including the future and later renowned Admiral William Fisher, then flag commander, who happened to be a cousin of Virginia's and Adrian's. Everything went off smoothly and solemnly. Gun salutes were dispensed with at the request of the "Emperor." The event would have passed totally unnoticed had not the author of the prank, in his vanity, leaked the story to the press. Headlines treated the masquerade as a great joke on the navy. Inquiries were made in the House of Commons. One member wanted to know whether "the joke was a direct insult to His Majesty's flag." The answer was not given, but the First Lord simply said he hoped he would not be asked to go further into a matter "which is obviously the work of foolish persons." Later the House was told "no flags were hoisted or salutes fired, and no special train was ordered by the Admiral."

Virginia's cousin was understandably furious, and certain officers of the navy considered the affair an affront. Duncan was spirited in a car to Hampstead Heath, where some naval persons wanted to give him a drubbing; but he was wearing his carpet slippers and seemed amiable and peaceable and was unwilling to fight. "You can't cane a chap like that," said one of the officers. So Duncan was given two ceremonial taps and naval honor was satisfied.

Adrian and Duncan went to the Admiralty to apologize. Virginia remembered that they were treated "as if they were schoolboys." Government rules were quickly made about casual telegrams from the Foreign Office, thus closing all possibility of other performances. The First Lord of the Admiralty, said Virginia, seemed "secretly a good deal amused, and liked the hoax, but didn't want it repeated."

The hubbub in the press soon died down, but it would be succeeded a few months later with a much greater hubbub of a different nature about Bloomsbury art. Quentin Bell tells us that "the theme of masculine honour, of masculine violence and stupidity, of gold-laced masculine pomposity" remained with Virginia; she had entered the Abyssinian adventure for the fun of the thing, but she came out of it with a new sense "of the brutality and silliness of men."

The public, we must remind ourselves, did not then think of the incident as "Bloomsbury." In retrospect, however, the historical connections would be made.

Vision and Design

Vanessa Bell met Roger Fry at one of Desmond Mac-Carthy's parties in Chelsea. And then one day in 1909 she and Clive ran into him on the train coming up from Cambridge. Fry talked about art with a breadth of experience and an enthusiasm that delighted the Bells. He had the air of being perpetually surprised by life. Painting was not a camera. Form was the outcome of feeling. Shape and color generated emotion. What a painter put on canvas was how he felt. The painter had to paint with a sense of craft, as well as vision, a knowledge of structure and design, if he was not to perpetrate a mere daub. Roger Fry held them spellbound. He could leap from the Italian masters to the Chinese; he redefined the Impressionists; he flew on magic carpets to Islam; he soared into the sublime, especially on the subject of Cézanne. Clive was carried back to his months in Paris when he had seen the new paintings through the eyes of O'Conor and Morrice. For Vanessa, Fry expressed thoughts she had long had, but for which she had never found words. Roger Fry, unlike many art critics, also painted. He painted stiffly at first; he put too many schoolmasterly ideas into some of his canvases. Yet he had a strong sense of form and color. Vanessa particularly liked Roger's warm humanity and his vitality. He had a genius for summing up the qualities in a painting—and in a painter. He was fresh from America, where he had been attached to the Metropolitan Museum of Art. He was also known for his art criticism in the *Athenaeum*. He clearly spoke the language of modern painting for Bloomsbury, and he was soon a familiar visitor.

Vanessa invited him to talk to her Friday Club in Gordon Square. Roger appeared before a small and select audience of artists and art lovers on 25 February 1910.

Virginia came to hear him. She saw a man with graying hair and strong deep lines in his face, as if some painter had put them there with a thin, hard brush. Roger seemed worn and seasoned, yet he was also bronzed and animated, "ascetic yet tough." Some inexhaustible source of energy fountained into his mind, spreading to nerves and muscles. He had restless hands. They were broad and supple. He picked up a vase; he shifted the flowers, recomposing them into a picture. He fingered a piece of china, set it down again. There was no interruption of his thoughts or words: "things played over the surface and were referred to some hidden centre." His voice was deep, "somber and majestic" (as Desmond would say), and also (according to Kenneth Clark) "grave and resonant." Clark said he was "the most bewitching lecturer I have ever heard." He had the power of transmitting emotion while transmitting fact. The Friday Club felt this in the voice, the hands, the black bushy brows, and the luminous and intent eyes behind his spectacles. In very little time he was a beloved Bloomsbury figure, although he was some dozen years older than most of the friends.

II

Roger Fry seemed at first glance, one is tempted to say, "standard" Bloomsbury. There had been Clifton (Thoby's school); then King's College at Cambridge (Maynard's college) and then the Apostles (Leonard, Lytton, Maynard, Desmond). He had all the male Bloomsbury credentials. He also had the oddity (like Leonard) of being outside their traditional "frame," for he came of a long line of Quakers. "Thoroughly," the motto of the Woolfs, might have been the motto of the Frys as well. They were God-fearing, puritanical. Roger Fry was first destined for science by his father, Sir Edward Fry, who had risen by degrees in judicial circles and finally represented Britain at The Hague. One might also find analogies between the early circumstances of Maynard Keynes and Fry—the closely woven family, a household of rules and disciplines, with the difference that Maynard was nurtured in friendliness and intimacy while Roger was brought up with chill reserve, a subordination of emotion and passion to the dictates of an invisible but presiding God and visible and omnipresent Quakerism. Maynard's accepting parents had ended by giving their son an almost inhuman but constructive intellectuality. In the Fry household the contradictions and ambiguities, above all the arbitrary authority of the mother, seems to have bred flexibility and rebellion, a spiritual mobility, which was at the very core of Roger Fry's being.

In Clifton and at Cambridge, Roger Fry's most intimate friends were men of strong mind and homosexual tendencies. For some years Roger had (so far as we can determine) a Victorian-Platonic friendship with G. Lowes Dickinson, an explorer and an exponent of the Grecian and Oriental ways of life—though himself, curiously enough, of the onanistic persuasion. An extant letter from Fry to Dickinson contains these words, "I love you and understand you," but adds, "It isn't the only kind of love I'm capable of." This was written after the young Roger had met an older woman, who initiated him into "the many ways of love." Roger married and had two children by the time he began to frequent Bloomsbury. In a striking and saddening way he was already in the position in which Leonard Woolf would find himself later—he was married to a woman whose mental instability gave rise to serious crises.

Fry had roots that reached back, given his age, to the mid-Victorian years. The others in Bloomsbury were late Victorians by birth, Edwardians at maturity. The quality he shared in common with the Bloomsbury friends was his refusal to accept the received ideas either of the Victorians or the Edwardians. He had a way of propounding "incredible theories" with an air of perfect reason. He set his course early at Cambridge. He began by fulfilling his father's wishes and taking a first in the science Tripos. He then dashed family hopes by choosing art as his vocation. There were many family pressures, but Roger was strong and resilient. He ended in Italy studying the masters. He might have rivaled Bernhard Berenson had he pursued these studies further, but he wanted to be a painter. He accordingly went on to Julien's in Paris. While painting, he also became a critic and began to write a series of papers and reviews of exhibitions which won him, very speedily, a reputation on both sides of the Atlantic. New York beckoned; and he spent some years helping the Metropolitan Museum acquire certain masterpieces, at first with the blessing and later with the hostility of J. P. Morgan—for Roger Fry could not always condone the brutal compromises practiced by Mr. Morgan between his personal acquisitions and those of the Museum. Virginia and Vanessa, when they listened to Roger at the Friday Club, little knew that in this year of 1910 their speaker had reached a serious crisis in his personal life. He had parted company with the Metropolitan as a result of Morgan's hostilities. His wife was finally pronounced "incurably insane" and institutionalized. Roger was left footloose in the very middle of his life and, for the moment, deeply depressed. He dreaded shutting himself up, he said, "in the imprisonment of egotism." But he was too mobile and on occasion too volatile for such imprisonment. His appetite for painting, for ideas, for museums was much too robust. He had always to be up and doing. By a mixture of circumstances, at this crucial moment he was asked to mount an exhibition of "modern art."

III

To understand Roger's famous show of "Post-Impressionist" paintings—it was he who found the name—one must know the evolution of his knowledge and taste in art, the steps by which he landed on the doorstep and in the house of "the modern." During the 1890s, the years of his training, he had studied Italian painting closely. His first book was a work on Giovanni Bellini. In subsequent years his articles in the *Athenaeum* and the *Burlington Magazine* espoused the importance of form and design. He looked at the Impressionists with some skepticism. They seemed to him to be denying the fundamental structures of nature. In a word, he was on the side, more or less, of the art establishment in Britain. He first saw Cézanne's work in 1905 and in 1906, the year of that master's death. Fry seemed to have reached the point at that moment when the full meaning of the French modernism swam into awareness. He saw a Cézanne still life with new eyes—the intensity of bright color, the handling of greens and grays, treated with insistence on decorative value, in which light and shade were subordinated to color. And then in a Cézanne landscape Fry found the same decorative intention and a magical handling of "the illusion of the planes of illumination." The world then still laughed at Cézanne's "crude" painting and dismissed him as a failure. By looking at the seeming crudities and color violences of Van Gogh, then also a subject of ridicule, Fry began to understand how Cézanne had been a stalker of design and a painter of infinite precaution and subtlety. He ultimately called him the "tribal deity" of the modernists. "By some mysterious power he was able to give to the mountains, the houses, the trees, all their solid integrity, to articulate them in a clearly felt space and yet to sustain a rhythm of plastic movement almost unbroken from one end of the canvas to another." And Fry added that "only in the very latest of Titian's work can I find something akin to this, a similar shortcircuiting, as it were, of all ordinary methods of expressing form."

That final remark about Titian suggests to us the ultimate stature of Fry in art criticism. By knowing the old, he could understand the new. He ranged from the art of Paleolithic and Neolithic man to the Greco-Roman vision, and on to the symbolism of Christian art and the great journey to Byzantium. "For the six centuries which lie between the years 1300 and 1900 the history of European art may be described very largely in terms of the increasing power of realizing the ideated space of the picture and the plastic perfection of the volumes it contains." And then he could take his readers from Rembrandtesque chiaroscuro into the world of the Impressionists in which "the artist's eye deliberately recovers the long lost naiveté of the new-born baby's."

> . . . by a charming paradox the artist, who has succeeded in seeing the actual world as a meaningless mosaic of flat patches of colour, finds, when he records this vision on his canvas, that the flat surface takes on the whole curvature of the visual hemisphere and objects spring into clear relief. Never

before was the flat surface of the picture more completely suppressed.

In these leaps through the history of art—that is, the record of man's struggle with form and color—Fry was ahead of his time. English art had stopped in the tracks of the "representational," even in its Ruskinian Pre-Raphaelite moment and later in William Morris's attempts to decorate the functional things of life. Sentimentalities and moralities were attached to the splendid skills of the Victorians. All this was now irrelevant. Fry, at the beginning of the new century, could not take the public taste with him. He was a harbinger of the future. What happened in late 1910, and again in 1912, in the art world of Britain projected Roger Fry and some of his Bloomsbury friends into the center of the artistic stage. They created unexpected excitement and controversy by a coalescence of ideas in painting—and literature—which would ultimately be a part of "the modern movement."

IV

The art explosion occurred in a very innocent and businesslike way. The Grafton Galleries, having no exhibition planned for the autumn and early winter of 1910–11, offered its facilities to Roger Fry, who had urged a show of modern foreign painting. He was given a free hand and, as the impresario, he took no rewards. Nor did the gallery expect revenue. However, at Roger's suggestion it engaged Desmond MacCarthy to be secretary of the exhibition and paid him for his services. He also had the promise of a percentage. The history of Roger's and Desmond's journey to the Continent to collect the moderns is well known. Desmond himself wrote it. He described Fry's boundless energy and how pleasantly cooperative the Paris dealers were—there was not, after all, great demand for some of these *outré* painters. Fry had two things in mind: to show England certain artists who had already revealed an "innovative" spirit in Paris, and to place before the British art-viewing public works which illustrated his mature aesthetics. Desmond was an amateur with no knowledge of the financial side of art. He simply guessed; and when he asked for 20 percent of the proceeds, the French dealers seemed glad enough to accept. Later he learned that in other circumstances they would pay no more than 11 percent. Doubtless they figured they should not look a gift horse too closely in the mouth.

Then came the naming of the show. Roger wanted to speak of these particular painters as "expressionists"—as distinct from "impressionists." Urged by the press to explain, Roger said, "Oh, let's call them Post-Impressionists; at any rate, they came after the Impressionists." The final title was "Manet and the Post-Impressionists." This was not historically accurate, and Walter Sickert and Jacques Blanche would insist on being more historical and literal; after all, Cézanne was a contemporary of the Impressionists—he did not come after them. What Fry was trying to say, however, was that Cézanne did not paint like Claude Monet or Camille Pissarro and should be attached to the realism of Edward Manet and the tradition which belonged with Post-Impressionist creation. At any rate, when their little tour was over Desmond and Roger had several hundred paintings from which to choose. Desmond had obtained a particularly good haul of Van Goghs from the painter's sister in Amsterdam, including the now famous sunflowers and the celebrated postman, since calendared around the world. There were twenty-one Cézannes, thirty-seven Gauguins, twenty Van Goghs, some of the *fauves,* among them Vlaminck and Rouault, and Derain, Friesz, Picasso, Matisse and Maurice Denis. Fry showed indecision in the hanging of the paintings, and Desmond had the difficult job of numbering and renumbering the catalog. But the moment came when the doors had to open. By that time Desmond had written a preface in which, attempting to explain Fry's aesthetics, he put together a sentence that would be endlessly quoted: "There is no denying," wrote Desmond, "that the work of the Post-Impressionists is sufficiently disconcerting. It may even appear ridiculous to those who do not recall the fact that a good rocking horse has often more of the true horse about it than an instantaneous photograph of a Derby winner."

One expected *The Times* to take a stand in behalf of convention. Sir Charles Holmes accused the painters of gaining simplicity by throwing overboard "the long-developed skill of past artists." The primitive, said Holmes, belonged to primitives, since their art came into being unconsciously. But "deliberate" primitivism seemed to him regressive. Sir William Richmond said that Fry was leading a bunch of asses—"exactly his right place." The abuse mounted. "A bloody show," said the freewheeling Augustus John. John Singer Sargent had a frown on his face. He was "absolutely skeptical as to their having any claim whatever to being works of art." He did have a word of praise for Gauguin's colors. Sir Arthur Conan Doyle, imaginative enough to have created Sherlock Holmes, could not find the imagination for Post-Impressionism. Always a reflector of the philistine, he spluttered like a British colonel. The painters were rogues and charlatans. They were quite mad. Wilfrid Blunt, as we learn from his diaries, considered the show a bad joke, even a swindle. He called it "pornographic." His was perhaps the most innocent of judgments in terms of the marketplace: one might, he said of a group of canvases that would sell for millions in our time, pay five pounds in order to put them on a bonfire. But the pictures sold even then: the gallery made money. Desmond got an unexpected windfall out of his percentage, some £500.

Years later he would call the show "the Art-quake of 1910." The public, scenting fun from the critics, began to pour into the Grafton Galleries. Four hundred persons came daily to laugh at the pictures or to grow angry because things were not the same as they had always been. The Manets were acceptable. They might shrug their shoulders at the Cézannes as bad painting; the Gauguins were exotic and had a certain appeal; the Van Goghs aroused derision and were treated as the work of a madman. The works of Matisse were wholly outside British experience. If the attitude of Walter Sickert, as a frequenter of Paris *salons*, was that this was old stuff, especially the Cézannes and Manets, Robert Ross called the show "pretension and imposture." Matisse was "mere discords of pigment." In a sense the British were back in the period when Ruskin accused Whistler of flinging pots of paint in the public's face. The history of the exhibition is described by Virginia Woolf in her life of Fry; it figures in the biographies and memoirs of other artists. But in retrospect what can be seen is Fry's great success, particularly as an irritant; or as Virginia put it, the paintings had "the astonishing power to enrage." One critic of the time said, "Art suddenly became a vital matter."

Roger Fry enjoyed the excitement in the press but had to ask himself what kind of public he had been leading. It listened to him with profound respect on the masters; it venerated art; but now it felt betrayed by his attempt to reveal what had been revealed to him. He had himself come to modernism late, as Sickert reminded him. This led to accusations of "charlatanism." Fry's reputation as a critic went into immediate decline. The corollary of this was that he found himself, in middle age, a leader of the young—those artists who were themselves experimenting in England and to whom "modernity" was being revealed in a striking way. Time has handsomely vindicated Fry far beyond the quibbles of whether the show was rightly or wrongly named. A few months later he would hold a "Post-Impressionist" show of British painters, and in 1912 a second exhibition.

Kenneth Clark has summed up Fry's role, saying that he "ceased to be a learned expert and became the champion of modern art." And in Bloomsbury, where Vanessa and Duncan had been finding the language of design and decoration in painting, Fry became a catalyst. He gave to Clive Bell, who had seen these new painters in his Paris days, confidence to launch himself in art criticism. Clive brought to it his robustly logical mind as well as his rage against stupidity. He could express in more journalistic terms the unverbalized feelings of Vanessa and of Duncan; and he could be a loyal disciple to Roger. In this way Bloomsbury ranged itself with the modern in painting, as it would be ranged later with the avant-garde in the novel, in modern biography—and we might add, in economics and political science.

A Journey to Byzantium

Roger Fry's arrival in the houses of Bloomsbury distinctly contributed to the emergence of the friends as a "group." Virginia Woolf would say much later that Bloomsbury "produced" Roger. It gave him a circle in which he was understood and appreciated, and there were reciprocal influences among the painters. Vanessa put it another way—and she was probably thinking of the nonvisual members such as Lytton and Leonard. Roger, she said, helped them to be "more directed to painting than the meaning of 'the Good.'" However, success still lay ahead for the younger generation, then in its late twenties or early thirties, while Fry in his mid-forties was riding the tempest of modern art. Far from being "produced" by Bloomsbury, it might be said that he helped to produce it.

Roger Fry gave Bloomsbury a center and a focus in art between 1910 and the outbreak of the war. Bloomsbury art would attract the public's attention long before the same public found itself reading Bloomsbury's books; indeed, before these books were written. Roger appeared among the friends as an alert partisan of modernity. He was fascinating—almost spellbinding—in his talk; he had abundant vitality and an interest in the minutiae of life, while always seeing the essentials. Some years earlier he had declined the directorship of the National Gallery. He was now offered that of the Tate. But he chose not to be of the British art establishment. The Grafton Gallery, after the success of his show, was available to him for future autumns and he threw in his lot with the avant-garde. He was by no means a "dictator" of British art, as some tried to make him out to be. He had simply attracted national attention. There were other active groups in London—the Camden Town Group, the Allied Art Association, the New

English Art Club—that espoused their own forms of modernity. There was also Wyndham Lewis, who would soon publish his journal *Blast* on behalf of the Vorticists. There was Walter Sickert with his lively brush and lively tongue. But Roger nonetheless had made a particular place for himself, and younger artists, as we have seen, looked to him for leadership. He derived great joy, Desmond said, in discovering unrecognized beauty. This endeared him to a wide circle, as it did to Bloomsbury.

II

When the Post-Impressionist exhibition closed, Roger was exhausted and felt he needed a holiday. He began to talk of going to Turkey. There were the great mosaics which Duncan had seen during his recent trip with Maynard. Duncan also talked of the great churches and their architecture; the Hagia Sophia in Constantinople, he said, was unsurpassed. Under Roger's spell, Vanessa and Clive decided to travel with him, although Vanessa had had another confinement a few months earlier (her second son, Quentin). She felt, however, that the children would be in safe hands in the Gordon Square nursery. The party ultimately consisted of the Bells, Fry, and the Cambridge mathematician H. T. J. Norton, a friend of the Bells and one of Vanessa's circle of admirers. They set off in April across Europe and the Balkans on their journey to what had once been Byzantium.

Like the journey of the Stephens to Greece in 1906, the visit to Asia Minor—to Constantinople and beyond—had its treacheries. When they first arrived in the ancient city, Roger and Vanessa were in a state of constant delight: it was a new world of color, sound, smell, filled with opportunities for the painter. They looked at the mosaics in terms of Seurat's "optical painting." Bloomsbury artists would later attempt to "mosaicize" subjects, as in Duncan's *Queen of Sheba* now at the Tate—that is, paint disparate squares of color as if they were copying a mosaic. Vanessa and her three admiring males journeyed from Constantinople to Brusa in Anatolia, a city of some 76,000 composed of Moslems, Christians and some Jews, as remote from modern London as was Leonard's Ceylon. They proceeded there by boat across the Sea of Marmora—a long, slow voyage—and then went by a pottering train to the lower slopes of Mount Olympus. Here lay Brusa, divided by its three ravines. Mountain streams and mosques, almond blossoms and tombs, cypresses and bazaars made Vanessa and Roger reach at once for their sketchbooks and paints. Brusa had clean streets and a long history. While the two painted, Clive and Norton studied composites of civilization around them and went to the bazaars. They relished the crowds, the architecture, the textiles, the exquisite silks. One day Roger set up his easel alongside Vanessa's outside a weaver's house, and they painted a Turkish cemetery in the middle distance with its row of cypresses. The weaver was a gentle and kindly man; he took an interest in these strangers from afar. He brought them Turkish coffee and invited them into his garden, where a little stream bubbled. He had beautiful manners and an antique hospitality. It was a scene of remembered tranquillity.

The English travelers stayed in a ramshackle inn. They were sufficiently experienced to put up with whatever was available. But with the emotion and excitement of discovery and strangeness, Vanessa began to complain of great physical weakness. She was usually a hardy person, but suddenly she had fainting spells. Clive was helpless in such matters; Norton was wholly inexperienced. But the resourceful Roger was available and ready. There were no doctors and no nurses—only a local chemist (very much like the situation of the heroine in Virginia's *The Voyage Out*, who became helplessly ill in a remote foreign town). What had happened, it was soon ascertained, was that Vanessa had left on the journey in an early state of pregnancy. She had now had a miscarriage. The arduous trip had unwittingly been undertaken at the wrong moment. In London, Virginia began to have anxieties. She read between the lines of letters telling her not to worry. She remembered how Thoby had died of typhoid he contracted during his travels in 1906. With a show of energy—and a touch of panic—she rushed across the Continent until she reached Brusa.

Virginia later vividly re-created Roger's remarkable response to the emergency. He had a doctor's interest in drugs and a painter's interest in the human body. He improvised. He consulted books. He ventured into the kitchen of the inn to concoct dishes. When the patient was resting, he was out in some courtyard painting a tree or a fountain, while consulting a Turkish conversation book. He took Virginia for a drive and expatiated on the Turkish hills. The light was real light, he said, "not pea soup dissolved in vapor." Some women were carrying pots to the wells. He stopped the driver. Where could he buy such pots? Soon he was in a native quarter bargaining for artifacts and colored handkerchiefs. His hotel room was littered with stuffs, silks, a chess set, medicines, bottles, pottery, paint boxes. Somehow he managed to get all this packed. A week after Virginia arrived, her sister was carried on a litter of Roger's design to the train station, where at the scheduled time they boarded the Orient Express. Roger ousted a truculent colonel to obtain an ideal corner for the patient. And so the two sisters, the male companions, and a freight of fragile china, pottery, and paintings sped into familiar Europe. Presently Vanessa was back in Gordon Square, attended by British doctors and nurses. She was ill, depressed, and convalescent for many weeks.

III

Before their return, Vanessa and Roger knew that they had fallen in love. There had been the intimacy of their outings—a romantic moment in a carriage in Constantinople, and the romance of their sketchings-together. Her convalescence that summer, in a cottage not far from Roger's home, was probably prolonged by feelings arising from her troubled marriage. Much of her life with Clive had been valuable and constructive, although she could not share his worldliness and was troubled by his infidelities. And he could not share her self-contained regality. Her greatest interest lay in home, family, art. Clive's ceaseless flirtation with Virginia, however much it repeated Virginia's old attitudes, was painful. At this moment Vanessa feared (as her son tells us) "that her much loved but agonisingly exasperating sister might set herself to charm Roger" as well. Virginia always wanted what Vanessa had —she envied her men, children, paintings. Between the summer of 1911 and the outbreak of the war, the marriage of Clive and Vanessa, which had started with considerable depth of feeling but certain strong incompatibilities, was gradually converted into a *mariage de raison*. So it would remain to the end.

Roger stirred her in different ways from Clive. He gave her a quality of tenderness that she had lacked ever since the death of her mother. He was himself maternal. His care for Vanessa at Brusa had shown this. There was also their common devotion to and practice of art. These qualities counted heavily with her and made her respond to Roger with passion; they also became the destructive element in their relationship. Vanessa did not need mothering. She was capable of being mother to all Bloomsbury. And she preferred silence to talk about painting, especially at work. Roger was very much rooted in his selfhood, endlessly articulate and enthusiastic. Two strong wills were thus temporarily united.

Profound feeling existed between them. Observing friends later said that it was clear in Gordon Square how centered Vanessa had become on Roger. Occasionally the two would slip away, when they could, to some obscure place for a weekend of quiet if uneasy domesticity. In those early months Roger gave Vanessa strength and peace, authority and judgment. He could be her voice. Years later she could still catch the sense of the time when to see him every day "most of the day sitting near him, reading, talking, looking . . . I first realized fully what an absolutely enthralling companion had come into one's life. Our feelings jumped together at each new sight; for the first time there was someone who could convey his feelings and show that he understood mine. Such sympathy was so delightful, so complete, so quick that in itself it gave one as it were new senses and apprehensions. Not only that, however, but also such fascinating speculations and trains of thought, such imaginings seemed to spring continually from some inexhaustible source that one felt here was a prospect of endless delight ahead." Vanessa could return, even after years, to emotional truth. In her biography of Roger Fry, Virginia refers to their love elliptically in Roger's terms: "There was the new friendship with Vanessa Bell, who, as painter belonging to the younger generation, had all the ardor of the young for the new movements and the new pictures and urged him away from the past and on into the future." Roger's feelings are abundantly present in his love letters to Vanessa:

> . . . the queer silkiness of the palm of your hand and your throat that swells like a great wave when you throw your head back for me to kiss it, and the little waves of hair that ripple round your ears, and your torso that's hewn in such great planes and is so polished . . .

He told her she deserved more than he could ever give her. He spoke of "this miracle of rhythm in you." He compared her physically to the noted swimming star of the time (who also was appearing in early movies), Annette Kellerman, a woman with ideal physical measurements, as of a Venus de Milo.

Clive, in spite of his own infidelities ("Chastity is not his line," said Vanessa), had occasional twinges of jealousy. These would be more acute later, when Duncan succeeded Roger. But he was sufficiently civilized to face the strains and stresses and at the same time share in common joys— their growing sons and the art world in which Roger was his master. It was a "triangle." Clive, however, had created other triangles; and Virginia had been a complicating element. Quentin Bell describes the situation of his parents with careful truth: "On the whole the break-up of the Bell marriage, that is to say its transformation into a union of friendship, which was slowly accomplished during the years 1911–1914, made for a relaxation of tension between the sisters and a slow dissolution (never quite complete) of Virginia's long troubled relationship with Clive."

Virginia, he adds, having envied the domesticity of the Bells, had no need to envy it any longer: "It was ceasing to exist, things were changing."

Bloomsbury: The Third Phase

Things were changing—and not only in Gordon Square. The lease in Fitzroy Square was expiring; and after five years of domestic life together, the Stephen brother and sister wondered whether some new design for living might not be found. Quentin Bell tells us that Virginia and Adrian were tired of their "long and quarrelsome tête-à-tête" and now proposed what he called "a domestic revolution." This was that they should find an even larger house and invite others to share it with them. Maynard and Duncan fell in with the plan; and when Vanessa recovered from her illness, she helped search for the ideal dwelling. A big house in Fitzroy Square, with splendid Adam rooms, was rejected. "Elegance is becoming rather tiresome," Vanessa said. A house in Bedford Square was briefly considered. Had they taken it, there would have been some kind of neighborly link between Lady Ottoline's salon, which flourished in this square, and expanding Bloomsbury.

What they finally found, however—and it suited them all—was No. 38 on the north side of Brunswick Square. The large ground-floor sitting room had a fine spread of curving wall at the garden end, opposite the street. Duncan painted a lively mural on it, a London street scene depicting a collision of horse-drawn cabs, which gave free play to his sense of humor: women hanging out of windows, animals, police, street urchins. He used his Seurat-Byzantine style, which Vanessa labeled "Duncan's leopard style." The mural was distinctly English, distinctly cockney and Brueghelesque. The sitting room shared with Maynard showed Duncan's hand not only in his mural but also in the rugs, yellow and green stuffs thrown over chairs, a decorated vase on the mantelpiece. On the first floor lived

Adrian, and he had his mural as well, a tennis game in the style of Matisse painted by Duncan and Frederick Etchells. Adrian himself, who had an amateur's talent, added several nudes to various cupboard doors. Virginia's rooms were on the second floor and resembled those she had in Fitzroy Square. Designed for repose and writing, they were book-strewn, casual, most often in a state of disorder. At the top were smaller rooms for one more tenant. Thus one segment of Bloomsbury became what we would now call a "commune"—a modest one. It harbored a future genius in economics, a future genius in the novel, and a man destined to be one of England's experimental painters during the great length of the twentieth century.

"We have spent a month discussing how to live," Virginia wrote to Lady Ottoline in November of 1911 when they were making the move from Fitzroy Square to Brunswick Square. "We are going to try all kinds of experiments." Brunswick Square represented the third and final phase of Bloomsbury's emergence. The first phases had been social and artistic—parties, readings, literary evenings, charades, discussions of art. With this new house—"so quiet and a graveyard behind"—there began the process of "living together": separate existences and shared expenses. The Bloomsbury friends had long talked of ideal societies, "pantisocracies" of friends. During the first summer of her marriage Vanessa, in the full glow of physical love, had advocated "a circle founded on the principle of complete freedom of sexual intercourse." But neither Vanessa nor Bloomsbury was quite as promiscuous as that. In fact, the centers of Bloomsbury were decorous and domestic. Whatever sarabands of love might be danced at different moments, whatever changes in partnership might occur, there seemed to remain a desire for stability. They were only spiritual bohemians. They liked creature comforts; and then, bohemianism interfered with intellectual and artistic pursuits. Clive Bell once wrote to Molly MacCarthy, with whom he had one of his minor love affairs, "It seems absurd that people who are fond of each other shouldn't all live together always. What's this modern notion of pairing off instead of living in rookeries?" Clive himself would have been the last to accept the democracy of a rookery. With its modest town houses and its country retreats,

Bloomsbury was both serious and playful, cooperative and sensible—hardly libertine. The bourgeois underpinning always remained.

II

The *modus vivendi* in Brunswick Square—the "experiment" of which Virginia spoke—was well organized. The Stephen domestic sense combined with Keynesian logic to make the kitchen work of life function smoothly. The servants—a cook and a maid—"seemed prepared and rather amused than otherwise" by the whole idea. The "Scheme of the House" provided breakfast at 9:00 A.M. The help was notified each day on a "Kitchen Instruction Tablet" who would be in for lunch or dinner: lunch at 1:00, tea at 4:30, dinner at 8:00. Meals were placed on trays in the hall; they could be eaten sociably in one or another set of rooms or in solitude. "Inmates are requested to carry up their own trays; and to put the dirty plates on them and carry them down again *as soon as the meal is finished*." Vanessa has recorded how pleasant she found the arrangements of the two neighboring houses—Gordon and Brunswick Squares.

> Rooms were decorated, people made to sit for their portraits, champagne was produced (rashly left unlocked up by Maynard Keynes who was half the time in Cambridge), to while away the morning sittings—all seemed a sizzle of excitement. Brunswick would come round to Gordon when tired of the tray system of meals, and in those easy days the larder always held enough for two or three unexpected guests, and servants seemed to welcome them with delight. So it was natural to say "stay to dinner" and to sit and talk as of old till all hours, either in the familiar room at No. 46 or in the [Brunswick] Square garden.

"All sorts of parties," she said, "at all hours of the day or night happened constantly." The arrangements made for considerable spontaneity.

The Gordon and Brunswick Square houses, in the months before the war, established in this way a pattern for a casual kind of communal life among the Bloomsbury friends. Asheham House in Sussex, which was discovered at this time, came to be the kind of house they used as a retreat from London; for some years it was a valued and much beloved resort. It had been built in 1820 and stood isolated on the Downs: it had two large sitting rooms on the ground floor which gave on a terrace through large French windows; there were four bedrooms on the second floor and a large attic. Leonard Woolf uses such words as "romantic, gentle, melancholy, lovely" to describe Asheham and its small disheveled walled garden on one side. Leading from it were rows of elms, and below the terrace the field swept away, joining with the Ouse valley to meet the Downs, "a sea of green trees, green grass, green air." The house itself was perhaps too much in the shade, for it was built against a hill. Modernity had not touched it. An earth closet, water pumped by hand from a well, an oil stove, candles and oil lamps at night: pastoral Bloomsbury could shrug its shoulders at comforts later considered indispensable. But then they had all been reared in the pre-electric age. And so between this country spot and the urban houses, Bloomsbury worked and played and entertained during the war-burdened years ahead.

Pericles and Aspasia

Leonard Woolf's six and a half years in Ceylon came to an
end early in 1911, a few weeks after the Clive Bells, Virginia Stephen and Roger Fry completed their journey in
Asia Minor. They recrossed Europe at the end of April;
Leonard crossed the Indian Ocean at the end of May. He
was on a year's leave. In characteristic fashion, he fulfilled
all his duties to the last detail before he sailed. As Chief
Government Agent at Hambantota he calmed an outbreak
of Buddhist and Moslem strife: with calculated impartial-
ity he fined the Buddhists for using their tomtoms without
a license and the Moslems for disturbing a religious proces-
sion. It was not easy to relinquish his high authority—his
power to arrange the affairs of thousands of people. He
was accustomed to hard work. He did not welcome idleness. He had spent many lonely, dreary months in the
outpost, but he also enjoyed being a white sahib. He might
brood on the evils of colonialism, yet he had been its
functioning and efficient instrument. Widely read in political science, he held to those principles of law and justice,
freedom and society, that he had discovered long ago in
Thucydides. He always cherished the immortal words of
Pericles about "the unwritten laws of humanity and civilization." The great funeral oration of classical antiquity was
the cornerstone of the civilization he had helped carry into
Ceylon. He had lived the myth of the builder; he felt
himself an architect of city and state. He had learned his
Thucydides as a mere schoolboy and under the worst possible conditions—in an ugly classroom smelling of boys
and ink, with dog-eared books around him. He had sat at
an uncomfortable desk, the slow tick of the clock making
monotonous counterpoint with the voice of the master.

And yet the glorious words of civilization in "the language of bare beauty peculiar to the Greeks" had entered his being and reverberated there all his life. "I can never read it even today," he wrote when he was old, "without an uplifting of the heart."

For almost seven years he had lived these truths of the Athenians in the tropical remoteness and the jungles—the world of matter and of spirit. Preoccupied with the material things of a primitive society struggling for subsistence, Leonard's mind had dwelt on reason and law, a social and psychological system of logic and justice, in which man used power for the good of all. Greece would seem to Leonard Woolf the starting point for the new *Principia Politica* that he would someday write. In the dim mythic way in which we cling to heroes of our past, he would remember the words of Pericles. Seeking a mask for Virginia Stephen's name in his diaries, he called her Aspasia, who had been the consort of Pericles and was said to be one of the wisest women of her time. The classical model for Leonard's myth of himself as a wise governor and leader linked to a woman of wisdom was the age of Pericles: a dazzling sun on the marble of Athens at the moment of the city-state's greatest effulgence: Pericles and Aspasia.

II

On the last day of his rule in Hambantota, Leonard inspected two schools, one of which he had built. In his official diary he noted there were signs that "some knowledge" was being driven into the heads of the native youth. He sailed the next day from Colombo. Less than a month later he landed at Marseilles. He returned to London with misgivings. Everything seemed diminished; everything seemed shrunken. In his mother's home in Putney he was conscious of his depression. The ceilings seemed low; the rooms were small after the palatial windowless rooms of his official residence in Ceylon. He could still hear the sea pounding outside his door; he could feel the unending jun-

gle around him. He escaped from "family" to his old fa-
miliars in Cambridge. Lytton Strachey was staying in
King's Parade, and for a few days Leonard relived his
student days. He attended a meeting of the Apostles. The
eternal questions were still being discussed. And there were
new faces, among them the young Rupert Brooke, who
looked like an Adonis *aetat* twenty-three. Leonard felt
middle-aged. He had gone to Ceylon at twenty-four. He
was now thirty-one.

His melancholy dissolved slowly, and he was in comparatively good spirits early in July 1911, little more than a
month after his return, when he went to dine in Gordon
Square with the Clive Bells. He had last been at No. 46
seven years earlier saying anxious farewells before leaving
for the unknown. Thoby had been alive; the Stephens had
just moved into Bloomsbury, and Vanessa and Virginia
had presided over their new hearth with the charm and
exalted beauty Leonard saw in them. They had remained
his dream of fair women during all his colony years. He
had found himself returning in memory to the happiness of
May Week in 1903, and the exquisite English womanhood
in Thoby's rooms at Trinity. Now Vanessa was married to
Clive. Leonard did not approve of their marriage; he considered Clive to be Vanessa's inferior—"a bright service-
able little mind." Meeting the Bells again, Leonard was
carried back vividly to his youth. Whatever his remote
roots as a Jew who had lived in Putney, he felt that he was
"still a native of Trinity and King's." He was a reserved,
cautious, sophisticated Cambridge intellectual; and he was
in his familiar world that evening at the Bells'.

Virginia was not at the dinner, but she came in from
Fitzroy Square afterward with Duncan Grant and Walter
Lamb to greet the returned exile. "What was so new and
exhilarating to me in Gordon Square of July 1911,"
Leonard said, "was the sense of intimacy and complete
freedom of thought and speech, much wider than in the
Cambridge of seven years ago, and above all including
women." What was new, in effect, was "Bloomsbury."
They called one another by their Christian names. There
was often a kiss instead of a shaking of hands. Leonard was
made aware that certain Victorian residues had dropped

away during his absence. He found a new and continuing life of which he could once more be a part. He later said that this evening of reacquaintance was the origin of Bloomsbury "so far as I was concerned." The man who later would be referred to as the *éminence grise* of Bloomsbury became the last of the "originals" to reenter its ranks.

He was not yet one of Virginia's suitors. But when she came in that evening, he found himself stirred by her ethereal beauty and the quality of her voice—he apparently thought of the French words *l'harmonie la plus douce est le son de la voix de celle que l'on aime.* He was not yet in love with Virginia, but he was in love with the idea of loving her. That idea had taken shape in his correspondence with Lytton when he was still in Hambantota. Lytton had described to Leonard how in a moment of talk he had impulsively proposed to Virginia. He had no sooner spoken when he wished he could bite his tongue. He felt "it would be death if she accepted me." This kind of "death" came instantly; Virginia did accept him. Both were aware that they were playing some kind of love-game, a *folie à deux* between an ardent homosexual and a virgin. "I was in terror lest she would kiss me," Lytton had written Leonard. Calm thought followed the insanity of the moment: the engagement was broken off within a day or so. "Do you think Virginia would have me?" Leonard wrote. "I'll take the next boat home."

Leonard did not take the next boat. In the two intervening years, however, Lytton assumed Cupid's role. "You could marry Virginia . . . she's an astonishing woman." And again, "You must marry Virginia . . . she's young, wild, inquisitive, discontented, and longing to be in love." Leonard mused on his future. What was love? We have seen how he believed more than 90 percent of it to be simply a desire for copulation. And copulation itself was for him but a moment of "frenzy."

Now, sitting in Gordon Square, he looked at Virginia and she looked at him. Both knew they were "candidates." It had been one thing for Lytton to shoot his sly and safe arrows across miles of ocean. It was another for the two to be face to face with the concealments and gallantries of courtship.

III

Virginia's thoughts had been on marriage, as we know, ever since she first moved into Fitzroy Square. She had no lack of suitors; however, not one of them had seemed "right"—Lytton least of all. He was as much accustomed to being taken care of as Virginia was. They were both complete egotists. Neither would have been able to rise to the mutual responsibilities of marriage. There were moments in the midst of Bloomsbury sociabilities when Virginia had a feeling of horror that she might end up a Victorian spinster. "I hate pouring tea and talking like a lady, and realise my own inadequacy without Nessa. However it has to be faced." And to Vanessa, who had disapproved of one of her suitors, she wrote, "Am I to have no proposal then? If I had had the chance, and determined against it, I could settle to virginity with greater composure than I can, when my womanhood is at question." What was Virginia's womanhood? "How can a virgin be expected to understand?" Lytton asked. In her first novel Virginia wrote, "Marriage, marriage, that was the right thing, the only thing, the solution required by everyone she knew." She certainly wanted this solution for herself.

It is doubtful whether Virginia, during her many months in Fitzroy Square before Leonard's return, gave much thought to the exile in Ceylon. Lytton had told Vanessa of Woolf's interest, but it is not clear whether Vanessa told Virginia. Vanessa, given her delicate relation with her sister, may have remained silent; she spoke only when her opinions of various suitors were asked. But it is hardly likely that Virginia was unaware of Leonard as a potential suitor. Other suitors had swarmed: even when they were homosexuals, they were attracted by Virginia's "distance" and her fancy, which in conversation at the right moment could have vertiginous flights. We need only list those who sought to marry her to see the variety of men she attracted. There had been Walter Headlam, a Hellenist; H.T.J. Norton, who had been on the trip to Turkey and was really in love with Vanessa; Saxon Sydney-Turner, who seemed on the surface not interested in anything so active as being a husband; Walter Lamb, who was interested, but thought

Virginia lived "in a hornets' nest" and told her, "Marriage is so difficult." He said to Virginia "Will you let me wait?" and she replied, "Don't hurry." Finally, just before Leonard, there were Hilton Young and Sydney Waterlow, the Cambridge prodigy who was in the Foreign Office. We might include Lytton Strachey, although after their brief comedy he relapsed into friendliness and their consistent dialogue of wit and aggressivity. Her problem was her need to receive love, without the ability to give it. This is considerably documented in the ambiguous wooings depicted in her second novel, *Night and Day*, written after her marriage. Her heroine, Katharine, has Vanessa's beauty but also Virginia's sexual coldness. The leading couples become engaged not out of love, but out of confused feelings. There was something regal about Virginia. Her years of illness, her life lived on the border of insanity, contributed to this. She felt herself motherless—and she would deprive most of her heroines of their mothers. Her low self-esteem made her dependent on a large circle of maternal female friends. Quentin Bell has listed for us the lowly animal nicknames she chose for herself: goat or monkey, a half-bird (Sparroy), mandril, a cocker spaniel. She could not imagine herself a tigress, a panther, a bird of paradise. "These animal *personae* safely removed from human carnality and yet cherished, the recipients indeed of hugs and kisses, were most important to her, but important as the totem figure is to the savage," wrote Quentin Bell. She characterized herself thus in the animal kingdom and showed her ambivalent feelings about marriage. She could appeal to a homosexual like Lytton, since her aloofness offered no womanly threat. But one other kind of husband was possible—a husband who would replace the absent mother and take care of her. Leonard Woolf, the man farthest removed in his heritage from that of the Stephens —member of another tribe, another caste—would thus be brought into innermost Bloomsbury.

IV

Some time earlier, Virginia had leased a small house at Firle in Sussex, which she had named Little Talland House after the Cornwall house of her childhood. She had been using it as a country retreat from Fitzroy Square and Adrian. She now invited Leonard to come for a weekend: this was her appropriate gesture of welcome to Thoby's old friend. Leonard delayed acceptance. It was midsummer; he was scheduled to go to the Continent. He was involved with his family in Putney, and there seems to have been some young woman there to whom he was attracted. This became the subject of a novel he would write two years later about Bloomsbury and its presiding graces. He called it *The Wise Virgins*, and in it the hero, a young Jew, is divided between his love for a Virginia character, beautiful, cold, intellectual, and a suburban middle-class young lady, who is sentimental and aspires to be an Ibsen heroine. In the novel the hero is unable to extricate himself and is forced to marry within his own social caste. In life the opposite occurred.

Early in September Leonard paid the postponed visit to Firle, Marjorie Strachey being the other guest. He and Virginia had met only four times before and in the most casual manner. Now he took long walks on the Downs with his hostess, and they talked intimately far into the night. They seem to have been cautious and in a way shy—perhaps made self-conscious by Lytton's hyperactive matchmaking, but also by their different worlds and temperaments. She had known no Jews. Although Leonard's background and education were quite as English as those of Virginia's brothers, she thought of him as an outsider. She had to become accustomed to the idea of marrying someone who did not belong to her own tribe. She was troubled by Leonard's mixture of intelligence and gloom— or, as he makes her say in his novel about the wise virgins, "You want to go away into a corner and quietly ruminate on the eternal discomfort of the universe." It was true that Leonard was a very serious young man: he brooded as only some young Jews can brood, on the state of the world, the need for wisdom, the plight of the poor. There was something of Virginia's father in him: both had the stance of a Hebrew prophet, and Leonard Woolf had the tenacity and carapace of his people. She felt comfortable in the fatherly side of Leonard, but found Leonard's sense of fun buried behind his high seriousness. Leonard embodied all that she had known best in men (she had known them at their worst in her half brothers). And then Leonard had a Jewish quality of which Virginia was only becoming aware: he was one of those Jews who, when touched by civilization, as Jews like to be, remain hard as nails, inflexible in principle, exigent in ethic—so had the race remained in order to survive. Some were coarsened by this process, and literature seemed to show them as coarse. Others were refined and as eloquent as Shylock. Behind Leonard's will to live lay a love not only of life, but of the despair of life: an eternal melancholy—as of the wailing at the sacred wall in Jerusalem for the perishable things of this earth. All this is implicit in *The Wise Virgins*, where we can see that Leonard Woolf was more deeply troubled about caste than he reveals in his autobiography. And then he found Bloomsbury inclined to be frivolous. He did not have the aristocratic ability to "play" as well as work.

If Virginia was troubled by the aura of intelligence—and gloom—in which Leonard moved, Leonard in turn was troubled by the fact that the Stephen sisters seemed to live in a world of words. In *The Wise Virgins*, the young Jew explodes, "You talk and you talk and you talk—no blood in you! You never *do* anything." And when the male character to whom he speaks asks, "Why do you think it's so important to do things?" the answer is "Why? Because I'm a Jew, I tell you—I'm a Jew."

Leonard develops this argument between himself and the society in which he moves not on racial, but on sociological, grounds. The British of Virginia's class, or Clive's, lived in a "settled" world—a world *made* for them, into which they were born and lived at their ease. The British Jews, on the other hand, had had to find their way. They needed money "and out of money, power." The hero of Leonard's *roman à clef* is explicit:

. . . knowledge, intelligence, taste. We're always pouncing on them because they give power, power to *do* things, influence people. That's what really we want, to feel ourselves working on people, in any way, it doesn't matter. It's a sort of artistic feeling, a desire to create. To feel people moving under your hands or your brain just as you want them to move. Admiration, appreciation, these are the outward signs. They make you swell with pride and happiness. . . . Then of course we get an acquired pleasure in the mere operation of doing things, of always feeling oneself keyed up and absolutely alive. . . . You must admit that our point of view implies imagination.

In his hero's vehemence, Leonard not only revealed the alertness of some Jews to action and social reform but also expressed the powerlessness he himself felt, divided as he was between Putney and Bloomsbury—he who had been a quasi-ruler of thousands in Ceylon, "working on people." As George Spater and Ian Parsons say, the difference between Leonard and Virginia, which the two examined in their book on the Woolfs, was in reality not that of Jew and Christian, but "between professional middle class and cultured and leisured upper-class intellectual." Leonard was of a tradition outside Virginia's high-fenced upper-class mores. That she ultimately chose him as against a large group of Anglo-Saxon suitors suggests that there was no trace of bigotry in her, although some critics have accused her of what is today called "racism." In both Leonard and Virginia there was a strong desire to free themselves from tribal bondage. This was one way of Virginia's taking her "voyage out." Her ambivalence was reflected in the fact that while she had removed herself from the Stephens and Duckworths and the "mummification" of her past, she did not need to divorce herself from her class; her roots would not be torn up. It was Leonard who was uprooting himself. In Bloomsbury, however, he could remain the social reformer, the political scientist, the planner of a better world.

The phrase "the voyage out" is used by the Virginia character in Leonard's novel. She tells the hero she wants "the romantic part of life . . . it's the voyage out that seems to me to matter, the new and wonderful things." But she also says, "I can't give myself: passion leaves me cold. You'll think I am asking for everything to be given and to give nothing. Perhaps that's true."

V

They saw a great deal of one another after a while, for Virginia invited Leonard to occupy the empty rooms at the top of No. 38 Brunswick Square. She was saying to Leonard, in effect, "Come live with me and be my love"—spiritual love, as we know. Leonard joined the Bloomsbury commune shortly after it was organized and regularly brought his lunch tray to Virginia's rooms on the second floor. "There is something very like Thoby about him, not only his face," she would write to Violet Dickinson. Thoby remained for both sisters the male touchstone. In his rooms at the top, Leonard worked on his novel *The Village in the Jungle*. Virginia, on the floor below, was rewriting *The Voyage Out*. It is perhaps a detail, but just after he moved into his new home, in December 1912, Leonard began to make certain secret entries in his diary, in a personal code invented by using Sinhalese and Tamil symbols for the English alphabet.

A period of intense mutual appraisal between the two lovers now began. If they got tired of their meals in Brunswick Square, they wandered over to Gordon Square, where Vanessa—herself involved with the passions and stresses of her affair with Roger—was sufficiently well organized to feed family and friends. Leonard's leave from Ceylon was shrinking, and London had never seemed so attractive. It was a period of much happiness for the lovers, mingled with hours of misgiving and doubt. The two or three Seasons before the outbreak of the war had an intense art-life that had been flowering since the end of the Victorian era. There had been many years of peace. Britain and the Continent seemed at a peak of civilization. Old forms, old fetters, were being broken. New experiments were being tried in art and in living. Out of Muscovy came the Russian ballet to delight the West: the fairy tales of *Scheherazade, Swan Lake* and *The Firebird*, Nijinsky, Diaghilev, Bakst (the designer), Stravinsky. Roger had shown London the meaning of modern painting. The English stage, revitalized by Ibsen and Shaw, was now seeing Chekhov for the first time. This world seemed made for Virginia and Leonard in their hours of courtship, and each night unrolled some new fantastic fable or myth. "Modernism" was being born under their very eyes. Ceylon, for Leonard, had been all work and strenuous bridge games to relieve boredom. He now felt free as never before. His life during 1911 and 1912, he said, was a "kaleidoscopic dream." When he was not with Virginia or at his writing, he went riding in the parks or visited Cambridge and the Apostles.

VI

We have seen that Leonard gave a name to his beloved out of the age of Pericles. A document of the highest value exists in which Leonard tried to set down a "character" for his "Aspasia," he being perhaps in imagination a kind of Pericles, intent upon bettering the world. He was a socialist, brooding over ways in which statesmen might learn to keep peace and use logic and above all common sense. Aspasia is mentioned in an ancient dialogue, the *Menexenus*, attributed to Plato (but regarded as apocryphal): "Truly, Socrates, I marvel that Aspasia, who is only a woman, should be able to compose such a speech, she must be a rare one." There is no doubt that Leonard considered Virginia "a rare one." In Greek history Aspasia is described as a courtesan, but Leonard was thinking not so much of Aspasia's body as her mind. She aroused in him, if we are to go by his novel, "a curious excitement of the mind, rather than the body." Pericles made Aspasia his mistress and recognized his son by her as legitimate. The comic poets spoke of her as adviser to Pericles in his political actions. Perhaps Leonard's choice of the name had the most meaning in terms of the dialogue by the Socratic Aeschines. In this work Aspasia criticizes the manners and training of women. Without pressing the classical analogy too hard, we can recognize that, in disguising Virginia as Aspasia, Leonard was foreseeing the writing of *A Room of One's Own* and *Three Guineas*. He compares his Aspasia to hills against a cold blue sky—in other words, she is a chilly landscape. But he warms to "the glow of her mind which seems to bring things from the centre of rocks, deep streams that have lain long in primordial places beneath the earth." She generates "an air of quiet and clearness." He also finds that her mind is astonishingly without fear. "She is one of possibly three women," wrote Leonard, "who know that dung is dung, death death and semen semen." Who were the other two? One was probably Vanessa. It little matters. This was the Virginia he saw, and the Virginia we know in her moments when she was most in touch with the palpable world. He ends, however, with a surprising observation: "And her heart? . . . Sometimes I think she has not got one."

Leonard, then, saw very clearly during his wooing the troubled side of Virginia: her self-absorption; her inability to love. He saw her as a creature who lived on Olympus: and since when did the Olympians have to deal with mortal demands? It was they who made demands. "I feel no physical attraction to you," Virginia-Aspasia said, not without a certain candid cruelty, "yet your caring for me as you do almost overwhelms me." This was certainly true. Leonard cared deeply for Virginia. And in the other sense of the word "care," he would indeed care for her to the end.

Let us read more of what Leonard wrote with great and deliberate insight into his Aspasia: ". . . to think of her is to see her sitting, lying back in immense chairs before innumerable fires. . . . I see her sitting among it all untouched in her quietness and clearness rather silent a little aloof and then the spring bubbles up—is it wit or humour or imagination? I do not know but the thought has come from strange recesses, life for a moment seems to go faster, you feel for a moment the blood in your wrists, your heart beat, you catch your breath as you do on a mountain when suddenly the wind blows. The things that come are strange often fantastic, but they are beautiful and always seem somewhere far below to have touched, even to have been torn, from reality. . . . She asks too much from the earth and from the people who crawl about it. I am always frightened that with her eyes fixed on the great rocks she will stumble among the stones." After wondering whether Aspasia-Virginia had a heart, Leonard added, ". . . she is made merely of the eternal snow and the rocks which form the hidden centre of reality. And then I swear that this cannot be true, that the sun in her comes from a heart." This was his inner debate. He cut through Virginia's verbal fireworks of the mind to see a series of hard images—hills against a cold sky, rocks, snow. The landscape of love contained a distinct element of hardness and chill. Reading the "character" of his love, we can wonder why Leonard decided to marry Virginia, after such a circumstantial appraisal. He had the courage to show her what he had written, perhaps in the hope that she would say something and help him make up his mind. "She read it slowly in front of the fire. I forgot that she was reading it in the pleasure of watching her face and her hair; she must have sat silent thinking for some time when I heard her say: 'I don't think you have made me soft or lovable enough.' " She was reading the imagery correctly. And her use of the word "lovable" rather than "loving" might have indeed given Leonard further pause.

VII

Leonard Woolf proposed to Virginia little more than a month after moving into Brunswick Square; that is, in January 1912. She asked for more time. She was, as a matter of fact, in a state of turmoil and was having one of her little "episodes." Or, as she frankly told Leonard, "a touch of my usual disease in the head, you know." On the edge of a breakdown, she entered a nursing home. Leonard's diary tells us he went to see Virginia's doctor, Sir George Savage. What the interview was about is not recorded. Savage knew as much as did most psychiatrists of the time. Medicine was resisting Freud, whose diagnostic and therapeutic discoveries would make their impact only by degrees after the war. The visit to the doctor was on 21 March 1912.

Leonard also saw his own doctor about his trembling hands. He learned that this condition was congenital and not incapacitating. It could simply, at times, be embarrassing. It was during this period of the sounding out of their potential physical health that Leonard wrote his private "character" of Aspasia. Love was, however, stronger than doubt. And Leonard had to face a serious personal decision. Virginia was keeping him waiting, and his leave would soon be up. He applied for an extension, and his superiors asked the grounds for this request. Leonard was too reticent to say, even though he was assured of the utmost confidentiality. Deciding to gamble on his future, he resigned. He would not return to Ceylon.

At the beginning of May, Virginia wrote him with a candor for which she apologized. "As I told you brutally the other day I feel no physical attraction in you. There are moments—when you kissed me the other day was one— when I feel no more than a rock." Leonard, nevertheless, burned his bridges. He was confident that there could be accommodation between them—and he was deeply in love. He had savings in the amount of £600 to £800 (he had won a sweepstake when in Ceylon). He would discover whether he could live by his writing. Virginia had a modest income and her earnings as a reviewer. It would, from her point of view, be a far from brilliant match, especially in the light of her inbred sense of class distinction. For him it was love above all—and perhaps also, in a subterranean level, a feeling that he would be even less of an "outsider" (something he had never consciously admitted to himself). He would try to bring her into his world of social reform. She would bring him into the heart of the world to which he aspired.

About a month after Virginia had told Leonard of her doubts, she suddenly changed her mind. She announced that she loved him. This was on 29 May 1912. They were lunching in her rooms in Brunswick Square. As Leonard described it, "I think we both felt a strange happiness of being for a moment alone together in an empty universe."

Virginia Stephen and Leonard Woolf had looked into each other's eyes and had seen the truth. He knew that she had great warmth and was capable of the deepest kind of feeling. He knew too that somewhere within, in her physical being, she was sexually cold, with a frigidity she could not explain. He must have hoped that this could be overcome, that his own passion would melt all resistance. They were married in spite of what they discerned because they wanted each other. They expected to bridge great distances, because she was drawn to a man who desired to control, organize, rule, even as she on her side wanted the comfort and strength of such rule, as she had been ruled by her dictatorial father. Also, she knew that if she lost control, as often happened, he would always remain, tenaciously, in full charge. Virginia translated this into her need for love, for being loved. But in a hidden way she too ruled. She dominated by needing to be cared for. There were, then, two kinds of dominion involved in this marriage, two kinds of power. The struggle between Leonard and Virginia resided in a delicate balance of inner psychic needs and "interpersonal" strength based on these needs: an extraordinary marriage of two kinds of egotism.

VIII

It had been a year's wooing. And they were not in a hurry. Virginia's letters to her women friends announcing her engagement contain a curious mixture of apology and self-denigration. She stressed to all that Leonard was a Jew and that he was penniless; this was not the most desirable match for a lady of position like herself. To Violet Dickinson she broke the news as "a confession." But then Violet had seen her through difficult illnesses. "I feel I shall get fearfully spoilt—but at the same time he'll keep me in good condition as far as other things go." She thus forecast accurately one aspect of Leonard's marital role. She attached importance to his surrender of his career in the colonies "for love—he gave up his entire career there on the chance that I would agree." Years later she would remember "How I hated marrying a Jew."

Leonard took Virginia to meet his mother. Virginia developed a headache. "Work and love and Jews in Putney take it out of one," she wrote to Violet. It was indeed a "plunge." To her old Greek teacher Janet Case she admitted that at first "I felt stunned." The decision had been unsettling; the conflict had been great. Leonard would become for her not only parents and siblings, but also doctor and nurse and (like her father) intellectual and literary mentor.

We must remind ourselves that by this time Virginia had passed her thirtieth birthday. She was eager for marriage. The wedding was set for August. They gave themselves time to adjust to their changing lives—and they wrote a postcard to their bearded Cupid, simply the words "Ha! Ha!" and their signatures. Virginia's low self-esteem and competitive sense came out in her remarks to her friends. "I don't think I'm nearly worth what he is." To Violet she wrote: "We're going to work very hard."

They were married on 10 August 1912, at the St. Pancras Registry Office in the midst of a thunderstorm. The two Duckworth half brothers were in attendance in formal regalia; also Vanessa, who seemed to be daydreaming. She forgot herself and interrupted the formalities by asking about renaming her second son. "One thing at a time," the officiating clerk told her. Duncan Grant came in borrowed finery, a top hat and a silk coat; he brought the painter Frederick Etchells with him. Clive, Roger Fry, Saxon Sydney-Turner, and an aunt of Virginia's completed the party. We know that Clive did not think Leonard would be a good husband for Virginia. He still had a certain proprietary feeling. The wedding breakfast was in Gordon Square. For Vanessa, the marriage of her too-lively spinster sister was clearly a relief. Leonard was now taking over responsibilities she had carried for too long. "God!" exclaimed Virginia as she signed "V.S." to her letter inviting Duncan to the ceremony. "This is the last of S." It was by no means the last of Miss Stephen, for she would remain a spiritual virgin. The name of Woolf, however, would carry her very far indeed.

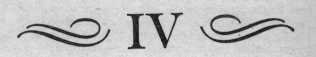

IV

A Crystal Moment

Bloomsbury was becoming an influence in England. The centers of energy originally confined to the Squares on either side of Tottenham Court Road radiated strength and knowledge, power and well-being on the eve of 1914. "A certain receptivity to new ways of thinking and feeling" was Clive Bell's way of putting it, and he added, "A mind at least ajar." Leonard Woolf, years later, said, "We were out to construct something new." He was allied with the idealists. "We were in the van of the builders of a new society which should be free, rational, civilized." So were the Fabians and many other groups in many parts of England and the world. We must not see Bloomsbury as embattled and alone in the prewar avant-garde, but it had its singular aspects as a group of singular individuals. "How full of life those days seemed!" said Vanessa. "Beauty was springing up under one's feet so vividly that violent abuse was hurled at it." She also said, "A great new freedom seemed about to come."

The momentum of this freedom can be seen in the murals Duncan Grant painted in 1911 in the dining hall of the Borough Polytechnic near the Elephant and Castle. Roger was once again the moving spirit behind this project. He gathered a number of young and lively painters around him; they painted their theme of "London on Holiday" with a fine show of color and design. Duncan elected to do football players and swimmers. His long, lean players move in concert as in ballet; their bodies display great energy and well-being. The rhythm and speed of football, and a love for the male body, are in the murals. In the accompanying aquatic scene, muscular males swim, dive, clamber into a boat; and again the spectator is aware of strength of limb and muscle and nerve, a beautiful mobility within the movement of the water. The London press rightly said that Duncan had depicted "the act of swimming rather than the individual swimmer." Another critic saw the athletes as "primitive Mediterraneans in the morning of the world." Still another remarked that "the effect of the whole gives an extraordinary impression of the joys of lean athletic life. It makes one want to swim—even in water like an early Christian mosaic." These observations from a press often casual about matters of art suggest that Duncan succeeded admirably in capturing both movement and emotion. His lyrical murals were a skillful representation of the spirit of the youth of England, that same youth which a few months later, helmeted and uniformed, would be swarming like football players out of the trenches in a game of horror, a dance of death.

The sense of joy the press found in Duncan's panels seemed to be universally experienced at that moment—the moment of peaceful pause before war—throughout England. The Seasons were benign: days of great clearness and beauty as the country went through its rituals for the new reign of George V—races, rowing, riding, games, crowds in the parks, the splendid social panoply of Britain in its all but final Imperial hour. Bloomsbury mingled with the grand and bohemian *monde* of Lady Ottoline. David Garnett, barely twenty, was introduced into Bloomsbury at this time by Adrian Stephen and found himself dazzled by the worldliness and elegance of some of the parties in Gordon Square. A certain high polish had been applied to the old "at homes." Duncan arranged puppet shows, creating large figures whose Racinian accents were pronounced by Gallic Stracheys with all the cadences of Bernhardt. There might also be music by the three D'Aranyi sisters, while Lady Ottoline rustled in her exotic garb, adding luster and humane questions to the gatherings. Clive was a genial host. There were boisterous occasions when Duncan in his masquerades might dress as a pregnant prostitute, or Marjorie Strachey defy convention by attiring herself exclusively in a medallion. Maynard, increasingly affluent— his applied economics yielded high dividends—staged lively dinner parties at the Café Royal preceding the Bloomsbury evenings and dispensed champagne amid inbred wit. The

Victorian insularity that had made London seem for decades an outpost of the Continent gave way to an invasion of Russian dancers, German singers, Wagnerian operas, poets who talked of French symbolism—such as the middle-aged William Butler Yeats and the jaunty young American Ezra Pound, who proclaimed "Imagism" in poetry. The English artistic world reached across the Channel. France, in its own way quite as insular as England, now turned to England, inviting Duncan to design costumes for Jacques Copeau's production of *Twelfth Night*—an adventure which led Duncan and Vanessa into the salon of Gertrude Stein and to meeting with Picasso and Matisse, whom Duncan already knew fairly well. The French actress Valentine Tessier, then young and exquisite—whose radiance would continue into middle age in the plays of Jean Giraudoux—found herself at Bloomsbury parties, where Clive aired his modern French quite as smartly as the Stracheys aired the classical—

> Never were the plane trees loftier, leafier
> the planes of Belford Square,
> and of all that summer foliage motionless
> not one leaf
> had fallen yet, one afternoon
> warm in the last world-peace before
> the First World War.

So William Plomer would write long afterward, remembering a time when aristocratic and bourgeois London alike tasted of the new enchantments and freedoms. Lady Ottoline describes in her journals how she came out one day into Bedford Square with Bertrand Russell, Nijinsky, and Leon Bakst; they saw Duncan Grant and other lithe young men playing tennis in the Square. *"Quel décor!"* murmurs Bakst, who had created the *décor* for the Russians. Nijinsky echoes him. And Plomer wrote in his poem:

> That moment under the plane trees (*quel décor!*)
> ... a crystal moment.

England's—Bloomsbury's—crystal moment.

II

Roger Fry staged his second Post-Impressionist exhibition in 1912. This time it was not a solo performance, aided by Desmond, as in 1911. It could be called a "Bloomsbury show." Roger wrote the preface to the catalog. Duncan and Vanessa designed the posters. Leonard, back from his honeymoon, found temporary employment in the job Desmond had filled, that of the exhibition secretary. Leonard was struck by the raucous laughter and indignation of the spectators; and by Roger's patience with them; and with the slightly bewildered and fussy Henry James, nearing his seventieth year, to whom Roger gave a quiet cup of tea in the gallery basement, patiently explaining that Picasso was doing for art what Flaubert had done for the novel. The first show had used Manet as point of departure; the second was directly focused on Cézanne. The walls were covered with his canvases. But other artists, including Matisse and the *fauves* and Picasso, were well represented. London was beginning to accept Cézanne; it still laughed at Matisse. This time Roger also arranged a corner for the British Post-Impressionists, not least Duncan, Vanessa and himself.

Before the exhibition ended, Roger had extended himself into further enterprises: a trans-Channel show of British painting and the creation of the Omega Workshops in Fitzroy Square. He brought into this project a number of young artists who lived from hand to mouth amid accumulated unsold canvases. His idea was to put British painters to work, to demonstrate that all life belongs to art. There was, after all, the precedent of William Morris. All art—and especially decoration—became Omega's dominion: interior decoration, modern design for furniture, patterns for carpets and china, murals in private homes. Virginia, envious and disparaging, commented: "The furious excitement of these people all the winter over their pieces of canvas coloured green and blue is odious. Roger is now turning these upon chairs and tables; there's to be a shop, and a warehouse next month." The Omega Workshops reflected Roger's genius for improvisation and organization and his dedication to the ways in which art illuminates living. The cooperative enterprise acquired a certain vogue in spite of quarrels and secessions and survived the greater part of the war. Some artists, among them Wyndham Lewis, resented Roger's idea of maintaining strict anonymity in the works. Roger wanted a group-sense, the objects to be impersonal like the French cathedrals or the reviews in the *Times Literary Supplement*. Some of the painters may have rightly felt that Roger was himself hardly anonymous. He signed his prose in the *Athenaeum* even though he might feel he should not sign his *objets d'art*.

The Omega struggled valiantly. Its visitors were always surprised by the novelty, the strangeness, the inventiveness of the artists turned loose on furniture and carpets. In one of his novels Arnold Bennett describes a shop like Omega and captures the spirit of its work. "The walls were irregularly covered with rhombuses, rhomboids, lozenges, diamonds, triangles, and parallelograms; the carpet was treated likewise, and also the upholstery and the cushions." Bennett wrote that the place resembled "a gigantic and glittering kaleidoscope deranged and arrested." And he went on to say that "every piece of furniture was painted with primitive sketches of human figures, or of flowers, or of vessels, or of animals." At the front of the mantelpiece Bennett describes a painting that might have been the work of Duncan or Vanessa: "two nude, crouching women who gazed longingly at each other across the impassable semicircular abyss of the fireplace." Fry described to Bennett how much trouble he had inducing industry to make rugs to his designs, but how public interest was forcing them to lower prices. "I gradually got to like a number of things," Bennett noted. He was not alone. One may read Virginia Woolf's account of the Omega's history in her biography of Fry, and Richard Shone has fully documented this enterprise in his *Bloomsbury Portraits*.

III

Bloomsbury books were also appearing. The first work to be published by one of the friends was Desmond MacCarthy's, and this was ironical, for he would produce so few in the years to come. In 1907 he collected his series of drama critiques in *The Speaker* devoted to the Court Theatre and the developing reputation of Bernard Shaw. After that came Lytton's potboiler in 1912, *Landmarks in French Literature*, which showed his gift of summary and his ability to write clear suave prose. Leonard's *Village in the Jungle* and his *Wise Virgins* appeared soon after, while Virginia was making final revisions to *The Voyage Out*. In 1912 Maynard Keynes assumed the editorship of the *Economic Journal*, a center of power he would hold for the next twenty-five years. He also brought out his first book, a work on Indian currency. Then, to the surprise of those of his friends who called him a "lightweight," early in 1914, Clive Bell published his first book, which he titled very simply *Art*. "Are you waiting for Clive's book to come out to know what to think on Art and every other subject?" scoffed Lytton to Duncan. The book, however, emerged to general applause. Sickert said it was "an illuminant to thought on painting," containing some of the "profoundest, truest and most courageous considerations." Roger described it as "a breath of fresh air." Other reviewers treated it as a manifesto. His "brilliance is vastly entertaining," said the *Manchester Guardian*. All agreed that Clive Bell had brought certain important aesthetic questions into focus and in a manner accessible to all. Even Virginia, critical of Clive, said the book was "clear and brisk," though a bit "too smart."

Clive had begun with a secret ambition to write a *magnum opus* (like Moore's *Principia*) on "modernism." He had an ambitious title, "The New Renaissance." After a while (he confessed) he came to his senses. Realizing that what was really needed was a manageable small book on modern aesthetics, not a huge treatise, he quarried *Art* out of his larger manuscript. The public had been looking with bewilderment at the new paintings and asking for explanation of "method" and "meaning." Clive provided the necessary catchword; it had all the magic of a slogan, "Significant form." Significant form was simply "arrangements and combinations that move us in a particular way." At this late date in the century the label is old and worn. Kenneth Clark has called it a "catchpenny phrase." But when it was newly minted, it had a bright luster. Gallery-goers realized, thanks to Clive, that colors harmonized in a certain way did not have to look exactly like flowers; they could suggest floral attributes and provide emotions akin to seeing an actual vase filled with actual flowers. In 1914 this was, for the British—and later for the Americans—a new, and even revolutionary, idea.

In his 300-page book Clive explained that "significant form is the only quality common to all and absent from none of the works of visual art that move me." He glanced lightly at art works through the centuries, drawing on his own early Parisian exposure and his travels in Italy and Asia Minor. If he was a trifle abrasive in his remorseless logic (as was his manner) this could be forgiven, for he argued a cause and was replying to the strident laughter of the viewers. The book proved a useful and indeed incisive performance. It set Clive Bell upon a straight path as art critic. With Roger Fry, Clive helped create an often resented Bloomsbury hegemony over art opinion in England during the next twenty-five years—and even beyond.

IV

Whether *Art* was intended by Clive, within the Bloomsbury circle, as an answer to Leonard's and Lytton's disparagement of him, we do not know. But it certainly had that effect. Leonard, in *The Wise Virgins*, had treated his brother-in-law with a certain brutality. In the fictional form, Clive was presented as having "a fat, round body, and his little round, fat mind . . . one of those men so small mentally and morally that anything which took place in his little mind or little soul naturally seemed to him to be one of the great convulsions of nature." Apparently neither Leonard nor Lytton could understand that such "convulsions" in persons who have come late to certain kinds of culture contain within them a contagious enthusiasm. Clive was more in tune with the uniformed public than was either of his critics; and what he found for his book were simple words to express his own strong emotions. He says as much at the end of *Art*. "For those who can feel the significance of form, art can never be less than a religion. In art these find what other religious natures found and still find, I doubt not, in impassioned prayer and worship. . . . He who goes daily into the world of aesthetic emotion returns to the world of human affairs equipped to face it courageously and even a little contemptuously." Clive's religion of art was easy to accept and he had many converts.

On a deeper personal level, Clive Bell's book was an act of self-assertion both in art-journalism and in the intimate love-complexities of Bloomsbury. He seems to have been more disturbed than he knew by Vanessa's love affair with Roger: he was caught in an ambiguous position. He loved Roger and looked upon him as his mentor in the world of art, and at the same time he had no alternative but to accept him as his wife's lover. And then he was troubled by Virginia's marriage to Leonard. During his prolonged and self-indulgent caprice with Virginia, he had come to feel that she belonged to him and to his relaxed private "harem." He felt that Leonard would drag the mischievous, scintillating Virginia into a drab world of dreary cooperatives and political committee rooms. Clive would have liked to keep her as his playmate, even if she was virginally exasperating; for she was also provocative. He had lost Vanessa; it was in part his own fault; but Virginia might still have been his spiritual "concubine." Now he had lost Virginia as well. Both sisters had seceded from him. He faced this reality and wrote to Virginia with his characteristic gallantry as she left for her honeymoon, "You must believe that, in spite of all my craziness, I love you very much, and that I love your lover too." And it is true that Clive, in his raucous and guffawing way, was capable of much affection. He was not a man to harbor a grudge. In producing his book, he may have been suggesting that he was as much of a man of art as Vanessa's lover, and that he possessed much more than "a little round, fat mind."

Shortly after this he began to find solace in an attachment to Mary Hutchinson, née Barnes, a cousin of the Stracheys, the young wife of a successful lawyer, St. John Hutchinson. In neither household was there a desire for divorce. The males had indulged in their infidelities; they had to accept the modern view that women were entitled to have theirs as well. Elizabethans might have called Clive a cuckold. Later generations might have said he was "complaisant." The "civilized" Bloomsbury of these arrangements lay in the recognition that, if there was to be sexual freedom, it could not be the sole property of the male. Clive loved and admired Vanessa; he adored his sons. Vanessa's needs were simple and clearly defined. She could not share Clive's pretensions to the *Grand Monde*. He was gregarious, a gourmet, a lover of parties and social talk. Vanessa preferred solitude, quiet, the domesticity of a household in which she could rear her children and above all paint every day. She was addicted to "still life" in art and she wanted life to be still—but not static. We have observed that the shapes of "things spoke to her more eloquently than humans did. And so the Bells in the years to come maintained a *status quo*—a kind of family "still life": it is painted by Vanessa in the Nativity mural she created in the old medieval church of St. Michael and All Angels at Berwick in Sussex, not far from where she lived. The painting, into which she introduced some of the faces of her children, is tranquil, "set," motionless, a "still life" of family.

Clive continued his forays around London, his journalism, his long hours of reading and writing, and his life with Mary Hutchinson, who in due course was reluctantly accepted by Vanessa. Clive and Mary sometimes had rooms in Vanessa's Charleston house for the weekends Clive spent with his children. Mary Hutchinson had bright eyes, a high forehead, a small mouth; she was thin, and dressed elegantly. Virginia first saw her as a shy "somewhat unforthcoming" woman. Later she said that she was "nice" behind "a fuss and exquisiteness of dress and get up." But then the carelessly dressed Virginia believed that all women fussed too much over clothes. In later years her malicious pen turned Clive and Mary into a couple of bright-colored parakeets or cockatoos. "We had a visit from the two Cockatoos in their brightest plumage." Again, "the amorous Parakeets are flourishing. Why, when they're together, do they produce such an atmosphere of the Brighton pier? Something brazen and yet sterile; nothing but double asters and lodging house windows." Later when Clive had further involvements, Virginia could write to Vanessa, "Is it true that Clive is chased around Paris by both the female cockatoos, one outdoing the other in elegance and artifice, and he remains cool as a cucumber, talking at the top of his voice about art and civilization and drinking enormous bumpers with his male companions?" In spite of Virginia's aviary-comedy, a series of truces were in the making on the eve of the war: between Clive and Vanessa, Leonard and Clive, Virginia and Vanessa, Clive and Roger. Certain crises and stresses had been surmounted. The war would soon blot out much private life. The Bloomsbury energies would remain. For the time being they would have to be rechanneled.

Between the Acts

Virginia Woolf returned from her honeymoon in 1912 in a state of high stress and showing symptoms of one of her breakdowns. Leonard knew of her trouble, but he was witnessing only the anxious preliminaries. He would learn later the meaning of her state of excitement and euphoria, her "high" that preceded headaches and insomnia, these the prelude to dissociation, hallucination, abstention from food and sometimes a lapse into indifference and a catatonic state.

Her new signs of illness came at a moment when Leonard and Virginia had been looking forward to founding their home and perhaps a family. Virginia had married, as we know, in a state of anxiety. She was, in reality, not designed for marriage. Her entire childhood—the particular misadventures with the Duckworth boys apart—had frustrated psychosexual expression, made her one of those Victorian girls from whom all sexual knowledge had been deeply guarded or, as she put it, such a girl had been taught "a very strict moral code, which in childhood prevented her from kicking up her legs in the presence of the other sex; and as she grew older, prevented her from being alone in the room with them, from standing at an open window in her nightgown, from saying anything or doing anything which could suggest even remotely that she felt physically or ideally attracted by them."

With her sexual ambivalence she found herself now married to an intense, powerful, passionate man. She was emotionally unprepared. Her mind acquiesced; her body resisted. Moreover, her responses to love and to sex were now such as to short-circuit natural impulse and warmth of feeling. Certain emotions had been frozen, and it was doubtful whether a lifetime of knowledge could bring a thaw. During her honeymoon Virginia had discovered— she was face to face with it—that her physical relationship with Leonard left her frigid. It brought none of the joys Vanessa had experienced. Virginia's letters are sufficiently explicit. She wrote to one of her women friends, "I might still be Miss S. Why do you think people make such a fuss about marriage and copulation?" And she added: "I find the climax immensely exaggerated." Leonard, on his side, wrote half-humorously, but also ambiguously, to Molly MacCarthy, "I don't feel like a married man." Virginia's worries about her frigidity are confirmed in a letter from Vanessa to Clive. The Woolfs had closely questioned Vanessa: "They were very anxious to know when I first had an orgasm. I couldn't remember. Do you?"

The sexual problem was the most striking element in the long emotional "conditioning" which brought on Virginia's relapse into illness. There were not only the accumulated anxieties and melancholies of her years, but the still-present shame and guilt to which her half brothers had exposed her, as well as the memories of "that house of all the deaths" and the sealed-in emotions of the time. Leonard learned in due course that doctors thought it wise Virginia should not have children. Given her state of health, her swings of mood and mind, this, he felt, was the wisest thing to do. But men—doctors—were always telling Virginia what *not* to do. She was supposed to rest, to take food, be sensible, sleep a lot, and not become excited. To mundane deprivations was added the supreme deprivation of motherhood. Her sister had a husband and wasn't denied children. Virginia had always believed that Vanessa had all the advantages, and she now felt more worthless and defeated than ever.

She did not have a breakdown after Thoby's death because doors seemed then to open upon life. But marriage, instead of being a "voyage out," seemed to close these very doors. Marrying a man who reminded her of her father as well as her brother, who represented the male world to which she was alien, proved a ruder shock than anyone might have expected. And then Leonard, doing all he could to help her, found himself in a policing role as he carried out the doctors' prescriptive orders. Virginia began to experience revulsion and horror, and terrible rages.

Just after her honeymoon, she completed her much-revised novel *The Voyage Out*. This too seemed a termination, a closing door, although the book had been quickly accepted. Edward Garnett, David's father, a celebrated reader for publishers, praised it. Virginia, however, was tuned in more to failure than to success. She seems also to have believed that the book's publication might reveal her madness. Rereading what she had written, she lived through the emotions of her heroine's sudden death. Death for Virginia had always been unmotivated and unexpected. As omniscient author, she could have given her heroine the victory and life implied in her book's title. But to make a voyage out—into the world—was a dangerous thing. The voyage in the story becomes a voyage into death. Virginia's decision to kill Rachel Vinrace—with a vague tropical fever—was in a deeper sense a killing of herself. Marriage now came to seem that kind of voyage. On 9 September 1913, when Virginia and Leonard were staying in Adrian's rooms in Brunswick Square, she discovered that Leonard—usually watchful—had left her medications unlocked. She took a lethal dose of veronal. The presence in the house of Maynard's brother Geoffrey Keynes, a doctor, and Leonard's rapid mobilization of nurses and emergency help, saved Virginia, but she was very close to death at 1:30 the following morning. Her survival was in part a result of the other side of her ambivalent inner world—her tenacious will to live.

Leonard, after this, was not himself for a while. He too was on the edge of a breakdown. He had violent rage headaches and a period of depression. Lytton helped him; and Roger, whose own wife was in an institution, gave strong support. Woolf's strength and will carried him through. He ultimately learned Virginia's symptoms and by degrees established a way of life for her which was controlled and beneficent. During the next twenty-four years she would lead an active and productive existence and fashion the career the world now knows. Virginia's slow recovery did not occur until after 1915. By that time Leonard and his friends were deeply engaged in the war.

The personal disaster in the marriage for the time merged with universal disaster. Thus one of the most remarkable literary marriages of our time had to wait for peace. Not until the war's end would the Woolfs find practical solutions to their life-dilemma, the compromises and avoidances that made for harmony and creation.

The War

On 2 August 1914, Bertrand Russell encountered Maynard Keynes in the Great Court of Trinity College. Russell had been discussing what was to be done if war were declared. One gathers he would have welcomed some moments of talk with Keynes. The latter, however, was in a great hurry. He was wanted at the Treasury. The war panic would push up the bank rate. This had to be avoided at all cost. Maynard would not give a kingdom for a horse, but he was eager to find a motorcycle. "Why?" Russell asked. There were, after all, plenty of trains from Cambridge to London. "Because there isn't time," Maynard answered. And he rushed off to his brother-in-law, A. V. Hill, eminent in medical research. Hill not only had a motorcycle, but offered to drive Maynard in the sidecar. Traveling at high speed, he delivered the economist to the Government, dropping him off a short distance from Whitehall. A motorcycle seemed to both a ridiculous vehicle from which to descend in front of the Treasury.

"War, war, war," wrote Lady Ottoline Morrell in her journal. "All that is left is war." Her pen seemed choked with tears—and rage. Her husband, Philip Morrell, M.P. for Burnley (with its factories and weaving sheds), had protested in the House. It was monstrous that England should go to war. There were cries of "Sit down." He finally made his pacifist speech—and ended his political career. On 4 August 1914, Ottoline and her lover, Bertrand Russell, walked the streets of Bloomsbury in profound depression. Few persons seemed to show any sense of horror; they encountered rather a sense of elation. People were flushed and excited. Outside parliament Lady Ottoline sat on the stone seat that ran along the wall, watching the members going in. Lord Ridley came out and told his brother (Lady Ottoline overheard) that it was "all right." Lady Ottoline, never one to hesitate, asked *what* was all right. "Why of course, Sir Edward Grey has sent his ultimatum." And Ottoline wrote in her diary: "I looked at his face, flushed and happy, and marvelled that anyone could look or feel happy at such dire news."

On August 4, Leonard and Virginia Woolf were at Asheham. They walked six or seven miles, beginning in the Ouse valley across the river, up through Southease, on to the Downs, and then over the top of the Down to the sea. They looked at 500-year-old Itford Farm. They passed the church in Southease, unchanged for 700 years. In the tea-room at Telscombe Cliffs, in the Post Office, they ran into Jack Pollock, son of the eminent legal light, Sir Frederick Pollock. The son and his friends were greeting the war with cakes and tea. Leonard found the scene dreamlike. "The war would never have begun had not certain human beings thought certain thoughts, desired certain ends, and willed certain acts. It might have ended at any time during those four years of painful and sordid glory, by a change of human thoughts, desires, or wills." So Leonard would write later in his study of the psychology of war. But on the fateful day, both Leonard and Virginia felt that, once the step was taken, England had to fight. Could one allow the Germans to invade England and do nothing? Virginia noted: "Rather like Napoleonic times."

David Lloyd George, Chancellor of the Exchequer, looked at Maynard Keynes's memorandum on specie payments. Who was Maynard Keynes? A don in Cambridge, he was told, who knew a great deal about economics. "Monstrous," said Lloyd George. Why, he asked, did outsiders need to be called in? But, added Basil Blackett, writing in his diary, Lloyd George read Maynard's document. The next day, "Lloyd George has at last come down on the right side. . . . He has clearly imbibed much of Keynes's memorandum and is strong against suspension of specie payments." Five days later Keynes wrote to his mother, "Where money can be spent on capital improvements, a large part of it going in payment of labour *which might otherwise be unemployed,* the argument for spending it is very strong." The great theories were beginning to take form.

On August 6 and 7, Maynard, Duncan Grant and Adrian Stephen went to Lady Ottoline's in Bedford Square. The pacifists Bertrand Russell and Ramsay MacDonald were there. "That satyr Keynes, greedy of work, fame, influence, domination, admiration," wrote Lady Ottoline. But Maynard, she also noted, was "very sympathetic to the ambitions of young men. . . . His intellect is of a fine steel-like quality." Maynard said the banks were "timid, voiceless and leaderless." He wrote that some international regulation of the gold standard might be forced on the principal countries of the world as a consequence of the war. Gold, he said, should be reduced to the position of a constitutional monarch and "a new chapter of history will be opened."

Leonard Woolf, after conferences with Beatrice and Sidney Webb, set to work on a study of "international government." Like Maynard, he moved in his thoughts at this time beyond immediacies into the interrelatedness of nations. He was foreseeing some great League, some union, that might make war impossible. "I was, in a sense, 'against the war,' " wrote Leonard. "But I have never been a complete pacifist; once the war had broken out it seemed to me that the Germans must be resisted and I therefore could not be a conscientious objector." In due course, Woolf was medically examined. The doctor found an "inherited nervous tremor which is quite uncontrollable." He exempted Leonard (whose nerves of steel and capacity for endurance would have made him a good soldier) from every form of military service. This was just as well. Virginia needed much of his attention. And he was free to pursue his Periclean labors in behalf of enlightened government among the nations.

Lytton Strachey was at work on his essay on Florence Nightingale. He had just completed his prose portrait of Cardinal Manning. Only too aware of his sickly physique, he was untroubled by questions of service. "God has put us on an island and Winston has given us a navy," he said. "It would be absurd to neglect those advantages." And again, "The only hope is to appear anti-German and also for peace." Where France was concerned—and Lytton seemed more concerned about France than about England—his sympathies were clear. "The real horror is that Europe is not half civilized, and the peaceful countries aren't strong enough to keep the others quiet." He expressed a different horror in his occasional verse—the horror of the sacrificed young men whose bodies he loved, dying in the mud and filth of the trenches . . .

> What comfort, when in every lovely hour
> Lurks horror, like a spider in a flower.

Lytton said that physically fit intellectuals should fight for England, but he added, thinking of himself: where were the intellectuals who were physically fit?

His ultimate appearance before the Tribunal when conscription came was a planned Stracheyesque comedy. Suffering from hemorrhoids, he brought a rubber cushion which he inflated as if he were blowing a bugle. His friends testified on his behalf. A military interrogator said he understood that Lytton had a conscientious objection to all wars. "Only this one," Lytton replied. The same questioner asked Lytton what he would do if a German soldier attempted to rape his sister. Lytton's homoerotic being provided the prompt answer. He would "try and interpose my own body." The Tribunal reserved judgment pending Lytton's physical. He sat, reading a history of England, in a congerie of unclad youths destined for the trenches. The doctors pronounced him unfit for service. He returned to the writing of *Eminent Victorians*.

For Maynard the war was a challenge, a matter of attacking and solving problems as they were encountered. But before he went to the Treasury he saw the other side of war, the side of human attrition, death and grief. "I am absolutely and completely desolated," he wrote to Lytton. "It is utterly unbearable to see day by day the youths going away, first to boredom and discomfort, and then to slaughter. Five of this college [King's] who are undergraduates or who have just gone down, are already killed. . . ." Later, in 1916, Virginia spoke of the nightmare: "Two cousins of mine were killed last week, and I suppose in other families it's much worse." In 1917, Leonard's brother Cecil died in action and another brother, Philip, was wounded. Maynard's biographer, Roy Harrod, has some interesting words about the differences between the First and Second World War. Even though during 1914–18 there was not the continuous danger from air raids as in the next war, there seemed less risk of defeat, for the Kaiser was not "such a black fiend as Adolf Hitler," and the austerity did not come until mid-1917. But he added, "There were more widows and mothers that lacked sons. Perils could be borne with courage; the long casualty lists were facts and the burden of sorrow was heavy."

Clive Bell, in his characteristic manner, reacted with anger against the war. For him it was "the end of civilization," and he would ultimately define what he meant by civilization. He would write a book about it. Clive expressed his anger best with his pen, and his pen in due course fashioned a pamphlet entitled *Peace at Once*. How could one be the professional connoisseur of life in the midst of a bath of blood? It took, however, a certain kind of courage, which Clive possessed, to issue such a pamphlet, which went against the grain of a nation already plunged into mourning for lost husbands and sons. Clive's abrasive manner even wore on Lady Ottoline's nerves when she invited him to be a farm laborer on her farm in lieu of service. "Clive only wants to say something smart and shocking," wrote Lady Ottoline. But Garsington proved a refuge. Virginia mocked: "The war has done some funny things among our friends." Clive "sits in a farmhouse and occasionally turns over a vegetable marrow." The Lord Mayor of London, with that insouciance about freedom of the press which great countries show when they wage wars, ordered Clive's pamphlet publicly burned.

For Roger Fry the war posed no problem. He was overage, almost fifty. He continued to devote himself to the Omega Workshops, feeling that the standard of art, and all it stood for, had to be kept flying even in times of war. However, with his Quaker background he found himself working on the side of peace; and for a while he served with the Quakers in France. His fellow artist Duncan Grant, the youngest member of Bloomsbury—unless indeed we include the late recruit David Garnett, who was even younger—first thought he would join the Artists' Rifles; but he was, given his nature, ill suited for fighting. One remembers his passivity before the irate members of the navy who wanted him to duel with them after the "*Dreadnought* Hoax." In his passivity, Duncan, encouraged by Vanessa, did nothing until conscription was voted. At that moment he and others could face the Tribunal as conscientious objectors.

There remained Desmond MacCarthy, who was thirty-seven when war was declared. Desmond, in keeping with his essential humanism, decided at once to enroll with the Red Cross as an ambulance driver and stretcher bearer. In the autumn of 1914 he appeared in the drawing rooms of London in his khaki uniform, looking very elegant and handsome, as he said his farewells. He was scheduled for an early departure. The Red Cross assigned him—perhaps because he spoke French—to serve with the French Army. He turned up at Henry James's one day in Cheyne Walk. The Master was finding the war a crushing burden that he felt, at his age, he should not have to bear. He wrote that when he dipped his pen into ink all he could smell was blood. It cheered him to see Desmond, alert, pleasant, loquacious, and he remarked that his service "can only contribute hereafter to his powers of conversation." James's niece, the daughter of William James, who was staying with her uncle, and was then just coming of age, fell girlishly in love with the beautifully spoken and enchantment-weaving Desmond in uniform.

Vanessa's attitude toward the war was that it was the stupid work of politicians and unprincipled men. She was not interested in governments and their use of words to excuse their violent actions. All her life she had fought a stubborn defense of the Self. The war made no difference. In any event 1914–18 was still a war which had no role for women save that of nursing or odd jobs on the civilian front. Vanessa quite naturally would have none of these. She had her two sons to rear. She had the elderly Roger and the young Duncan as her artist-companions. She took active steps to create a rural Bloomsbury.

As for Virginia, illness made the first two years of the war seem like a mysterious dream; and then she emerged into the realities of the last two years, with the zeppelins, the blackouts, the falling bombs. She absorbed through her mental and verbal antennae the atmospheres of suffering and survival, as her pages on the war show in *The Years*. During the period of her recovery, she began to write her remarkable diaries.

Bloomsbury, wrote Virginia in March 1916, "is vanished like the morning mist." In June of the same year she was even more emphatic. She used the imagery of war. "Bloomsbury is pretty well exploded." What she meant was that the friends were scattered—as it turned out, permanently. The commune in Brunswick Square had only briefly survived Leonard and Virginia's marriage. Maynard moved first to Great Ormond Street, then to Gower Street, and finally to Clive and Vanessa's Gordon Square house. The Woolfs settled at Hogarth House in Richmond. Lytton had always maintained an establishment apart. He would set up his own country seat before the war was over. Bloomsbury, it might be said, would never be the same again. It had lost its original impulse and spontaneity. It was now involved in sharing the common burdens of England; and then the friends, all except Duncan, were reaching middle age. The war for Bloomsbury was very like the chapter Virginia Woolf named "Time Passes" in *To the Lighthouse*. What came afterward would somehow stitch itself to what had gone before. There was a continuum, but there was a break in time "between the acts." The curtain had gone down in the very middle of the play. It would rise on a new play altogether, but with the same characters, all a bit older and much changed. Between these disparate acts there was mainly the question of endurance and survival.

Desmond in France

During the winter of 1914–15 the British and French soldiers discovered that military life is not all heroic cavalry charges and splendid assaults on battlements, but simply mud, eternal damp, endless shellfire, misery and death. The Germans too found that when the element of surprise had played itself out, they were equally bound to the trenches and massive firepower, death and desolation. The new war seemed less of an adventure than a trial of endurance. The cumbersome machinery of Government adjusted itself with little flexibility to new conditions, new technologies. Britain still remembered Waterloo and the Charge of the Light Brigade.

Desmond MacCarthy, volunteering for service in the Red Cross, found himself transferred from London's pleasant drawing rooms to tiny villages in northern France. Their names, hitherto unnoticed, stood out in the daily communiqués. Desmond's task was to carry battered and bloody human freight, the wounded and the dying, from the fields of battle—from the jungle of slaughter—into the human warmth and care of improvised hospitals. Of the Bloomsbury friends, he was the only one to see the war, in its initial stages, at close quarters. He worked near the lines. The Germans were often a few yards away. There were sniper fire and gunnery. He discharged his doleful duties with alertness and skill through November and December of 1914 and the freezing months of the deep winter of 1915.

Hope ran high in the early stages; perhaps the war might be over by February. But February came and passed and the terrible battles of position continued. Life went on as if Desmond were living in Dante's Hell, a *perpetuum mobile* of exhausting action interrupted by brief leaves. Within earshot of the enemy one tried to keep some order, some memory of the old life, some attempt at cleanliness, a few shreds of civilization. Near Ypres, in a long low convent room in which Desmond and some fifteen or twenty of his fellows ate, slept, cooked, washed, smoked, shaved, sang, read, talked, mooned, joked, argued, warmed themselves and dried their clothes—the enumeration was his—he swept out the rubbish when his turn came and performed other menial tasks which are as much a part of war as actual fighting. He made short work of fragments of shell and bomb splinters, along with potato peelings and cigarette butts. "He's gone and thrown all the souvenirs into the dustbin," a comrade shouted. And Desmond realized that these souvenir scraps of metal had to be restored to their owners. They were like scraps of the war, a kaleidoscope of the life and death to which his days were committed. In London his days had been devoted to talk of men and books, and gossip that prolonged itself from lunch to dinner; agreeable clubs; evenings at the theater; deadlines he had to meet in composing rooms for the *New Statesman* and other journals. At Ypres and Montdidier life was simplified—the sweeping out of a room, or the gathering up, in dim darkness, in pelting rain and into the sky-filtered dawns, of shattered human beings. There was little time for the why and the how. One coped with immediacies between periods of idleness.

At Montdidier, five or six miles from the trenches, he lunched in a dining room between midday and two o'clock. Always the same faces—the men in uniform, the women in black. The civilians were nearly all relatives of soldiers; many came simply to visit neat mounds in the open field annexed to the local cemetery, or to visit the wounded in one of the hospitals. Or they were waiting to meet some soldier on a two- or three-day leave from the trenches— waiting in hope and in fear. The dining room was insufferably hot. Flies still circled, although there had been snow and frost. Desmond moved among the French civilians; he gathered information, he took notes, he observed. He kept trying to find out how the Germans behaved in towns later retaken by the Allies. At one hotel the lady in the glass box told him that they had been very stiff and peremptory but *convenable*. "I, of course, was very cold."

He noticed one house in Montdidier inhabited by a woman who had not left the town in fifty years. She would hardly allow a war, let alone some intruding German soldiers, to budge her. The soldiers knocked on her door at night. Face to face with several tough-looking male specimens, she listened as they asked her to let them in. With the courage that comes to civilians in life-and-death situations, she coolly said, "Your officers are already here." The men fled. When Desmond congratulated her on her presence of mind, she told him, "It has taken years off my life."

Montdidier was a red-and-gray town; it reminded Desmond of Rye in Sussex. A French Impressionist might have painted it. The older houses, residences in the past of the French nobility, seemed to Desmond now to shelter lives more keenly private than ever. If one rang the bell, some little old woman in silent slippers and meager black would answer. But the next day the same woman, who had seemed like the mousiest of servants, could be seen treading her way with dignity to early mass—a lady; and Desmond realized how these quiet lives continued to be lived on the very rim of battle. As he walked the cobblestones of the lampless streets at night, the sky seemed full of restless stars. His footsteps echoed between silent houses. Desmond MacCarthy, in his peaked cap and khaki, felt that the moon was putting little ghosts into the clean, black panes of the windows, and the skeleton shadows of trees fell on the street as clearly defined as upon snow. He was distant indeed from the theater of Ibsen and Shaw and Chekhov.

II

Desmond had gone to France expecting to endure hardships, wishing to take part in the most humane side of the common experience. But there were many hours when he found himself idle in little hotels in Boulogne, in Amiens, in towns that brought him closer to the mud and ruin. Then there would come nights when every hour was crowded with action until sleep filled his eyes and he kept on moving as in a dream amid horrors that had become commonplace. They got up quietly on such nights, the specific detail, so as not to wake the others. Desmond listened to their gentle snoring. The room was stuffy; it was cold. He had tried to dry his socks; the moment he put them on, the familiar chill traveled up his legs. He had been told that it would be an "all-night job," and he heard the officer in command ask the man on the watch to have hot cocoa ready for their return. The cannon had been booming all evening. Desmond got extra blankets for the stretchers; he filled bottles with boiled water; he crammed cigarettes and chocolate bars into his pockets. The detail was composed of three vehicles. They had to remember the shell holes. The road was deep enough on each side to bog down a heavy ambulance. They drove nervously. One had the image of the vehicle sunk in a hole and the horror of upsetting a load of wounded in open country. They drove with their headlights off, knowing vaguely that the German lines were on their right. After a while they seemed to crawl. The tiny taillight of the vehicle in front looked like a burning cigar in the total darkness. Then they lost it. The wind pressed on their eyes. The vehicle sloshed, skidded, seemed drunken in its lurchings. One wasn't sure of the road curves. Intermittently Desmond used his flashlight. It showed a yard or two of mud and stones, and the brief moment of light left him dazzled when he extinguished it. At moments there was a sudden green glare—a German rocket: two flaring stars, then blindness again. Desmond got out and walked in front of the car feeling for holes. More rockets. The commanding officer suddenly appeared in the dark, his flashlight pointing to a crater. They maneuvered into a village. A shattered church. A lonely crucifix in a shrine bespattered and chipped by shrapnel. Ghostly men moved about—French marines in blue overcoats, wearing round flat caps. A glow of a cigarette lit up a bearded mouth, a scarf, a thick hand.

The floor of the room in the house they entered was covered with straw, but the straw was nearly all hidden by the spread of the wounded. He heard low moaning and voices in quiet talk. Near the door a surgeon on his knees was dabbing at a red hole in the side of a half-naked man who was propped up by knapsacks. Desmond looked into the face and saw apprehension and relief "as a frightened child shows when it is at last being cared for." In another corner he saw a young soldier in a fetal position talking rapidly to himself. Those whose wounds had been dressed were laid out at the further end. To reach them, Desmond picked his way between broken legs, bleeding heads. As he helped put men on the stretchers, they often cried out in pain; there was little room in which to shift feet for the lift. At the door French soldiers helped, murmuring words of kindness to their comrades: *Courage, mon vieux, bon voyage.* Some remarked on the superiority of the English ambulance. Whatever its qualities, it could not provide a smooth ride; the return was a bumping along in liquid mud. The summer lightning of the guns shone on the stark winter landscape; the wind continued to blow their sound away—only the purr of the car's engine, the swish of the mud, the agonized moaning broke the silence when the vehicle lurched.

After what seemed an interminable time, they could turn on their headlights again; however, the vehicle still crawled over the oblong cobbles as they watched for the red lights of the hospital. It was located in what had been a small cabaret. The barroom was already full; there were beds upstairs and mattresses on the floor. Through an open door Desmond saw two surgeons hovering over an operating table. An elderly doctor stood looking as if he had been hypnotized; when Desmond politely greeted him, he tapped his forehead and answered, "Sleep, sleep—not for two days and nights now." Some of the wounded had to be taken to the next hospital. Then Desmond went to the kitchen and drank coffee laced with rum. Back they went over the same roads for another load. As Desmond later put it, "The bodies of the wounded were just consignments marked 'fragile,' to be handled and delivered with care." The work continued all night. The barroom of the cabaret seemed emptier on later runs. There had been deaths. The sleepy doctor was bending over a man lying loosely with eyes shut. Desmond had more coffee, more rum. A hard light, as hard as sapphire, announced the dawn. Everything seemed telescoped in a weird dream of phantoms. Finally he was back in the original room; the sleepers still snored quietly. He crawled between the blankets feeling as if he had passed a night of "tumultuous and distressing dreams."

And he later added, "There is sometimes an almost mystic comfort in the touch of a pillow."

III

The following spring, when the war seemed settled into a kind of stagnant permanence, Desmond was back in London. A man of feeling, articulate, watchful (the painter Mark Gertler called him "a most peaceful and quiet personage"), with the imagination of language, he set down his memories of his work in France in a series of twelve pieces—set them down as if he had spent nights in theaters but had himself been one of the actors. It was all vivid, low-keyed and filled with an after sense of hurt and violence. In the pages of the *New Statesman* he told of the passive courage of the civilians; the dry humor of their talk; the blind suffering of the men; the nights of human freight-carrying; the compulsive talk of some of the French, as if their words, feelings, and thoughts could be released only in long apostrophes of words and gestures; of the way in which everyone depended on "pretty words," cushion words, to muffle the pain of the communiqués; of long cavalcades stretching a mile or two; of French cuirassiers riding abreast along the frosty road, as if they were on their way to Moscow at the bidding of the emperor rather than taking part in a modern war; of smeared stretchers propped against a wall to dry in the sun; and how he used to watch the ambulances being emptied, always hoping the bandages would not be across the stomach or the face. He described his visits to the wards in the hospitals; the young servant where he was billeted making his bed and suddenly giving way to a fit of weeping—her husband had been killed three weeks earlier. Then she recovered and went on with her work. He described how he became aware that the men did not want to talk about what had happened; that one had to be careful about the compassion that hurts, the empathy that makes for nervousness, the delicacy of communicating with those who have known horror and are trying to obliterate it. There was also the danger of becoming desensitized. "The more completely you realize them as individuals, the less likely are you to be merely nervously sympathetic [he wrote]. If you think about their wounds, and you are not a surgeon or dresser, you may be frightened or sickened and become indifferent."

Some time later, Virginia Woolf described Desmond Mac-Carthy's coming to dinner with Leonard and herself. He had "the hard seaworthy look of an old salt, cased in stiff black, with a few gold scrolls about him, and boots made out of plain leather." Virginia was describing Desmond's uniform. He was now on the staff of Naval Intelligence at the Admiralty, with the rank of lieutenant in the Royal Naval Volunteer Reserve. Within this military garb Virginia found him "as tender and vague as ever." Desmond might be "vague" in social situations, but there had been nothing vague about his writing of life at the front. Virginia's record is of 1918—three years after Desmond's Red Cross service. The war had by then grown stale and monotonous. Desmond's mind at the dinner had "a factitious spryness about it, as if still working under the official eye." Later in the evening he picked up the typescript of Joyce's *Ulysses*, which the Woolfs were reading—it had just been offered to the Hogarth Press—and he read aloud the scene in Eccles Street when Leopold Bloom fries the breakfast kidney and talks to the cat. Desmond imitated the Joycean rendering of "Mkgnao!"—"milk for the pussens." In the book the cat replies, "Mrkgnao!" Desmond would find in Joyce "only nerves and haunted imagination." On this evening he lingered; later he agreed to spend the night, talked about books "and rambled off quite out of time for his office" in the morning.

He had had his haunted vision of the war and of life behind the war. There remained with him the feeling of "a man who has taken a bad header into deep water." He retained the spectacle of a long stream of muffled figures hurrying on their way to the front. He had shaken hands with some and wished them *bonne chance*. A little later in the eerie dawn, the sky turning pink and gold and blue, he met some of the soldiers (as he drove his ambulance) and they were already limping and bleeding—the very ones "who a short time before had hailed us in the lane." So it went during 1914–18 until the day of the Armistice.

Love among the Artists

Vanessa Bell had begun her affair with Roger Fry during 1911, the year of their journey to Asia Minor. As the months passed, she discovered that Roger mysteriously wore on her nerves, and she recognized that she was "absurdly depressed." At first she felt this to be her fault. Roger had done nothing to change their relationship, which had had many moments of intensity and passion. He remained the busy, outgoing, creative man of art, a marvel at organization, a walking compendium of art history—but a faltering painter. He did not always have painterly feelings, although he had a skilled eye for the "architecture" of plastic creation. He was thirteen years older than Vanessa, and in her life it was she who had been always "the older one." In the reiterated patterns of her being, Roger fell more into the role of Leslie Stephen than into that of a lover; in his affectionate way he was fatherly; and he was demanding—a man of standards and accounts. How could she have been so mistaken? She felt a strange guilt; she thought she was being very selfish. Her depression persisted. Roger was kind and gifted; he responded to her with masculine strength and much tenderness. They went to secret meetings in obscure towns, but each time Vanessa ended by feeling herself imprisoned rather than liberated. She said of Roger's painting (they were abroad), "It's even more difficult, I think, than in England to like what he does." She also said, "He does manage to reduce it all to such a dead, drab affair."

A dead, drab affair . . . the words were spoken of his painting, but they expressed what she truly felt. Their affair was by now drab; romance had fled. During the months before the war Vanessa gradually faced this painful confusion of feeling. Escorted by Clive, Roger and Duncan, she had gone to Italy in May 1913. Clive and Roger were strenuous tourists; they were indefatigable; they discussed aesthetics continually. Vanessa, after a bit, announced that she would look at not more than one thing a day; artistic surfeit was like any other kind—the spirit as well as the body rebelled. She wrote to Virginia, "I find that Duncan sympathizes with me . . . if he and I had the conduct of the party on our hands we should settle down somewhere for a month and spend most of our time loafing." One must read "painting" for the word "loafing." Vanessa and Duncan invariably reached for a pencil, a piece of charcoal, a brush.

Vanessa found that her depression lifted considerably during the hours she spent with Duncan. He was six years younger; being her junior, he brought her back to her earliest needs: he could be a younger brother and she could be wholly in tune with him, as she had been with Thoby. That he was in love with Maynard Keynes mattered little either to Vanessa or to Duncan. Duncan's androgynous affections were all-embracing and the two had in common their love of painting. Duncan was the sentient artist; Roger was the learned craftsman. He was constantly asking Vanessa to see and think; Vanessa wanted to see and *feel*. She was not interested in the higher criticism or philosophy of art, to which, it seemed to her, Roger reduced so much feeling. She shared with Duncan what seemed to her a simple desire—to paint with feeling. And it was a delight to paint with a man from whom she learned so much—not the erudition on which Roger drew, but the sense of color and of voluptuous shapes. She shared this to such an extent with Duncan that later there were times when their works were taken for each other's. This is not to say that their talents were not individual; and there were times when Vanessa's more sober approach to painting suffered from exposure to Duncan's facility and made her feel inadequate. He could be a discouraging man to work with. Still, a careful observer could easily recognize that Vanessa spoke clearly in her art out of her own world and her own skills. And Duncan had a kind of virtuosity that marked him as a stylist—an influence among the new painters. The two felt in complete harmony when they worked at the decoration of houses and apartments. Most often time passed quickly and without burden when they were together; and it was even amusing to paint the same subject and see what differences there were in their angles of vision, their feeling for form, their sensual use of design. Duncan was lighthearted, inclined to be a bit mischievous, boyishly playful, full of easy natural laughter; and he made few demands. It took very little to keep him contented. He had the same painter's joy in the "ordinary" things of life that Clive had remarked in his Paris days when he was with Morrice.

After a while the two knew that their feelings for one another were strong. Vanessa, at first almost imperceptibly, and then without hesitation but with some caution, turned from Roger to Duncan. Fry was not able to listen when she suggested this distancing as best she could, and with as much delicacy as possible. Vanessa had brought great riches into his life. He had found himself lonely and in a flirtation with Lady Ottoline when Vanessa had taken over the foreground of his affections. He could not easily let her go. As late as 1915, when Duncan and Vanessa had arrived at a durable pattern of life and work, Roger complained—ironically enough to Clive—about Vanessa's always being with Duncan. It was as if Clive had consented to have Roger as his wife's lover and they were supposed to unite against the intruder. Roger wrote to Clive: "In painting Nessa and Duncan have taken to working so entirely together and not to want me, and altogether I find it difficult to take a place on the outside of the circle instead of being, as I once was, rather central, so that I can't see life in London very easily just now. But exactly what and how and where I shall exist isn't clear to me." He complained directly to Vanessa: "You dodge all my openings and give me safe kindly generalities." He spoke of his loneliness but said it was "better than making believe with people." He also wrote, "I don't like myself any better, but I'm no longer disgusted . . . for not being exactly like you or what you like or admire."

Even when the truth was clear to him, he still clung to some hope of a change. "The fact is, my dear, I can't put up with anyone [else] for a very close or long intimacy." But reality gradually asserted itself. Before the end of the war he could write to Vanessa, "You have done such an extraordinarily difficult thing without any fuss: cut thro' all the conventions, kept friends with a pernickety creature like Clive, got quit of me and yet kept me your devoted friend, got all the things you need for your own development and yet managed to be a splendid mother. . . . You give one a sense of security, of something solid and real in a shifting world. . . . You have genius in your life as well as in your art and both are rare things, so you can feel pretty well pleased with yourself."

Vanessa had, in effect, surmounted and kept intact husband, lovers and family, as long before she had taken hold of the disorganized Stephens in Kensington and kept them unified. Small wonder that Bloomsbury called her "monolithic."

II

The war found Vanessa seeking to unravel the threads of her complicated life. She responded to the conflict with her firmness and her ability to act when decisions were needed. Her primary desire was to leave undisturbed the relation she had formed with Duncan and to protect him from the peremptory demands of conscription that might interrupt the delicate balances of her life. In 1915 they lived first at a house called Eleanor, the home of the St. John Hutchinsons, near West Wittering, Sussex, to which she moved her children. Then she and Duncan settled in Wissett Lodge, Halesworth, in Suffolk, where Duncan was a fruit farmer in the interest of the national endeavor, and a painter on the side. Eleanor was too small a caravansary for Bloomsbury. Maynard on occasion slept in a caravan—for he had to be worked in as a visitor along with Clive, who slept in a room in the village when the house became too crowded. Duncan slept and worked for a while on a studio boat. Together Vanessa and Duncan redecorated Eleanor, leaving their designs on its dining-room doors. There were awkward war comedies too. Duncan's dark complexion and quiet manners gave rise to rumors that he was a spy. Clive for a while fell under local suspicion as well.

The record of the subsequent life in Suffolk has been written by David Garnett, who aided Duncan in the fruit farming. Wissett Lodge was a Victorian farmhouse; the quarters were more commodious than at Eleanor, but the Victorian clutter had to be cleared away. The rooms were dark. But once again the place was given the benefit of the Duncan-Vanessa interior decoration. Virginia and Leonard, Maynard and Roger, came to visit—and later Lytton. The children had the country to roam in; there were a pond, a vegetable garden, flower beds. "Deep in the country with her children and Duncan, and with uninterrupted hours for painting" (as Richard Shone describes it), "Vanessa had periods of calm and relative happiness." Virginia poked fun—and would continue to mock Vanessa's and Duncan's love of country life. She described Duncan as picking bugs off the currant bushes for eight hours a day, sleeping all night, painting on Sundays. "Nessa is going to keep house for him all summer." They had to prune trees; they augmented their food supply by raising chickens and ducks; they kept rabbits. It was at Wissett that the household went through several months of great anxiety, for Duncan and Garnett were summoned to the Tribunal. They had visions of themselves in jail. The Tribunal rejected their plea that they were conscientious objectors. But on appeal they were granted leave to work as farmers. The Tribunal also ruled that they could not be self-employed, as they had been at Wissett. They would have to find an employer and have their work supervised.

III

Virginia Woolf had a gift for discovering interesting houses. It was she who found the desired farm and the ideal house. "I wish you'd leave Wissett and take Charleston," she wrote to Vanessa. She had noticed the house just below Firle Beacon. Leonard had gone over it very carefully. The place had a charming garden, a pond, fruit trees. It was "very nice, with large rooms, and one room with big windows fit for a studio." There was a w.c. and a bathroom but only cold water. "The house wants doing up—and the wallpapers are awful." Virginia's discovery came at a propitious moment. Arrangements were made for the occupation of Charleston and work with a nearby tenant farmer. Vanessa promptly inspected the place and pronounced it "absolutely perfect." Charleston was "very solid and simple," a mixture of brick and flint, flat walls, flat windows in the walls, and a fine tiled roof. She thought the pond beautiful with its willow at one side. There was a wall edging the garden and a little lawn that sloped and had formal bushes on it. There was also a small orchard and another lawn and a wall of trees. Charleston had seven bedrooms: that would take care of the whole Bloomsbury family. One large chamber was indeed suited to be a studio —light and large with an east window. The house had a splendid dignified setting. It was remote and removed from public transport. Thus Vanessa's lover was provided for, even though he and Garnett worked strenuously under the young farmer. Domestic arrangements greatly facilitated their life, and Asheham House was not too distant. Vanessa thus set up a Bloomsbury center in the country—in Sussex—one might say for the rest of their lives.

Charleston gave fuller scope than the two earlier houses to the decorative talents of Vanessa and Duncan. A visitor today can still see what the years achieved. There was little that the two left untouched, from the woodboxes, on which Duncan painted musicians and dancers, to the fireplaces and panels, doors and walls, which they covered with murals or paintings. In the garden broken dishes were turned into mosaic on various paths. On the walls there were athletic figures painted by Duncan, a continuation of his Borough Polytechnic and Brunswick Square murals; a good many Omega artifacts were also discreetly distributed. "An enormous dog appears below a window, an improbable bird above, daisies stand upright in pale blue goblets, a crouching angel of impish pink plays a lute on a logbox, a swimmer glides across a chest in kaleidoscopic water, women carry baskets through the panels of a door. Witty and fantastic postures were devised to suit whatever object or surface came to hand." Thus the historian of Bloomsbury's art describes the slow but definite metamorphosis of Charleston. Here Vanessa and Duncan would work in the years to come. Here Julian and Quentin grew up, cavorting naked as little savages during the summer. Here their child Angelica was born just after the war ended and became sister to the Bell sons.

Roger participated as much as he could. Visits were difficult for him. It was not easy to see the rival lover ensconced. Clive, on the other hand, came and went cheerfully with Mary Hutchinson, always happy to be with his children, bringing toys, and also bringing cheroots and good wines for the farm laborers. Duncan worked in the fields, covered with mud and manure. They had to cart dung. They hoed ten acres of beans. The winters were hard. David Garnett has described them, and many bucolic incidents. He tells an astonishing story of how an infuriated cow charged Duncan one day. At the last minute, by adroit use of a shovel, Duncan deflected its horns. "Only the cow's shoulder struck Duncan and sent him reeling. His performance would have gained him," said Garnett, "a reputation in the Spanish bull ring." On another occasion Duncan cavorted balletlike with a cow—a dance of man and beast. The cattle could not always go into the fields in the winter; there was nothing to eat. The haystacks had been used up. There were months of frost. There were flocks of starving birds. Duncan and David had to dig drains across the pastures during extreme wet; they fought hordes of mice during the threshing—but this didn't prevent the affectionate Duncan from slipping one little bright-eyed beast inside his shirt to rescue it. The two laborers were paid ten shillings a week for their work and a few pence an hour for overtime. They worked a seven-and-a-half-hour day with a half day on Saturdays. The work, given their inexperience, exhausted them. The limited fat and sugar rations of the war were insufficient sustenance for physical labor of this sort. Garnett overcame the sugar ration by his beekeeping, which yielded large amounts of honey. Duncan, less stocky than Garnett, suffered more and lost weight alarmingly during the second winter. Doctors ordered him to work shorter hours. The variety of the farm work helped mitigate the monotony, and the hours of relaxation in the increasingly comfortable house helped. Virginia from her distance mocked as usual:

> Nessa and Duncan came over yesterday, having previously washed themselves, and then went back in a storm late at night to help ducklings out of their eggs, for they were heard quacking inside, and

couldn't break through. Nessa seems to have slipped civilization off her back, and splashes about entirely nude, without shame and with enormous spirit. Indeed, Clive now takes up the line that she has ceased to be a presentable lady—I think it all works admirably.

It worked admirably—but the war lay like a pall over England, and the conscientious objectors lost themselves in the labor of their days. Bombs fell in Sussex. At Firle Beacon, when the wind blew in certain directions, they could hear the guns across the Channel. There came a moment when Duncan received an offer to be a "war artist" —that is, paint in the national cause. He almost accepted. But when he discovered that he would have to wear a uniform and would be a major, he declined. He was a consistent pacifist. He could not even kill a mouse.

Virginia's diary records with her usual fine asperity a visit to Charleston during the later phases of the war. On a rainy day, when Duncan was free, they stayed indoors. Duncan painted a table. Vanessa copied a Giotto. Virginia "unpacked all my bits of gossip." She wrote: "They are very large in effect, these painters; very little self-conscious; they have smooth broad spaces in their minds where I am all prickles and promontories." Few people had "a more vigorous grasp or a more direct pounce" than Vanessa.

Roger praised Vanessa for her skill in arranging her life. Virginia saw her sister as a whole nature in use. Neither spoke of what Virginia also discerned—the "volcanoes" beneath Vanessa's sedate manner. Avoidances, discretions, silences—Vanessa practiced these, and somewhere she was paying a price: a deep store of grief, hurt, anger accumulated within the volcanoes. It was Vanessa's fate to live with shared love; she had none she could call her own. She had shared Thoby with Virginia; that had been an anguish of childhood. She shared Clive with his mistresses. She now shared Duncan with his lovers. Deep within Vanessa there resided the rage of Medea or the passion of Clytemnestra, held within the tight bonds of Bloomsbury's civilization.

The volcanoes finally exploded in the grief Vanessa experienced when her eldest son, Julian, was killed in Spain. Her mourning spiraled into illness and melancholy far beyond that of a mother grieving for a lost child. It was as if all the losses of her life were now exacting their due. Some said that from this time on she floundered in her painting. She doubtless had more failures, but she also had many fine successes. She had been splendid in her prime and, with the advancing years, there was a splendor in both her art and her life. Behind the much-praised facade there had been vulnerability; and she was now a noble presence. The "monolithic" was her mask of tragedy.

Eminence of Lytton

Lytton Strachey watched his Bloomsbury friends settle into their careers with despondent aloofness. Clive, Virginia, Leonard published books. His own little primer of French literature seemed trivial and academic by comparison. Keynes was moving close to the seats of the mighty. The painters were absorbed in their art. Lytton had scoffed at the second Post-Impressionist exhibition shortly before the war: "Why do people get so excited about art?" The show made him feel "cold and cynical." He found Roger Fry "a most shifty and wormy character." Clive strutted about the Grafton Gallery as if he owned it, patting a statue with his "fat little hand"—an echo by Lytton of Woolf's reference to Clive's "fat little mind." To Clive he said, in the manner of Henry James, "Can't you or Vanessa persuade Duncan to make beautiful pictures instead of these coagulations of distressing oddments?" Lytton was critical even of his old intimate Leonard, for putting himself on the level (the *niveau*) "of the Bloomsbury gang." This suggested that Lytton considered himself to be quite above the gang's level. What is clear, at any rate, is that Lytton's feelings about Bloomsbury were strong ambivalent. They continued to be ambivalent into the years of the war.

It would be too simple to ascribe Strachey's attitude to mere jealousy. The truth was that he, who had believed himself out in front of Bloomsbury, now felt himself, in a manner, bringing up the rear. His difficulties ran still deeper. He spoke of himself as a failure. He was well into his thirties. He still floundered. He had floundered ever since Cambridge refused him a fellowship and sent him into "exile." He still lived at home in Belsize Park Gardens, confined largely to his bed-sitting room. Whenever he could, he paid country visits; he felt much freer trying his wit on Lady Ottoline's friends at Garsington; and occasionally he made little journeys. He wanted to step forth into the demanding world, but a kind of morbid passivity kept him back. He had always been sickly, and he was now often ill. "If I had a decent health I should go into a garret and starve until I'd done something," he said to one of his sisters. It was amusing to his friends to think of Lytton starving in a garret for art's sake—he who needed his half-dozen glasses of warm milk daily for his delicate digestion. He might moan that he had "precious little" to show for his three decades, but what he showed most when he could not parade his wit was a tendency to chills, like a Victorian spinster, a need for a shawl or comforter, and long hours in bed. Max Beerbohm, seeing him at the Savile Club in 1912, wondered who this curious individual was, with his "emaciated face of ivory whiteness" above the square-cut auburn beard, the velveteen jacket, and his long body and arms draped around the table. Max took the measure of Lytton's angularities, as we discern in his cartoons. The face he portrays for us is always the face of the Knight of the Sorrowful Countenance.

This is not to say that Lytton's pen remained inactive. He fancied himself a great poet and a tragic and comic dramatist, yet all he could publish were literary reviews and historical essays in journals edited largely by relatives or friends. Occasionally he would talk of finding a house, of freeing himself from the maternal roof. There would be a flurry of house-hunting. Somehow he would never find a dwelling that was suitable. And his money was limited. So he kept up his reading; his scribbling, when possible; and his work was often interrupted by his peregrinations. When his friends suggested that biography rather than poetry or drama was more his métier, he demurred. "If I must write somebody's life it had better be Voltaire," he would say.

II

He talked often of writing a life of Voltaire. But he never did—for good reason, we may judge. Lytton Strachey had identified himself so early with the French genius of Voltaire that it would have seemed as if he were writing his own life. One might have said that he regarded his floating years as resembling Voltaire's—that his Caliban aspect was not unlike the wizened monkey face of the French wit; and Voltaire too had tended to be sickly, although he always rebounded with phenomenal energy. Lytton would have liked to be like Voltaire, the favorite of great ladies, perhaps even an intimate of emperors and kings; and at the same time the heroic and embattled enemy of the Establishment. An early Lyttonian essay admirably dissects the weaknesses of Voltaire's plays. Perhaps it was Lytton's way of saying to himself that his own literary dreams were in reality ineffectual. There were, however, other things to emulate: Voltaire's extraordinary mind, his life-style, his prose. Voltaire used his pen as if it were a rapier; he even dueled with the scepter of Frederick the Great. To be sure, Voltaire had been a "scoundrel." Lytton quickly added, "a scoundrel of genius"—and genius Lytton could countenance. He spoke of his own dream as "a little art, perhaps a little fame as well." He needed fame. The art could probably take care of itself. To write pointed, cutting, mocking sentences, to startle the world with a phrase, to take on Church and State—as Voltaire had done—and make his word feared, that was true greatness, true fame, true glory. And then to withdraw to some great good place like Ferney and be, to the end, intellectual master of Europe—or at least of England! We may judge this to have been Lytton Strachey's secret myth. He had assimilated to his own eyes the vision of Voltaire. The French master had looked on England and had seen its high achievements of the spirit and the mind—even if he had misunderstood Shakespeare. Lytton told himself that if he could not be "insatiably active" like Voltaire, he could use his mind with the same fierce authority, and temper it with clarity, coolness, elegance and humor, the arts he had long mastered. It was a matter of stance and style, of tone above all.

In his ultimate home, his Ferney, Lytton would place over the study mantelpiece a painting by Huber of Voltaire in old age surrounded by his disciples: his monkey-faced hero stands and holds his hand up in generous blessing. The picture symbolized Lytton's dreams of grandeur. There had to be admirers; and the admirers had to be well-built splendid young men, the pride of England's playing fields, to make up for his own cadaverous body. And he had to preside and be their father, their mother, their leader.

III

Shortly before the beginning of the war, Lytton Strachey decided that history was his field after all. He would for a time at least cease dreaming up tragedies and comedies and write a series of "silhouettes" of great Victorians—Cardinal Manning, Florence Nightingale, perhaps Darwin and Carlyle, and General Gordon; he drew up an imposing list. He was attracted by Cardinal Manning and started reading the writings of that Prince of the Church, whose power game Lytton could well understand. Had he not played his own modest games of power among the Cambridge Apostles? The moment he put his mind to a straight course of work, he discovered that his life simplified itself. Some of his friends believed in him and in his ultimate greatness. With a loan of £100 Lytton leased for a while a farmhouse in Berkshire. It was still not an ideal place, but he was able to have some months of consistent labor. There was another interval spent with his family, and still another journey, but he finally settled into a cottage near Marlborough for a stay that he prolonged into 1915. Here he completed the Manning essay and his portrait of Florence Nightingale. He sent the manuscript of Manning to Virginia Woolf. "How divinely amusing and exciting and alive you make it," she responded, and she added, "I command you to complete a whole series." He followed her command. By 1917 he had written a caricature essay of Arnold of Rugby and his long "End of General Gordon." He tried his portraits out on the "Bloomsbury gang" during visits to Asheham and Charleston. His friends continued to applaud— even Vanessa and Duncan, who, however, at the day's end, found it difficult to keep their eyes open as the voice of Lytton read on and on about the idiosyncratic Victorians.

Lytton Strachey was halfway through this series of portraits when his life took a strange and unexpected turn. During a visit to Asheham late in 1915—Clive, Vanessa,

Duncan and Mary Hutchinson were there—he met another visitor, a young girl, a painter who had studied at the Slade School. She had golden bobbed hair (some said she originated that fashion), bright blue eyes and a saucy manner. Her name was Dora Carrington, but she called herself simply "Carrington," as if she were a man. She hated being a woman. She had a woman's seductiveness and managed to look like a Florentine page boy. Lytton liked her. He accepted her boyish side, and in a moment of delight as they walked on the Downs he quite forgot her sex, for he embraced and kissed her. Carrington bristled with indignation. "That horrid old man with a beard kissed me!" Indignation turned to anger. Carrington (as we know from the much-told story) vowed that she would have her revenge. At dawn the next day she stole into Lytton's room carrying large shears to amputate Lytton's offensive auburn growth. The hairs had felt like straw on her lips. As she stealthily approached the bed, he opened his eyes. She saw them looking at her—gentle, kindly, hypnotic. And now it seemed as if Lytton's kiss had been like the *baiser de la fée*—he was the Prince and she was Cinderella; or she had Oberon's love spell in her eyes, like Titania, and was falling in love with Bottom. Carrington gazed at the beard, the pallor, the eyes, the long angular figure stretched on the bed; for the first time she knew what it was to have feelings of love for a man. Guilt and contrition made her creep away. Lytton's eyes closed again in sleep, and he was unaware that a turning point had occurred in his life.

Carrington's diary has a record of a later conversation:

> *Lytton:* But it's too incongruous. I'm so old and diseased. I wish I was more able.
> *Carrington:* That doesn't matter.
> *Lytton:* What do you think we had better do about the physical?
> *Carrington:* Oh I don't mind about that.
> *Lytton:* But do you mind me being rather physically attracted?
> *Carrington:* I don't think you are really. . . .
> *Lytton:* But my dear aren't you being rather romantic. You see I'm so very ancient. . . .
> *Carrington:* It's all right. It was my fault. . . .

> *Lytton:* I wish I was rich and then could keep you
> as my mistress.
> *Carrington:* (I was angry inside) It wouldn't make
> any difference.

Everything began to fall now into its scheduled Voltairean place.

IV

The story of this "love" between a mature homosexual with high literary gifts and aspirations and a saucy boy-girl from the Slade School with strong lesbian (or Sapphist, as Bloomsbury called it) leanings and marked ability as a painter has been told in minute detail by Michael Holroyd and in David Garnett's edition of Carrington's letters and diaries. Carrington was twenty-two; Strachey was thirty-five. Leonard Woolf said of her that she was in a way the classic female: if a male pursued, she ran; if the male ran, she pursued. Carrington pursued Lytton; but he was willing to be pursued, and as we have seen, he warned her that bedding was out of the question, although they seem for a time to have tried. His primary interests were elsewhere; hers resided not so much in sex as in a drive to power and manipulation. By degrees she took hold of Lytton's dreams and ambitions, and his mundane physical needs, as if she were his mother. She organized a household around him. She surrounded him with friends; she was an accomplished siren and attractive to certain kinds of men who in turn were attractive to Lytton. She brought Lytton his daily glasses of milk; she tucked him into his shawls and comforters, provided hot-water bottles, and learned to cook for him. She asked him to educate her. It was one of Virginia Woolf's little jokes that at Tidmarsh, where they set up house, Lytton and Carrington one evening withdrew from their company "ostensibly to copulate"; but when someone mounted the stairs, what was audible was Lytton reading Macaulay aloud to Carrington.

The "love affair"—if we want to call it that—must be seen not in the usual terms of courtship and cohabitation. It poses a number of questions that might be contained within the words "personal relations." The received opinion has been that Carrington immolated herself on Lytton's altar as the traditional "dutiful daughter" in quest of a father-figure. This was only a part of her intense neurotic needs. She had grown up with four siblings, three brothers and a sister. Her youthful environment had been almost totally male. She doted on her youngest brother, Teddy, whom she controlled and also cared for. He had been killed in the battle of the Somme. Her love for him was as powerful as Virginia's and Vanessa's for Thoby. Deprived of Teddy at the moment when she met Lytton, she found in him both the paternal and fraternal qualities on which she depended emotionally. Later she would find versions of Teddy in the men she teased and loved and decoyed into the Lyttonian lair. She kept an earlier lover, the painter Mark Gertler, dangling; he fitted neither into a fatherly nor brotherly role. She had an affair with the robust Ralph Partridge, who became Lytton's companion, and whom she ultimately married; and soon afterward she started an affair with Partridge's friend, Gerald Brenan. But even though she could be androgynous, her primary attitude was one of hostility to sexual relations with males. "None of That" was the title D. H. Lawrence gave to a story he based on Carrington. "At first there seemed something childish about her . . . rather round cheeks and clear eyes, so false-innocent. Her eyes were especially warm and naive and false-innocent but full of light." The repeated "false-innocent" touches the heart of Carrington. Her childish air of deceitful "innocence" carried her through the highly complex relations she created, the group of dangling men she liked to have in her train. She placed Lytton at the center of her tangled history. David Garnett, who knew her intimately, says that "like a child she found it hateful to choose . . . like a child she would tell lies . . . when caught out, or in an emotional crisis, she often behaved like a child, confessing her guilt, telling more lies and appealing to Lytton for help and forgiveness." If we translate this into its meaning, we can see Carrington as a strongly "manipulative" young woman, or, as Lawrence said in his tale, she was skillful "in making people dance while she pulled strings." She clung to her lovers as a child clings to dolls and teddy bears; and the animal imagery of her delightful caricatures in her letters are those which come out of a child's bestiary. She controlled people in the way some children learn to manipulate their parents. Lady Ottoline once described Carrington as "a wild moorland pony"—but there was little wildness in her calculated relation with Lytton. Ponies, after all, neither scheme nor seek to ingratiate themselves in the way Carrington did. She had no sense of self, since she despised herself as woman. She accordingly attached herself to others by imitating them. She quickly learned how to speak in Lytton's personal idiom; we can find in her letters diluted Voltairean malice and subterfuge, as if Voltaire had been refashioned in a nursery. She listened to the music of Lytton's ego and learned its tunes. And then everything she said could be consonant with his feelings. He read Shakespeare, Rimbaud and Donne to her; she quotes them in her letters to him. He taught her French and she became adept at using (if not spelling) French phrases. He always enjoyed the "mothering" process, as we have seen. He also felt mothered by her. In this way they gave each other strong primary gratifications. Ministering to his needs and making herself into a silhouette of Lytton, Carrington felt that she had become Lytton. It was therefore no accident that in later years she could mimic him to perfection and win a literary prize by parodying his biographical death scenes. In her mimicry there is always an enormous quantity of childish mischief and delight. She was probably the kind of woman Henry James's forlorn love-seeking Maisie in *What Maisie Knew* would have grown up to be.

In this complex of mixed identifications, like confronted like. Lytton, in his education of Carrington, compared himself to the centaur Cheiron, who in Greek mythology was an immortal. Where other centaurs were primitive and barbaric, Cheiron was wise and learned. Children of famous Greeks appeared at his cave to be reared by him—Jason, Achilles, Asclepius, Actaeon. On having the Cheiron myth explained to her, Carrington designed Lytton's bookplate: the bearded centaur holds a bow with his left hand; his right hand is on the right shoulder of a young Amazonian woman. She kneels beside him and has her hand on the bow as well, and it is she who is drawing the bowstring. Carrington learned rapidly how to shoot her well-aimed arrows.

The symbiotic drama of Lytton and Carrington has, in spite of its infantilisms, a certain liveliness and charm. It is charged with his humor and Carrington's playfulness. She had a child's love of nature, a child's feeling for its poetry, a certain clear eloquence. Her letters always cater to his moods. She titillates him with descriptions of young men; there is a kind of joyous frankness in her verbal "sexiness" which corresponds to Lytton's sexual humor whenever "the really interesting question" is raised. There was in the relationship a mutual irradiation of power. But there was a hint of pathos in their mutualities, an overtone of tragedy. What could Carrington do, as the *alter ego* of Lytton, when he disappeared? She was reduced to a hollow imitation of the dead, and life would turn to ashes. But this denouement lay more than a decade away.

By 1917, when Lytton was finishing "The End of General Gordon," Carrington had found The Mill House at Tidmarsh, near Reading, and made it into his home. It differed from Ferney in that he had to share it. Maynard Keynes, the Cambridge mathematician H. T. J. Norton, Oliver Strachey and Saxon Sydney-Turner agreed to pay £20 a year each for the costs of the house, with the under-

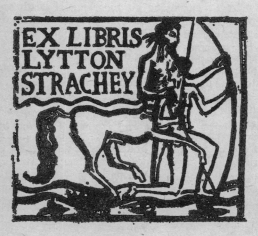

standing that they could use it as a country retreat: it was, however, basically to be the residence of Lytton and Carrington. It had three reception rooms, six bedrooms, a bathroom, a w.c., a very good garden and a shady grass lawn. The house was joined to the mill, and the river ran beside it. Carrington assembled furniture, bulbs, plants and artifacts and set to work to make a place in which her centaur might continue her education and find the peace to create.

Virginia Woolf, pondering the changes in Lytton's life, commented on his passivity: "Even in the matter of taking Tidmarsh, Lytton had to be propelled from behind, and his way of life, insofar as it is unconventional, is so by the desire and determination of Carrington." By the same token, it was Clive Bell who gave Lytton the necessary propulsion to assemble his four essays and send them to Clive's publisher, Chatto & Windus, *Eminent Victorians* was published on 9 May 1918, with an introduction that was a manifesto on the writing of history Lytton-style. If Bloomsbury by this time had attained a certain measure of modest fame, Lytton, who had been bringing up the rear, found himself suddenly in the vanguard. He was not only famous; he was a celebrity.

V

Lytton's manifesto on history and biography can be summarized: there is no excuse for dull biographies, those two-volume memorials with their funereal tone and tombstone size. History is an art, not a compilation written by journeymen. Biography has to be analytic, lively, human, and composed with becoming brevity. In modern times, with massive archives, it is no longer possible to write histories of a given age: instead, one can lower a small bucket into the great sea of documents and books and come up with characteristic specimens and symptoms; in a word, the whole can be deduced from the parts. In this way Lytton, by publishing only four "characters" out of the Victorian era, characterized the era. His book was an instant success during those final months of the long First World War. Everything had come to him at once: celebrity, money, a home, an efficient—an eager—mistress (in name at least) and adulation. His Voltairean dreams had come true.

Why did *Eminent Victorians* capture the imagination of war-weary England? Taine's theory of the race, the environment and the moment—*la race, le milieu et le moment* —as combining to produce a significant work may very well be applied to Lytton Strachey's book. Strachey challenged and mocked Church and State and the military. He did this not in criticism of the immediate war effort, but within the safety of the past—the recent past which England still remembered. It was a consolation and a relief for Britons to see that in this war they had shown the same toughness, the same resilience, and had made the same mistakes. Lytton had said that Voltaire grinned most when he was in earnest, and the grin of *Eminent Victorians* made it an earnest as well as an amusing book. His readers were prepared to overlook Lytton's mannerisms, his inaccuracies, his wantonly imagined details, and to accept his characterizations. The Church harbored ambitious and power-seeking individuals; the military had generals with an exalted notion that Bible and sword were the justification for their existence; the schools had great schoolmasters of platitudinous proportions. In his vivid portrait of Florence Nightingale, Lytton also paid homage to the toughness of English women and their ability to confound Downing Street. From now on he would paint English queens—Victoria, Elizabeth—who had in them the very stuff that produced the Victorian Miss Nightingale. Moreover, the essay on "The Lady with the Lamp" exalted the common soldier and spoke on behalf of his fate in compassionate and humane terms. England was at this moment filled with soldiers who knew the pain of their wounds and had experienced the benefits of Miss Nightingale's revolution. The urgencies of war had exposed Britain to all its institutions, and Strachey held up these institutions in the light of gentle (and at times even savage) ironies. Thus he fulfilled for his readers Taine's dictum: the English race, the beloved land, and this crucial moment helped create one of the greatest literary successes of the century.

There were few readers who realized that Lytton Strachey had done more than present a palimpsest of British history in which Britons could read their present into

the past. He had written his book in a new kind of ink—
the ink of Vienna, of Sigmund Freud. He had read certain
of the master analyst's primary books: and his brother
James Strachey would later be analyzed by Freud and
would become the translator of all Freud's works. Lytton
Strachey was the first practitioner of "psycho-history," and
he did it with direct use only of what in Freud was relevant
to his own work. The Viennese master himself could applaud him. When *Elizabeth and Essex* appeared, Freud
wrote a letter to Lytton saying that he had read all his
works and that he considered the book on Elizabeth an
exemplar of the psychoanalytic method applied to history.
Lytton had worked within "the incompleteness of our
knowledge and the clumsiness of our synthesis," but he
had worked with "boldness and discretion." Historians, unlike analysts, working with the personages beyond living
confrontation, were in the same position as "dreams to
which we have been given no associations." Lytton had
nevertheless been able to trace back Elizabeth's character
"to the impressions of her childhood." He thus "touched
on her most hidden motives." And Freud ventured to add
that possibly Lytton had succeeded in making "a correct
reconstruction of what actually occurred."

Lytton Strachey thus brought to the doors of Bloomsbury his high success: seven printings in the year of publication! But he brought hostilities as well, those of readers
who disliked his kind of wit and his sly disparagement of
English eminence. It was too easy to laugh at the past. And
it was too easy to take shortcuts with documents. Still, the
recent and esteemed Prime Minister, H. H. Asquith, during
his Romanes Lectures at Oxford in 1918, singled out Lytton's book for the highest praise. This was the accolade
Lytton needed most. A whole segment of the English public who would perhaps have ignored the book now fell upon
it with eagerness and excitement. "I remain calm even in
face of the praises of Mr. Asquith," the delighted author
told Virginia Woolf. And she (not a little jealous of his
sudden rise to fame and fortune) described him as behav-
ing like "a newly wedded bride." Lytton pretended that
fame was "uncomfortable" but, said Virginia, "he's obviously in a sort of rapture." He was indeed the man of the
hour—sought after by duchesses, embraced by elders in

their clubs, saluted by the press, treated as an oracle, he rode the waves of reputation with all the dignity he could muster, looking with fresh eyes at himself, the Caliban of the long beard and high voice. Surely this was what Voltaire had experienced! Speaking to the Apostles in Cambridge who feted his book, Lytton was at his most waggish —he readily agreed that "an eminent Victorian might be defined . . . as the sort of person whose life would be likely to be written by Lytton Strachey."

VI

Where lay the success of *Eminent Victorians* beyond the fact that it seemed to touch *la race, le milieu et le moment?* There were the Stracheyesque stance, the high irony, the intimate effect of using diaries as if they were the private thoughts of the characters and a host of new biographical devices including skillful *collage* and *pastiche.* And then there was the extraordinary economy of the prose, the flair with which vast amounts of dull material were reduced to a brilliant paragraph or sentence of description. Lytton Strachey had dared to do what other biographers feared: to interpret his materials courageously, to say what things meant. Biographies crammed with fact, he observed, were tasteless; a fact had no meaning unless some attempt was made to interpret it. Lytton's book—and we must not blame him for his imitators—gave rise to a whole series of "debunking" biographies in which the famous were knocked off their pedestals. But he also had disciples: André Maurois in France, Van Wyck Brooks in America. Brooks borrowed an entire methodology from Strachey— not always with happy results, but with considerable public success. What Strachey understood, for all his abrasiveness, was the principle of human volatility; he knew that the ego seeks at all costs its basic defenses; and he knew what other biographers had not learned—that a biographical subject is consistently ambiguous, irrational, inexplicable, self-contradicting; hence, it truly lends itself to irony and to delicacies of insight and sentiment.

How did Lytton Strachey convert all the negatives of his own experience into positives of achievement? The answer lies in the synthesis of his life myth. He was able to meta-morphose his ambivalence toward his mother, the Queen of Lancaster Gate and Belsize Park Gardens, into histori-cal metaphors—Jane Strachey's mixture of feminine en-durance and feminine-masculine action to which he had always been exposed. Lady Strachey had been an inflexible, determined, unassailable woman, strong-willed (like Flor-ence Nightingale), smothered in domesticity with a house-ful of children (like Victoria), yet always regal and in control. Florence Nightingale had been the mother of an entire army of soldiers (how delightful it was to identify with her and have England's wounded manhood to con-sole!). In his books Lytton Strachey identifies only par-tially with the males; he is on the side of the queens. In his life of Queen Victoria (his most successful book) he deals with the two elements of power within himself, the power gratification required in his maleness, projected through the character of the Prince Consort, and the only power he actually knew, that vested in the woman, this time the queen. The relationship of himself to his mother found its perfect analogue in the relationship of Victoria to her Con-sort. Writing these books offered him the gratification of his double role in life, his androgynous quest for a place in the sun. We note how he ridicules General Gordon or Arnold of Rugby (versions of his gentle and elderly father). His men are the real butt of his wit; he could not identify himself with them save in his own ambiguous homosexual role. It is always the women who have to be strong—and what figures are stronger in symbolic power than England's queens? In the role of Essex, the male is undone by his own folly; he cannot manipulate the queen as Albert handled her at a later stage of history.

Strachey basked in his newfound fame. He frequented high society; he developed a whole new string of hostesses where Ottoline had previously throned in lonely power. Money was pouring in. *Queen Victoria* would make him sufficiently wealthy to buy his own Ferney without being dependent on the kindnesses of his friends. He paid his debts in cash and also in his dedications: *Eminent Vic-torians* to H. T. J. Norton the mathematician, who had provided funds for one of his houses; *Elizabeth and Essex* to Maynard Keynes, who had in a manner of speaking been one of the landlords of Tidmarsh. And to Virginia Woolf he dedicated his *Queen Victoria*. She in turn dedicated to him her first collection of essays, *The Common Reader*. It was Virginia who looked at Strachey's work with strong reservations. She liked his personal mellowness, his charm, his warmth. She did not like his prose. It was bright and brittle, all surface, and cliché-ridden, doubtless a form of brilliant journalism. We read in the opening pages of *Elizabeth and Essex* such sentences as "the blood flew through his veins in vigorous vitality" or "the new star, rising with extreme swiftness, was suddenly seen to be shining alone in the firmament." Such worn imagery, such time-rubbed words, caused Virginia to decide privately that Lytton wasn't "first-rate." And she in turn could mock the great mocker. It has not been noticed that her own historical pastiche, *Orlando*, which focuses attention on Knole and Vita Sackville-West, is also a brilliant parody of Strachey's historical prose. Lytton had a personal style in all he did; but no, decidedly, he was not a "stylist."

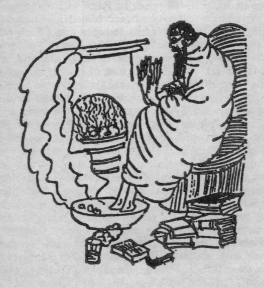

Maynard at Versailles

Maynard Keynes spent the war at the Treasury. He was brought in at the beginning of 1915 to write memoranda for the Chancellor's advisers. Lloyd George now referred to him as "a clever young Cambridge don." In a very short time he became the Treasury's expert on inter-Allied loans, and he invented a much-admired system of controls which the United States copied. By 1917 Keynes had moved into a special division at the center of the inter-Allied economic effort. After the Armistice in November 1918 he was named Principal Representative of the British Treasury at the 1919 Peace Conference in Paris with power to speak for the Chancellor. He also served on the Supreme Economic Council. These were the highest official posts he would ever hold.

The Government was quick to recognize that in Maynard it had, as one official put it, "an artist and a bit of a genius." He was supreme in his ability to translate theory into practice. Those who worked with him described him as a consummate chess player; he knew all the moves in advance. His power of persuasion was unusual; perhaps this was because he was always ready to explore all points of view and even to reexplore his own. He would persuade his colleagues that a certain course was justified; then he would find flaws in his own reasoning and reach a new conclusion, quite as persuasively. One Foreign Office official said his opinions were "in a perpetual state of progress" —but progress always to an ultimate workable decision. His mental *allegresse* represented a kind of "critical intuition only to be paralleled by great historians and scientists." These views might be summed up in the image of one observer—"in front of a large map he has the range of an eagle."

II

Keynes's work at the Treasury kept him more continuously in London and thus closer to Bloomsbury. He maintained his lifelong habit of working in bed when possible so as to have maximum repose. With his telephone at hand, and his papers spread before him, he was always master of a given situation. He immersed himself in his work, and he knew how to relax. He had his option to spend weekends at Tidmarsh with Lytton, and he was always welcome at Charleston. He would bring his work to Sussex and regale Vanessa and Duncan with "inside" stories of the war and the gossip of the great world in which he now moved. Sometimes, to take his mind off Treasury problems, he would work with Duncan and young Garnett in the fields, digging potatoes or helping in farm chores.

In London he made friends with Prime Minister Asquith and his family. He was never on such familiar terms with Asquith's successor, Lloyd George, who recognized his abilities but was always a bit suspicious of his bright mind. There were invitations to Downing Street and high London political society.

Keynes had to exercise his diplomatic skill on such occasions when the question of the conscientious objectors was raised. His sympathies were known. Lytton and Bertrand Russell challenged him very early in his new career: if Keynes was a pacifist, he should leave the Treasury. Was he not contributing to the war's continuation rather than the making of a peace? He seemed to be working for "the maximum slaughter at minimum expense." Keynes's answer was, "We are in it now and we must go through with it; there is really no practical alternative." He testified on behalf of his friends—James Strachey, Lytton, Duncan, David Garnett—when they faced the Tribunal. In his position on the war—that once it had started, it had to be finished—he was closer to Leonard's and Virginia's views than to those of Lady Ottoline's pacifist circle.

We catch two glimpses of him in Lady Ottoline's journals. He comes to dinner in 1915—"an interesting but rather dreadful evening," Ottoline writes. Keynes is "hard, intellectual, insincere—using intellect to hide the torment and discord in his soul. We pressed him hard about his purpose in life—he spoke as tho' he only wanted a succession of agreeable moments, which of course is not really true." This was Keynes in an epicurean mood. The "torment" to which Ottoline alludes was probably hers rather than Maynard's. She seemed to believe he was in conflict over his pacifism. It is doubtful whether Keynes ever was. He knew his own mind. He enjoyed his work at the Treasury; he entered into it with too must zest to want to give it up. Lady Ottoline also wrote on this occasion that D. H. Lawrence liked Keynes "but can't get on with him." She added, "I get on with him, but dislike him." She was troubled also by Keynes's bisexuality. Or, as she put it, "Lawrence has the same feeling against sodomy as I have." But on occasions she overcame this dislike. "His influence and his advices are always in favour of hard work, and point toward the high road of life, not to flights and dilettantism. . . . But his manner except to a few intimate friends is dominating and borders on the insolent." Still Ottoline responded to his "detached meditating and yet half-caressing interest in those he is speaking to, head on one side, a kindly tolerant smile and very charming eyes wandering, searching, speculating."

It was true that Maynard the epicure-"playboy" and Maynard the financial wizard—pacifist seemed contradictory and at odds. He reconciled these opposite sides of himself with greater ease than his friends believed and was usually at peace with himself. His "insolence" was another matter. It particularly disturbed those who were fond of him. Leonard, just before the war, had written privately of Keynes as "an effete and rotten old lecher"; he also said he was "clear and subtle and strong." But this was at the time when Woolf was being very critical and moral about Bloomsbury.

III

For a while Maynard took a house in Gower Street, with Middleton Murry and Katherine Mansfield as tenants. On another floor lived Carrington (before she went to Tidmarsh) and some of her Slade School friends, including Barbara Hiles (later Bagenal), who would work for Leonard and Virginia at the Hogarth Press, and Dorothy Brett, who was of Lady Ottoline's circle. In 1916, however, Keynes moved to No. 46 Gordon Square. Vanessa and Clive retained rooms in the house for use when they were in London. Thus Keynes was in possession of the "matrix" of Bloomsbury. No. 46 would be his London home for the rest of his life.

Perhaps one of the most amusing instances of Keynes's mental agility among his friends was his response to a bit of information Duncan Grant gave him at one moment during the war. Grant knew that some of the paintings owned by Degas were to be auctioned off in Paris. Maynard promptly recognized unexpected possibilities. Britain should bid for the pictures. It would provide the French with some much-needed sterling, and it was a chance to obtain for the National Gallery certain splendid works of art. With his power of persuasion, he obtained a government allocation of £20,000 and attended the auction with the head of the National Gallery. The Germans were shelling Paris that day; the auction was a nervous one; the bids were low. The National Gallery acquired (without spending all the allotted money) two paintings by Delacroix, a Gauguin, two Manets, three Ingreses, a Rousseau and some important drawings. Keynes bought a Cézanne and a Delacroix for himself and gave Duncan a Delacroix drawing. After returning to London, he was given a lift in Austen Chamberlain's car to Sussex. He deposited his luggage and various bundles on the road near Charleston. On entering, he told Duncan that there was a Cézanne down the way and that he had better bring it in. Incredulously, Duncan obeyed.

In 1917 Keynes went on a brief mission to the United States to settle outstanding Anglo-American financial questions. He crossed the Atlantic in a large convoy and negotiated a $50 million loan involving Canadian wheat. This was the first of his many crossings to America to attend international monetary conferences. And long before the war's end he had prepared his data on Europe and his blueprints for the postwar settlements. There would be the question of reparations. He was asked to provide information. The eagle perched over the map of Europe had long seen that Germany would have to pay a price—but how much? He recognized that what it paid, and the manner of payment, might gratify the punitive politicians but could be the ruin of Europe. To what extent could the militaristic Reich be dismantled without dismantling Europe's economy? Keynes had an economist's answers, but Lloyd George's answers were those of expediency and politics. The military establishment had narrow military answers. At these moments Maynard found himself at odds with the very institutions Lytton had described in *Eminent Victorians*. When Maynard left for the Peace Conference in Paris, the question of reparations, for which he had comprehensive humane answers, had been compromised by the politicians and the generals. Lloyd George himself went to the British electorate and was returned to office with the mandate that Germany must pay for the war it had caused. Keynes felt he was attending a parley whose conclusions had been prejudged.

IV

Maynard arrived at the Hôtel Majestic, seat of the British delegation, in the cold of the Parisian winter. It was January 1919. The Armistice was seven weeks old; the revelry of Armistice Day had given way to a general sobriety. Ways to a peace had to be found. The Majestic presented all the confusion of a newly established camp or a huge convention: British typists drank their tea; Scotland Yard men emptied wastepaper baskets and burned all scrap paper; red dispatch boxes circulated; familiar faces encountered familiar faces in the grand hotel dining room; other delegates explored Parisian restaurants. The atmosphere was one of "bored excitement."

Meanwhile, Maynard learned that the French were conducting quiet financial negotiations with the Germans under the umbrella of the Armistice. He demanded that he be allowed to participate, and here he confronted some typical paradoxes of the conference: How were the Germans to be fed (as had been promised) with the Allied blockade still in force and German assets and shipping frozen? This was the Gordian knot he tried to cut. President Wilson arrived at Brest on 13 December 1918, on the *George Washington*, the first American President ever to leave native soil for the high diplomacy of Europe. He brought with him his idealistic "Fourteen Points," speaking of "the concert of free peoples"—words which gave hope to the world. He spoke also of "self-determination"—the old American ideal for nations barely emerged from feudalism and economically ruined by war. How, it could be asked then (and now), could such peoples "determine" anything? Generous America, having established democracy in its own way after a revolution, seemed to believe that the ballot imparted national wisdom even to the ignorant.

Keynes sat at inner meetings of the world leaders, notably President Wilson, Georges Clemenceau of France, Orlando of Italy and David Lloyd George. He experienced no sense of awe before these representatives of the great powers. He had his own sovereign ease in his abilities, his mental reach, his superbly integrated economic knowledge. He studied the leaders in the harsh light of his own intelligence. They were interesting, even picturesque, men, and with his capacity for grasping detail and his ability for close observation he looked not only at what they wore, but how they sat or stood and their manner of gesture. Wilson, he noted at once, did not have the mental speed of the European leaders; Lloyd George seemed to him the intuitive one, with a strong feminine component in his makeup; and Clemenceau, called "the Tiger" by his people, lived up to his name. But his claws were hidden. Again and again Maynard expressed his frustration. He could not study Clemenceau's hands; the Tiger wore gray suède gloves. The three, he saw at once, were not their own masters; they listened to the national sentiment that had placed them in power and to the primitive passions that called for revenge and punishment rather than reconstruction. This was less true of Wilson, however. He had brought a group of American businessmen to be his experts. Keynes noted that Wilson's head and features were finely cut. The muscles of the neck and the carriage of his head were "distinguished." But, said Keynes, "Like Odysseus, the President looked wiser when he was seated; and his hands, though capable and fairly strong, were wanting in sensitiveness and fineness." He listened to the President and, perhaps because Keynes had a swift mind, he found

Wilson terribly "slow." The words "slow" and "slowness" are repeated four times in Keynes's later description: "His mind was slow and unadaptable"; "too slow and unresourceful"; "too slow-minded and bewildered"; his "slowness" was "noteworthy." The important distinction between Lloyd George and Wilson was that Wilson was insensitive to his environment while the British Prime Minister seemed to have extra senses; he moved, talked, experienced everything through his antennae that reached out and picked up the wavelengths of the others in the room. After listening to the former president of Princeton and now the President of the United States, Keynes decided that the American had "not much even of the culture of that world which marks M. Clemenceau and Mr. Balfour as exquisitely cultivated gentlemen of their class and generation." Clemenceau had lived in America when young and had married a New England woman; he could command the two principal languages of the negotiations. Wilson and Lloyd George possessed only their native tongues. But what chance could such a man as Wilson have against Lloyd George's "unerring, almost medium-like sensibility"?

In the drama of the conference Keynes paid close attention to Clemenceau. The old Frenchman spoke for a France that had twice, in half a century, fought Germany. France had paid heavy reparations to the Germans after 1870, and Clemenceau was determined that the Reich should now pay for everything and be leveled like Carthage. There he sat in a brocaded chair at the inner meetings in black garb, with his dominating walrus-mustaches —a fighter from the first. He had fought for Zola and Dreyfus long ago and had led France through endlessly intricate political mazes. Keynes observed minutely how he was dressed: his square-tailed coat of very good, thick black broadcloth; his boots of thick black leather, country style, sometimes fastened with a buckle instead of laces. He carried no papers, no portfolio. He was unattended by personal secretaries. Clemenceau was a very old man, conserving his strength for one thing: a dictated peace. France knew by experience that the Germans could not be allowed to be their equals at a conference table. One could not bargain with the defeated enemy: one dictated.

The three figures resolved themselves in Keynes's exploring mind into two admiring males—Wilson and Clemenceau—in attendance on a *femme fatale,* Lloyd George. They were "the President, the Tiger, and the Welsh witch" or "an old man of the world, a *femme fatale* and a nonconformist clergyman." The clergyman in Wilson was capable of delivering a sermon on each of his Fourteen Points, but he had come to this conference to decide the fate of millions with no facts, no research, no particulars for each of his points. Maintaining his imagery, Keynes likened Wilson to a fairy prince riding the barque *George Washington* to the enchanted castle of Paris, "to free from chains and oppression and an ancient curse the maid of Europe, of eternal youth and beauty, his mother and his bride in one." In this castle sat the old King (Clemenceau) with his yellow parchment face, a million years old, and with him an enchantress with a harp from across the Channel (Lloyd George). The enchantress sang the Prince's own words—the Fourteen Points—to a magical tune. "If only the Prince could cast off the paralysis which creeps on him and, crying to heaven, could make the Sign of the Cross, with a sound of thunder and crashing glass the castle would dissolve, the magicians vanish, and Europe leap to his arms."

This was the fairy tale Keynes witnessed for six months in 1919 in "the hot and poisoned atmosphere of Paris." The tale does not end happily—"the forces of the half-world win and the soul of Man is subordinated to the spirits of the earth." Keynes could not face the premises of the peace treaty, nor could he accept the idea of revenge planned in a way that would make not peace but another war. Already the nations carved out of new frontiers were coming to the British Treasury for loans—not for food and rehabilitation, but for armaments. It was, he wrote his mother, an "outrageous and impossible peace." It could bring "nothing but misfortune behind it." Years later Winston Churchill would say that Keynes did not understand political necessities; he only understood the necessities of world economy. The statement was accurate, perhaps, but then Churchill spoke out of his own political-military roots. What impresses us when we read Keynes on the peace treaty today is not so much his sketches of the leaders, which are clever and psychologically accurate, but the profound humanism and idealism that animated him, so that the question of whether he was pro-German or anti-German seemed irrelevant. He wanted to avoid a treaty that would make way for disaster—a disaster that could, as it ultimately did, spawn a Hitler. In that sense he was the prophet and the eagle looking at the map of Europe. Clemenceau and Lloyd George, looking at the same map, saw only politics and frontiers and the menace of the new and then hardly threatening figure of Vladimir Ilyich Lenin.

V

Keynes remained in Paris into June of 1919, sick in mind and body at the events he was witnessing, but he fought to the last for his principles; and "when it became clear that hope could no longer be entertained of substantial modification in the draft terms of Peace," he felt that he could no longer be a party to the proceedings. In a personal but significant gesture, he resigned and returned to England. He stepped back into his rooms at Cambridge; he was no longer a civil servant. And then he went for a rest to Charleston. Here in the Sussex rusticity, with his Bloomsbury friends around him, he wrote—at white heat—what he had just been through. The impressions, issues, conclusions of the Versailles Treaty were shaped by him into a series of lectures on the "Economic Aspects of the Peace Treaty," and these were delivered to overflow audiences of students that autumn in Cambridge. The students abandoned their other studies to hear this man who spoke out of his firsthand view of the Conference; and one who heard him remembered that he conveyed a "burning sense of the world's stupidities."

That burning sense was contained in the book he published before the year was out, *The Economic Consequences of the Peace.* (He paid for the publication of the book with Macmillan and paid Macmillan royalties to distribute it—as Bernard Shaw had done consistently with his publishers.) Thus within a matter of months a second member of Bloomsbury had produced a book that made a sensation. Strachey had asked readers to look at Church,

State, Education and the Military with wry amusement. Keynes's book was read by State and Military with strong feelings: he raised issues and described personalities of the moment. It was a fearless book, and it produced a profound impression on both sides of the sea. His sharp vignettes of the peacemakers were embedded in a thick mass of economic tables showing that to attempt to extract water from a stone would solve nothing. True, the Germans had been defeated; true, they had started the war; but in defeat, Maynard argued, it was possible to be magnanimous when magnanimity was wedded to the practical— and the practical showed that the peace treaty did not concern itself whether Germany was able to pay or not; moreover, in crushing Germany totally, European economy was being segmented. What had happened was that France had wrapped its Draconian terms in the language of President Wilson and satisfied him that "freedom and international equality" would be maintained. What would be maintained, Keynes saw, were inflation, death, disease, and an ultimate débacle. One economic center of Europe was being reduced "to servitude for a generation," and this involved the lives of millions of innocents. Clemenceau had seen the issues totally in terms of France and Germany, "not of humanity and of European civilization struggling toward a new order." The treaty degraded the lives of Europe's millions, and this, Keynes felt, "should be abhorrent and detestable . . . even if it did not sow the decay of the whole civilized life of Europe." Thus, he concluded, the three figures, "Clemenceau, aesthetically the noblest, the President, morally the most admirable, Lloyd George, intellectually the subtlest," had produced out of their disparities a "child of the least worthy attributions of each of its parents, without nobility, without morality, without intellect." He concluded his book by offering his solutions: revision of the treaty, settlement of inter-Allied indebtedness, international loans and reforms of the currency and close attention to the relations of Central Europe and the newly founded Communist State in Russia. In reverberating Shakespearean tones Keynes said, "We are at the dead season of our fortunes." He reminded his readers that "the true voice of the new generation has not yet spoken." The treaty had ignored "the problem of life and human relations, of creation and behaviour and religion." In making these affirmations, Keynes spoke not only as an economist but as one of the pacifists and humanists of Bloomsbury.

Leonard Woolf's "invisible" presence at Versailles can be read in documents. In 1915 he wrote a report for the Fabian Society on "international government." When he started this task, he discovered that no such document had ever been assembled before. With his characteristic thoroughness, Woolf read hundreds of Blue Books and White Books and annual reports dealing with such international organizations as existed—the Universal Postal Union or the International Institute of Agriculture. He interviewed civil servants who had attended conferences and congresses of these unions. In this way he assembled evidence to show the extent to which international cooperation is possible. What could be made to work for agriculture or the post office could be made to work in the service of greater problems still, and ultimately that of keeping the peace. Advocating an international authority to prevent war, Woolf published his report as a supplement to the *New Statesman*. Then he and Sidney Webb drew up a model international treaty establishing such a supranational authority. The two documents appeared in book form in 1916. The volume was used extensively by British Government committees in planning proposals for a League of Nations. Leonard's old Cambridge friend Sydney Waterlow drew up for the British delegation a report on "International Government under the League of Nations," and in the prefatory note he said that the facts contained in the first part of his report were taken almost entirely from Leonard Woolf's book. The task, he said, had been done so well that there was no need to do the work over again. We know that a copy of Leonard's book was also sent by U.S. Naval Headquarters in London to Colonel E. M. House, who helped draft the League of Nations Covenant. The memorandum said that Woolf "has collated, in a most scholarly way, a mass of data carefully sifted, of experiences and precedents for international government which may prove of use to you, as a scaffolding." In this way Leonard Woolf's work played its modest role in the writing of the Covenant of the League.

VI

Maynard Keynes had one experience at the Peace Conference which he did not describe in his public writings. He
disclosed it some years later to the Memoir Club, and it
was published only after his death. This was his account of
unofficial meetings with one of the lesser German experts,
Dr. Carl Melchior, a banker from Hamburg and, as
Keynes later ascertained, a Jew. We have seen that Keynes
intervened in the preliminary Armistice talks on the blockade of Germany. Marshal Foch was in charge and he
grudgingly took Keynes aboard his train to Trèves (Trier)
on the German frontier, where certain of the complicated
parleys were held. Keynes called Foch a "peasant"; his
military vision blotted out "nine tenths of the affairs of
mankind." The German delegates were unpleasant: "Erz-
berger, fat and disgusting in a fur coat . . . a General and a
Sea-Captain with an iron cross . . . and an extraordinary
resemblance of face and figure to the pig in *Alice in Won-
derland.*" They were exactly what the Allies meant when
they used the word "Huns." However, Keynes noticed in
the delegation a small, clean, neat man with a high stiff
collar, his head shaved to the point where his hair looked
like a bit of carpet pile. Dr. Melchoir spoke English slowly
and accurately. He did not stumble or hesitate, suggesting
to Keynes that he was mainly speaking the truth. He sat
"staring, heavy-lidded, helpless" and seemed to Maynard
"an honourable animal in pain." His face alone among the
impassive enemy faces "upheld the dignity of defeat." As
the deadlocked talks circled back to the same place on the
issue of how the Germans should pay for food and surrender their merchant ships, Keynes kept wondering why
they couldn't talk "about the truth and the reality like sane
and sensible persons." The reality was that civilians and
children were starving and that abundant food supplies had
arrived from the United States. The empty formalities of
the talks made human relations impossible. The French
mistrusted the Germans. The Germans kept trying to find
some way out of the maze. Nothing concrete emerged. The
military were in charge, since the negotiations derived from
the Armistice.

Keynes sought and received permission to approach the sympathetic German privately. He and Melchior had two meetings. On the first occasion they both stood up throughout the interview, aware that they were transgressing "the barriers of permitted intercourse." Keynes explained to Melchior that the Anglo-Americans understood Germany's need for food; a solution was imperative to avoid general starvation. Could not the Germans cut through some of the technicalities? Keynes asked Melchior to believe in his truthfulness and sincerity. As they conversed in quiet tones, in English, he observed that Melchior was "as much moved as I was, and I think he believed me." Melchior, at bay, had singular appeal. In a sort of way, Keynes said, "I was in love with him." He replied to Keynes with "the passionate pessimism of a Jew" that he would send word back to his chiefs, but he had little hope of success.

Nothing came of this first attempt at personal contact. Some weeks later Keynes tried again. By this time the urgencies were much greater and certain practical procedures had been worked out. The Germans were to start surrendering ships at the same moment as food shipments would begin. But the French were not satisfied. They wanted the Germans to state their "unqualified acceptance" of the ship surrender. It was simply a matter of their making a preliminary statement of what they had already agreed to do in order to satisfy the French, and no doubt French public opinion. Keynes was worried that the impasse had been so rigged that everyone would be waiting for a statement which the Germans did not know they had to make. He went in search of Melchior. They met in an untidy room. The beds were unmade; an unemptied chamber pot stood in the middle of the floor. Keynes told Melchior that, if the Germans would volunteer a statement on the ship surrender as soon as the next meeting convened, all would be well. The shortcut he had taken worked. The chief German envoy made the statement at the right time, and the deadlock was broken. In his direct way and to his own satisfaction Keynes had demonstrated that the impersonality of the talks could be breached. It was hard to deal with an enemy; but one could still speak to him in a humane way. His allusions to truth and sincerity, and the romanticism of his remark—"in a sort of way I was in love with him"—suggested attitudes of Bloomsbury rather than those of diplomacy.

The "artist and a bit of genius," by understanding the nature of pride and humiliation, defeat and surrender, by allowing himself to feel how his enemies felt, had achieved a simple solution—and not only out of his intricate mind and Cambridge economics but out of Bloomsbury's humanism.

Houses of Lions

Vanessa Bell found herself pregnant a few months before the war's end. It seemed to her a part of the fitness of things that a baby, a daughter, was born at 2:00 A.M. on Christmas Day, the first Christmas of the peace. In the Charleston of that Yuletide it was as if some Sussex Nativity Play were being enacted. There were assorted attendants and at least one Wise Man, Maynard Keynes, who helped the thirty-three-year-old father, Duncan Grant, during his hours of anxiety. Duncan's fellow farmhand of the war, David Garnett, was also still in the house; twenty-two years later he would marry Vanessa's only daughter, a little princess, as she seemed, of Bloomsbury, with her vast blue eyes and long fingers. In the frosty dawn, when her travail was over, Vanessa might have felt that hovering angels had attended, for she named her daughter Angelica. She said later that "it seemed rather extraordinary to have a baby then"—seven weeks after the Armistice. In the distance, as she lay in one of the upstairs front bedrooms of Charleston Farm, she could hear the farmhands going about their morning chores singing Christmas carols. It was a peaceful birth in a still world. The child of the love of two artists became the daughter of the Bell family and grew up with two fathers, Duncan, close at hand, and the visiting Clive, who continued to arrive bearing gifts and toys, always cheerful, always lively, always full of loud laughter. The two half brothers, Julian and Quentin, had been quietly removed from the house to stay with their Aunt Virginia and Uncle Leonard, who were now known in Bloomsbury as The Woolves (they even used the head of a wolf designed by Vanessa on their stationery, and also as the publisher's device for their Hogarth Press).

Virginia, denied by fate the opportunities of mother-hood, found that two boys, aged ten and eight, were more than a houseful. She delighted in the new small feminine being at Charleston. Bloomsbury uncles and aunts clustered around this very child of their *moeurs*, ideals, loves, art, humanism. The girl would grow up smothered in love and affection in a brilliant gregarious company. This no doubt had its benefits—and its difficulties. Certainly she had the smell of paint and turpentine in her nostrils from the moment she drew her first breath. And she would be aware of words, of wit and dignity—even in the eyes and beard of Uncle Lytton or the formidable seriousness in the lined countenance of Uncle Leonard.

The end of the war, with an angelic infant of the new time at Charleston, seemed to Bloomsbury to lift a curtain on another world. The old Bloomsbury of 1914 had been an informal group that met and parted, shared ideas and feelings and sometimes loves—and also jealousies and hates. The postwar Bloomsbury found the friends four years older, most of them in their middle and late thirties. They had lived through the deaths, the pains, the frustrations of the war years, which now seemed to them a kind of long dead winter in which the roots could barely be kept warm. Peace brought a radiant spring, and a flowering. They were free again. They had spread into the English countryside, although they still had footholds in London. Bloomsbury was now lodged in a series of houses or, in Virginia's image, a series of zoo cages, in which lions lived—and even The Woolves were on their way to becoming lions. In 1920, writing to Barbara Bagenal, Virginia spoke of Bloomsbury as resembling nothing so much as the lions' house at the Zoo: "One goes from cage to cage. All the animals are dangerous, rather suspicious of each other, and full of fascination and mystery." Virginia was thinking of the instinctive nature of the splendid beasts, their habits of pawing and mauling and clawing and bruising. She did not suggest that a lion's paw also harbors an excess of power—unconscious power. If the Bloomsbury friends seemed playful among themselves and occasionally scratched and clawed, that was a private matter; but how could the public not be aware now of Lytton's and Maynard's renown and of the pictures on the gallery walls and the reviews and articles in the public prints? This public saw the group as a single lion with a very powerful paw. The friends after the war might be a source of hypnotic fascination to some of the aspiring writers and painters, but to others Bloomsbury was seen as a parcel of snobs— dangerous snobs, because Bloomsbury seemed to hold in its hands so much authority in deciding which pictures should be hung and what new writers might be reviewed. Even Lytton, sitting in judgment on dead Victorians, had a curious negative effect on certain of the Georgians. Maynard's power belonged to higher levels; and Leonard's power, which was considerable, was less known, for he was a behind-the-scenes committeeman.

The Woolves spent the war at Hogarth House in Richmond, to which they moved shortly after their marriage. Here Virginia had her worst hours of dementia and tristimania—hours of storm and rage and then of catatonic withdrawal; and here Leonard had to grope in his own despair and desolation toward the special role he would have to play as husband. Bit by bit sanity returned. Virginia became Aspasia again and Leonard a modest modern Pericles. He worked endlessly, sitting through dull hours in dank fetid rooms, dreaming of new worlds and direct action to establish international sanity that would ban wars forever. Rational man had to learn how to rule his barbaric impulses. Publication of *The Voyage Out* in 1915 had given Virginia her first foothold in England's literary world; her place before this had been in the *Guardian* and the anonymous pages of the *Times Literary Supplement*, for which she now resumed her reviewing. In 1915 she started writing her second novel, *Night and Day*, as if she too had to relive her own recent nights and days, her marriage, her anxieties. The novel was dedicated to Vanessa, and Virginia projected a portrait of her sister—her beauty, her dignity, her unworldliness; but the portrait had much of Virginia in it as well. The world of Kensington is seen in relation to the world of Bloomsbury; and the Bloomsbury of earlier phases, the Fitzroy Square days, is described. The heroine wants a home of her own, but she also wants "something that hasn't got to do with human beings"—and here Virginia touched that part of Vanessa which wanted the perpetual "still life" of painting, the beauty and sensuousness of portraits and forms without life's volatilities. We catch glimpses of Lytton and of Clive in the novel; the hero has much of Leonard's integrity and selfhood; and we are given glimpses of the older Kensington world into which a Henry James figure strays or Virginia's eccentric aunt, Anne Thackeray Ritchie, who is lovingly and humorously portrayed. Like *The Voyage Out*, this novel is crammed with too many recent experiences; but unlike the first work it shows a Virginia restored to health, with a firm grasp of questions related to loving and living. Published in 1919, it represented a working out of Virginia's subjective problems to the point of enabling her to go on to the greater artistic freedom of *Jacob's Room*, her first truly characteristic novel.

Hogarth House was an ideal dwelling for Virginia and Leonard. Its well-proportioned rooms, its eighteenth-century paneling and chaste ornamentation, ministered to a sense of repose and peace. The two lived in this house from 1915 to 1924 and then decided that they wanted to be in London. They sold it and acquired a house in the heart of Bloomsbury, in Tavistock Square, the square in which one of Leonard's grandfathers had long ago made his home. In 1919 they also acquired Monk's House, Rodmell, near Lewes in Sussex as a weekend house within easy distance of Charleston. Asheham was given up.

At Hogarth House, Leonard had installed in 1917—on the dining room table—several cases of type and a handpress. This was planned as "occupational therapy" for Virginia, who otherwise would write herself into exhaustion. Setting type and a certain amount of printing provided a useful form of relaxation while keeping her hands occupied with letters and words, the stuff of her mind. Their earliest hand-sewn and hand-set brochures were in demand in their small circle. An essay by Virginia, "Kew Gardens," was praised in *The Times* and drew a flurry of orders; and by these stages the little amateur Hogarth Press, intended for "play," became after a time a serious business enterprise. Given their circle of acquaintance and their "modernistic" outlook, they soon had distinguished names on their list and switched from being printer-publishers to being regular publishers. To them T. S. Eliot brought his earlier poems, and Virginia herself set *The Waste Land*, in this way absorbing the poem letter by letter, word by word, so that some of its imagery crept into her novels at a later time. Katherine Mansfield brought *A Prelude*. During the next five years the Hogarth Press published nineteen books. James Joyce sought to have *Ulysses* printed by them, Harriet Weaver having approached them on his behalf. But printers in England would not set certain four-letter words, or anything mocking royalty. And then Virginia did not like Joyce's work; it was too close to what we now call "the media." She quickly absorbed its technical novelties, however, and even used them in *Mrs. Dalloway*. The press earned very little money to begin with; but at a later time it would provide adequate income, especially after Leonard and Virginia decided to publish all of Virginia's writings. This eliminated the stress Virginia experienced with publishers. Leonard became her sole editor. She relied on his judgment; and he knew the most beneficial ways of dealing with her sensitivities about her writing. Later still, the Hogarth Press published the writings of Sigmund Freud. From humble beginnings emerged one of the most distinguished publishing firms in England, which now continues to print Virginia's posthumous writings quite as if she were alive and providing copy.

No. 52 Tavistock Square had four stories and a basement. The press went into the basement, and here a succession of assistants and partners, from Ralph Partridge, Carrington's husband, to George Rylands, and later John Lehmann, worked with Virginia and Leonard at the tiresome tasks of distributing the books and keeping track of accounts. Leonard let the ground and first floors. He and Virginia had a fine flat on the second and third floors, which in due course Duncan and Vanessa decorated. There were panels and a rug of Vanessa's design and certain items of Omega furniture. The Virginia of her triumphant years is associated with this flat. There were long periods at Monks House as well. Both Leonard and Virginia worked without stopping—that is, their minds were on their work at every hour of the day. They wrote in the mornings; they read books and reviewed them. They kept up with public affairs and the world of art. They gardened for relaxation and they entertained. Virginia's diaries record her continual labors. She had some assistance in her house, but she often cooked and took care of mundane duties.

Leonard tried to enter active politics in the early 1920s, seeking a Labour seat, but was defeated and thereafter acted with increasing authority but in a less public way. William Plomer assessed his qualities when he observed that Leonard could have been a great force politically had he known how to appeal to the emotions of the voters rather than to intellect. He added significantly that one of the errors men of such high intelligence make is that they assume they are "addressing their equals." Other members of Bloomsbury did not suffer from such egalitarian illusions. Certainly Virginia, Maynard and Lytton knew that they could not tailor their creative selves to the "common man" and that it was necessary to educate him. If in this stance they earned the charge of being snobs, they succeeded nevertheless in going their own way—and maintaining their freedom. Leonard went his own way also. His *Coöperation and the Future of Industry* came out in 1918 and his *Empire and Commerce in Africa* in 1920. He wrote for the *New Statesman*, where Virginia, Roger and Clive also appeared and where Desmond was literary editor. Leonard for seven years was literary editor of the *Nation*, which Maynard reorganized financially. It can be seen that a great deal of literary and art reviewing—and the power of this branch of journalism—was exercised by Bloomsbury in the years after the war.

A different kind of power emanated from Charleston. Vanessa Bell and Duncan Grant had always painted essentially for painting's sake. Their careers had been more or less suspended by the war. In their newfound freedom they could take practical steps to become better known. Charleston remained their principal base, but in due course they took studios in London—Duncan again, as before the war, in Fitzroy Street. He had never had a one-man show. In 1920 when he was thirty-five he collected what he deemed his best recent work and displayed it at the Carfax Gallery in Bond Street, where it attracted considerable attention, attaching the postwar Duncan Grant to the prewar artist who had shown so much lyricism in his murals. Bloomsbury's art critics reviewed the show. There was nothing wrong with this, but it had its negative side and helped create the legend the Bloomsbury was a mutual admiration society. Clive Bell quite sincerely pronounced Duncan "the best English painter alive." The sweeping generalization was not accepted in some quarters, and one wonders whether it was true at a moment when other fine English painters such as Sickert, John and Nicholson had begun to show their work again. Clive said that Duncan's striking quality was "the ease with which he achieves beauty," and he also said that Duncan was "in the English tradition without being in the English rut." Roger Fry was more cautious and less belligerent. Duncan's show was without doubt an important event in the British art world, but Roger expressed some misgivings. He wondered whether Duncan's attempt to push his painting into various forms of "modernism"—his abstractions, his imitations of Parisian modes—had not resulted in the scrapping of some of his own distinctive qualities. These were Duncan's marvelous way of introducing his lively fancy into his canvases and his skill in giving an effect of improvisation. There was always his extraordinary ability in capturing the mobility of the body. The general public could not know how closely Clive and Roger—and the painter they reviewed— were linked by their love of one woman, and how closely they had lived and worked and traveled together. This was in reality irrelevant. Yet readers sensed the incestuous quality of the reviews, however honest they might be, and it reinforced their belief that Bloomsbury was a "clique." Bruce Richmond at the *Times Literary Supplement* signaled this danger when he hesitated to allow Virginia Woolf to review *Eminent Victorians* because she was Strachey's friend and she decided not to do it.

Vanessa, the high priestess of Bloomsbury and the presiding genius at Charleston (as she seemed to those who knew her), held her first show two years after Duncan's in 1922 at the Independent Gallery. She was then forty-three. The show was a success; she sold a goodly number of her paintings. Roger reviewed her with caution. He praised Vanessa's "gravity" and the sense of dignity inherent in her paintings. Vanessa, however, had the benefit of an independent review. Walter Sickert praised her "instinct and intelligence," and what he called the "scholarly tact" of her paintings. For the next four decades Vanessa and Duncan exhibited every year with the London Group. And both found themselves presently in great demand beyond Bloomsbury as muralists and decorators.

The painters and Clive reestablished their ties with Picasso, Derain and Matisse, as well as with other painters in the modern art movement. Some came to London when the Russian Ballet returned to dazzle the British as a sudden relief from the gloom of war. Diaghilev offered color and form, the lyricism and magic of the dancers—among the new ones Massine and Lydia Lopokova, whose tiny figure, and supple feet, whirling across the stage, filled London with rapture. Charleston entertained the French painters and Russian dancers in Gordon Square in co-operation with Maynard; and Maynard was irresistibly drawn to the ballet by the physical joy and strength of Lopokova, with whom he was soon deeply in love. The painters also traveled to the Continent, and particularly to France. Later there would be long stays in the south of France, at Cassis-sur-Mer, where Duncan and Vanessa founded a kind of miniature Charleston in a little farmhouse called La Bergère, set in the midst of a sloping vineyard under the exquisite skies of Provence. At the top of the sloping hill towered a strange rock formation in the shape of a roseate crown—Charlemagne's crown, the locals called it. In this vale of Fontcreuse, they spent certain months out of every year painting the land Cézanne and Van Gogh had painted, but distinctly in their own styles, and drinking the wine produced in abundance around them. Their artistic strength continued to lie in the sensuous use of color, the fullness of form. Vanessa would also perform a particular service to art in creating highly individual and lively dust jackets for Virginia's novels, decorating with her sisterly art Virginia's literary art.

Neither Vanessa nor Duncan sought fame. In their joy in painting, they tried simply to fulfill their need for their art and to earn enough for comfort. The world sought them out, however, and their days were filled with continual creativity. They had their imitators and their influence.

Roger Fry had been a center of power even before Bloomsbury, and during the war he had kept the Omega Workshops alive in the interest of an ideal. Gradually its influence was felt and even cheaply imitated by industrial firms. But in 1919, with the war ended, Roger finally closed Omega; he sold off what remained and found himself footloose and free. He was in his early fifties; most of the Bloomsbury friends were in their late thirties. He had been a center of power long before he had allied himself with Gordon and Fitzroy squares, and he continued to be—for he wrote and painted as always, painted indeed with a new intensity. His Omega experience had given him a pronounced distaste for the English view of the arts, its philistinism and caution; this still existed in the face of any creative flowering. In Paris he met Picasso with delight ("a man who constantly smashed his own reputations") and Derain and Charles Vildrac, who had a gallery. In 1920 Roger mounted a small Bloomsbury show in Vildrac's gallery—some of his own paintings, Vanessa's and Duncan's. Rouault came to see them, also Picasso, Derain, and others. Jacques Blanche praised them. Then Fry journeyed south into Provence, into that rosy and yellow glow of light on rock formations and the blue of its sky; he experienced a "sensation of color" that gave new vibrancy to his work. He painted Mont Sainte Victoire through the eyes of Cézanne; he formed new and abiding friendships with French intellectuals and painters, especially Charles Mauron. Provence liberated him, as it had so many of the artists he admired.

In England he reversed the pattern of Bloomsbury, which had spread itself into country houses. Fry gave up Durbins, at Guildford, which he had built in 1909, and moved into Camden Town, living with his sister Margery in a house at No. 7 Dalmeny Avenue. Here he arranged his collection of paintings and primitive masks and began to shore up his life's writings in *Vision and Design* and *Transformations*. Of his studio in Camden Town, Virginia Woolf wrote that it was "both an ivory tower where he contemplated reality, and an arsenal where he forged the only weapons that are effective in the fight against the enemy" —the enemy being those who wanted art always to be the same and who could not accompany Fry into his excursions into aesthetic values and criticism. He entertained his guests at a dinner table decorated by Duncan Grant and served the dinner from plates of his own making. They sat in chairs of his own design. And so, still writing in the journals, reviewing shows, helping the London Group mount their annual exhibitions, he remained a power in the art world to the end. Later he lived in Bloomsbury, near Russell Square. His own paintings, particularly his Provençal landscapes, showed a continuing growth and development. He was an old "lion" in Bloomsbury, and one much esteemed.

In old age he accepted the invitation to become Slade Professor of Art at Cambridge, having been repeatedly rejected for the professorship at Oxford. To the end he could fill Queen's Hall when he lectured on art: he spoke with tremendous effect, wielding his pointer over the slides on the screen as if he laid a huge magnifying glass on them. There was no question that out of Durbins and Dalmeny Avenue there radiated tremendous charisma and an extraordinary authority. "I continue to think him the plume in our cap," said Virginia, and by "our" she meant Bloomsbury's.

We have already seen how the other, the newly publicized lion, Lytton Strachey, at The Mill House, was waited on by his handmaiden. Lytton exercised a distinctive influence. In part it was negative, for he was quick to reject bumbling acolytes, and all too eager to ride the crest of his success in the *grand monde*. There was no doubt that Carrington, in her curious flighty way, but with practicality and adherence to the fundamentals of living, created a great stability for him. "You and Ralph and our life at Tidmarsh," Lytton wrote her, "are what I care for most in the world" —apart from work, he added, and "some few people." He enjoyed the picture-book letters of Carrington with their caricatures of his length, his beard, his awkwardness; she was inventive in finding names for him. He was her Yahoo, her buggerwug, her old egotistical humbug, her bearded gismonster, and also a toad in the hole. Lytton sat over the fire, the firelight playing on his red beard, his lambskin slippers on his feet, and a rug on his knees; three cats joined the ménage. Carrington assembled miscellaneous furniture. There was a wine cellar. They arranged the books in the library, for by now Lytton had a splendid collection and he liked to read aloud. Sometimes they played cards. But they were also often restless. There was inner tension in their mutual aggressive natures. Lytton would take flight in travel or country visits—there were many more he could now make—and Carrington carried on her complicated loves with assorted males and females. In this period, and with the regularity of his life, Lytton was able to work consistently and in a very short time write his *Queen Victoria*. The book emerged to extraordinary acclaim.

Roger, Lytton and Maynard were in a certain sense the three lions of Bloomsbury who were lone performers. Keynes's and Strachey's work overlapped; they were both human cartographers: Keynes of the living and Lytton of the dead. Both created, however, for the modern world.

We must remind ourselves of another kind of power which Bloomsbury wielded. This was exercised by Desmond MacCarthy, whose house at No. 25 Wellington Square in Chelsea was the one Bloomsbury center in London removed from Bloomsbury itself until Roger set up house in Camden Town. Indeed, Desmond and Clive Bell, the two hedonists of Bloomsbury, both had a large public following —Desmond in his humane and warm critiques of literature and the theater, Clive in his continuing popular art criticism. Clive was rough and hard on English painters and English taste. Desmond was urbane and Irish-warm. He had a genuine province of power as the literary editor of the *New Statesman*, which he exercised with generosity. He would have another when for a number of years he edited a review founded with a patron's subsidy, *Life and Letters*, a distinguished and widely esteemed journal. Desmond responded to literature as he responded to people. He moved through the great houses bestowing the blessings of his wit and the grace of his conversation. His home in Chelsea was a tall old building presided over by his wife, Molly. She had a gift for witty and delicate reminiscence, and her novel, *A Pier and a Band*, as well as her *Nineteenth Century Childhood*, found many delighted readers. Here this domestic couple, living as it were on the sidelines of Bloomsbury but very much of that circle, reared a family and maintained a center of civilization.

Clive, Desmond's fellow critic, in the field of the visual rather than the verbal or the dramatic, was *à cheval* between rural Bloomsbury and London Bloomsbury. He had an apartment at No. 50 Gordon Square, which Vanessa decorated for him. He was frequently at Charleston, and his life with Mary Hutchinson endured into the twenties. When they parted, he found himself adrift and experienced a crisis of loneliness and self-criticism at middle age. During this period he wrote his book on *Civilization*—much read and much criticized, an elitist's credo. He continued to go to Paris to meet the moderns; he was a friend of Picasso's; he encountered Proust; he retained his love for France and for the capital, as if his year in Paris long ago could now be replaced by a montage of new adventures, nearly always with painters. Fry said of Clive that he was "amazing in the quantity and flow of his mind," and he added, "The quality gets better." In his later years Clive was avuncular, much concerned as always with his *machismo* and, in his own more brusque way, as authoritative as Desmond.

It can be seen that the Bloomsbury friends led their different lives, followed different careers, yet were linked by old ties, old sympathies, old loyalties, old habits of thought, common opinions. They broke with the style of upper-class life, as Noel Annan has pointed out, and set new fashions in living. They scorned luxury, preferring cheap unfashionable town houses or flats and modest country houses. They subscribed to a bundle of beliefs that had evolved from their Victorian childhood into Edwardian liberalism, and these had suffered the shattering impact of the war. They performed the acts of life with an intensity and unselfconsciousness that derived partly from their comparative security. There was among them a mutual feeling of love and affection rare in such diverse and temperamental talents.

Yet they had one blind spot, and this proved a source of considerable pain to them. While they were aware of their individual strengths, they had no sense of their collective power. In a word, the totality of their endeavor, their power, became, in the minds of certain individuals and groups, a group power, and, to the more paranoid, a persecuting power. One can understand that, as literary editors, Leonard Woolf in the *Nation* and Desmond MacCarthy in the *New Statesman* had to choose certain books over others, take certain attitudes, show certain preferences. And young authors or young painters, as they watched Roger reviewing Clive, and Clive reviewing Roger, and Leonard reviewing works that appealed to him, and Virginia appearing increasingly in the journals—these writers and painters felt themselves not only discriminated against but victimized. Small wonder that Bloomsbury after the war was accused of "snob intellectualism" and of "puffing their own trifling productions." How explain that each of the friends was simply "doing his thing" on behalf of certain profound beliefs about aesthetics, or politics, or, in the case of Maynard, international problems. However much they disclaimed their "groupiness," they had ended up in controlling, by the power of their utterance, a great deal of space in the weeklies and monthlies, a goodly amount of wall space in exhibitions. And they had still other sources of power. Did not the group have, in a manner of speaking, its own press? What young dedicated gathering of fanatics in behalf of symbolism or surrealism or dadaism could boast a full-fledged printing and publishing apparatus such as the Hogarth Press? Bloomsbury published Bloomsbury —but we know it was not as parochial as that.

The now middle-aged individuals of Bloomsbury had solid work habits; they were productive. They put many of the young to shame. This was another reason why Bloomsbury was called a *junta* and a clique. Had not Lytton Strachey himself called them "a gang"? As early as 1919 Virginia writes that Clive tried to convince her that Vanessa, Roger, herself, Lytton "are the most hated people in London; superficial, haughty and giving themselves airs— that, I think, is the verdict against the ladies." And soon enough the newspapers began to convey an image of a special and malevolent power-seeking group, naughty in its attitudes toward sex, anarchistic in its view of life. Nothing was sacred. Lytton's frequently arrogant stance and debunking of the past was certainly at the root of much of the criticism. Some now also recalled the *"Dreadnought Hoax"* and other Bloomsbury capers. The Cambridge dogmatist F. R. Leavis would speak of "the Cambridge-Bloomsbury ethos" and refer to "the levity of so many petty egos, each primed with conscious cleverness and hardened self-approval." That was typical.

We can find echoes of even earlier attitudes. Thus James Whitall, an American who lived in London during the 1914–18 war, referred to Bloomsbury's reputation during those years. Even before *Eminent Victorians*, he said, Lytton Strachey and Vanessa Bell were "king and queen of the Bloomsbury group, powerfully ministered to (in the governmental sense) by Maynard Keynes, Roger Fry and Virginia Woolf." Whitall found Bloomsbury "frightening in the extreme." When encountered individually the friends seemed mild enough, although Lytton's vocal cords and baleful stare inspired a certain uneasiness. Lytton, in a manner quite different from that of bearded Bernard Shaw, had a Mephistophelian air when he entered a drawing room. And he liked to play the Bloomsbury ogre in public.

In sum, the public legend made them out to be rude busybodies in painting, politics, economics, the novel. They espoused "the new," it was alleged, more for oddity and sensationalism than anything else. They were always against the Establishment. They were bad-mannered egotists. They were self-indulgent. They were homosexuals or lesbians. They practiced free love. Small wonder that Leonard exclaimed one day when the writer of this account mentioned the "Bloomsbury Group": "Group, group! You mustn't ever call us a group! We were *never* a group!" Virginia, however, in the 1920s came closer to the truth by arguing that "if people, with no special start except what their wits give them, can so dominate, there must be some reason in it." William Plomer would later take this same view, saying of Bloomsbury, "They were rather superior people." To an American inquirer who asked about "the group," Virginia wrote in 1932, "The Bloomsbury group is largely a creation of the journalists.

To dwell upon Bloomsbury as an influence is liable to lead to judgments that, as far as I know, have no basis in fact." She was being, one feels, ingenuous and simplistic.

Clive Bell, in his memoirs published in 1956, took the same approach. He described the existence of the friendships, he named the friends—those of "Old Bloomsbury" and the newer generation that filled out its ranks—but he also published denials like a Foreign Office. As a group they did not act in common on any issues or initiate actions in the manner of classic bands of artists with manifestos. His essay titled "Bloomsbury" grew querulous: "Beyond meaning something nasty, what do they mean by 'Bloomsbury'? . . . Can a dozen individuals loosely connected be called a group? . . . For what did they stand?" His own answer was that Bloomsbury was "neither a chapel nor a clique but merely a collection of individuals each with his or her own views and likings." Now in the aftertime these accusations and denials are almost irrelevant, for we find Virginia's letters and diaries sown with allusions to "Bloomsbury." And we discover that Clive suggested to Roger Fry as early as 1917 that he should paint "a great historical group portrait of Bloomsbury." Even then, in the midst of the war, Clive had thought of Bloomsbury as belonging to history and worthy of having its pictorial record.

The Memoir Club

Roger Fry wrote to Vanessa of Clive Bell's suggestion that he paint a "historical" group portrait of Bloomsbury. Conscious that some might say they were taking themselves too seriously, Roger said he might introduce into the painting the non-Bloomsbury Sickert, peering in through an open door "with a kind of benevolent cynicism." Roger, however, soon dropped the idea; and it was Vanessa who later painted "Old Bloomsbury"—that is, the original friends—attending a meeting of the Memoir Club, seated in a circle in a drawing room. She did not finish this painting. It remains with the bodies of the friends shown in recognizable postures; their faces, however, are blank. Much later, when three of the friends were dead, she painted the later Memoir Club, with the younger generation in its ranks. The deceased members were represented in their portraits on the wall behind the seated group—that is, Lytton, Roger, Virginia. This picture Vanessa completed in the 1940s.

If the "historical" portrait, as Clive conceived it, was never painted, a durable historical club was formed—one of their numerous clubs—which testified to Bloomsbury as a group admirably conscious of its own past. This was the Memoir Club. The idea was Molly MacCarthy's. As a writer of reminiscences herself, it seemed to her that a Bloomsbury club devoted to personal recollections might yield much amusement and even some publishable works. Its success exceeded everyone's expectations—and for good reason. Of all the Bloomsbury clubs, beginning with the early Midnight Society at Cambridge and the later reading and art clubs, this was the one that touched the Bloomsbury originals deeply. They were in middle age. They had known each other in their nonage. They possessed in common their interest in private experience and in gossip, as well as the mutual understanding that had always given intimacy to their gatherings. They could explore their personal histories, their now tolerably long and active pasts, and do so in prepared papers written in their individual styles. And then Bloomsbury had always been obsessed with the writing of biography, ever since Leslie Stephen had reared, volume by volume, his monumental *Dictionary of National Biography*. Lytton wrote lives. Maynard sketched characters. Virginia came back again and again to biographical theory, writing a sufficient number of essays on the subject to fill an entire volume (if they are ever collected). Virginia would later write fictional biographies: *Orlando*, embodying Lyttonian biographical style and theory, and a study of the scent of things, her little whimsical history of Elizabeth Barrett's dog Flush. It would be she who would write Roger Fry's life after his death. Who knows how much more of Bloomsbury she might have memorialized had she lived? Also, in a sense Vanessa, Duncan and Roger, when they painted portraits, were creating visual biography. We have their portraits of all the Bloomsbury members. In organizing the Memoir Club, the group proved (in spite of denials) that it was an entity; that it belonged to history—literary and artistic and even economic and political; and that it had funds of common memory to draw upon. They had all read their Proust. (Clive would even write a small book about him.) This was their *recherche du temps perdu*.

II

The Memoir Club was organized at the MacCarthys' home in Wellington Square during February of 1920. The group drew up a series of informal rules. The club would listen only to reminiscence and memoir. The papers were to be drawn out of personal recollection and personal experience. No research in libraries, no secondhand material, no Lyttonian essays on figures of the past! In other words, the papers were to be strictly autobiographical. They were also to be "frank." Bloomsbury had always believed in "absolute frankness." Of course, as Leonard pointed out, the word "absolute" in such cases was relative; still, they would search for the truths of their past by trying not to conceal what had happened. They promised not to be "touchy"; not to be offended at what was said in the memoirs. Finally, they agreed (after the manner of old clubs) on privacy. Revelations were not to be spread about elsewhere.

We know that the first regular meeting of the club took place on 4 March 1920, appropriately in Gordon Square, where Maynard was host to the friends at dinner. They sat in the same room in which Bloomsbury had had its shy start in the young century, when Thoby Stephen was still alive. There were the nine, whose history we have told; and there were one or two others, including the silent member, Saxon Sydney-Turner, and the occasional Bloomsbury visitor, E. M. Forster. A little later David Garnett would be asked to join, and still later, as they grew up, the Bloomsbury children. The early meetings, however, were confined to the original friends.

Some notes made by Virginia Woolf after the first meeting provide glimpses into the club's proceedings. "Fearful," she noted. "Seven people read—and Lord knows what I didn't read into the reading." She does not always tell us the subjects of the memoirs. There was shyness at first. Vanessa and Molly interrupted their papers, overcome by some emotion: "Oh, this is absurd; I can't go on." And Virginia, after her paper on the Hyde Park Gate life of the Stephens, had her doubts; "Why did I read this sentimental trash!" Clive was "purely objective," but, as the sessions warmed up, he chose to relate and analyze an old love affair with a married woman named Raven-Hill, wife of a *Punch* cartoonist. The affair went back to Clive's eighteenth year, in Wiltshire, but his mention of later encounters with this woman caused Virginia to do some mental arithmetic. The affair "coincided with his attachment to me, then," she mused. She immediately rationalized: Mrs. Raven-Hill "was a voluptuary. He was not in love." In no time at all the Memoir Club became a club of mutual revelation and discovery, as well as of mutual admiration. After hearing memoirs by Lytton and E. M. Forster, Virginia noted, "Our standard is such that little is left for me to hint and guess at." She added, however, "They say what they mean, very brilliantly; and leave the dark as it was before." Lytton said, "We are as remarkable as the Johnson set."

Following Clive's confessional mode, Maynard read his paper on Melchior. This was in 1921 when the experience was still fresh in his mind. Virginia noted that she was "a little bored by the politics," but she was a good deal impressed by Maynard's character drawing. When he remarked that he had been rather in love with Melchior, "I think he meant it seriously," Virginia noted, "though we laughed." Duncan contributed a two-part paper on his art life in Paris. Desmond was in his element. In fact, Molly MacCarthy had in part organized the club, in the hope that Desmond would get a few memories down on paper, instead of talking them into the air. He did produce "A Memoir of Youth," recalling with great delicacy his first going to school. But he also foiled his wife by reading the paper E. M. Forster described—the one that he pretended was in his attaché case, but that was, to the astonishment of his listeners, a total improvisation. On another evening Desmond described the character of Wilfrid Blunt, but he used notes, not a finished memoir. It was "beautifully done," Virginia recorded, "and stopped when it might have gone on without boring us." Desmond said with a kind of enchantment, "We're not a day older, and we enjoy our society as much as we ever did." E. M. Forster, Virginia also noted, said he felt so fond of everyone, "I almost wept." Decidedly, the Memoir Club touched individual depths in calling up the past and renewed the group intimacy of earlier days.

Out of the Memoir Club would emerge much that we now cherish. The club stimulated Leonard Woolf to write his five-volume autobiography in his old age. Portions of David Garnett's memoirs were first heard there; Vanessa's memories of Virginia's childhood were read after Virginia's death—a moving and revelatory paper, together with her recollections of early Bloomsbury. Virginia herself was at her drollest in a series of papers—one discussing whether she was a snob, one recounting the first meetings of "Old Bloomsbury," and one drawing upon life at Hyde Park Gate and the efforts of the Duckworth half brothers to turn Vanessa and Virginia into society women. If ever the

Memoir Club papers could be assembled in their entirety, they would fill a very large volume and would be a remarkable record of Bloomsbury in the act of remembering.

On one afternoon in 1938 Maynard read a paper which particularly moved the club. He called it "My Early Beliefs," and Virginia noted (although her note may apply equally well to an earlier paper), "very translucent, I felt, very formidable, like a portrait of Tolstoy as a young man to look at, able to rend any argument that came his way with a blow of his paw, yet concealing, as the novelists say, a kind and even simple heart under that immensely impressive armor of intellect."

III

What Maynard did in his extraordinary paper on his early beliefs (since published) was to challenge those present— his old Cambridge comrades in particular—to reexamine what they had stood for when they were young. He humorously described them in their early Trinity College aspects: Strachey, even then "Voltairean"; Woolf, "a rabbi"; Clive, "a gay and amiable dog"; Saxon Sydney-Turner, "a quietist"; himself from King's College, "a non-conformist." E. M. Forster, he added, had been "the elusive colt of a dark horse." He began by recalling how D. H. Lawrence reacted after a morning's talk with Bertrand Russell and himself; and later the horror with which Lawrence characterized some of the younger generation, David Garnett's friends. They had made Lawrence dream "of a beetle that bites like a scorpion. . . . It is this horror of little swarming selves I can't stand." Lawrence found that "they talk endlessly, but endlessly—and never, never a good thing said. They are cased each in a hard little shell of his own and out of this they talk words." He was attacking, in reality, a young friend of Garnett's, Francis Birrell, and making side comments on Duncan Grant and Keynes. This was in 1915. He did not know the other members of Bloomsbury. But he wrote to Garnett, "You must leave these friends, these beetles, Birrell and Duncan Grant are done forever. Keynes I am not sure . . . when I saw Keynes that morning in Cambridge it was one of the crises of my life. It sent me mad with misery and hostility and rage." Yes, Lawrence, tied up in the knots of his own nightmare lower-class past, could not follow Keynes's nimble mind.

Maynard quoted these passages. They reflect Lawrence's personal problems: his fear of homosexuality—that is, his own problems of *machismo*, and his perpetual sense of inferiority in the presence of such less self-centered upper-class minds as Keynes's or Bertrand Russell's. Still, Maynard told the Memoir Club, Lawrence's words contained a criticism that might apply to the early beliefs of Bloomsbury. He reminded his friends of the days when their bible had been G. E. Moore's *Principia Ethica* and their delight in abstractions such as the Good and the Beautiful. He asked: "How did one compare the value of a good state of mind which had bad consequences with a bad state of mind which had good consequences?" "Was there a separate objective standard of beauty?" "Were all truths equally good to pursue and contemplate?" He added, "We were disposed to repudiate very strongly the idea that useful knowledge could be preferable to useless knowledge."

In this philosophical and almost Socratic tone, Maynard led Leonard, Clive, Desmond and others present to consider whether they hadn't all together "enjoyed supreme self-confidence, superiority and contempt towards all the rest of the unconverted world." This had been the world's later accusation. He now felt "it was hardly a state of mind which a grown-up person in his senses could sustain literally." To be sure, the "Moorist" air had been purer and sweeter than the air they now breathed—that of Freud-*cum*-Marx. What Moore had *not* done for them—or they hadn't done for themselves—was to make them aware that there was a distinction between "goodness as an attribute of states of mind, and rightness as an attribute of actions." Here spoke the Maynard Keynes who had watched the great international game of political action stripped of all thought of Goodness or Beauty. He spoke as a practical man of affairs, a man of wealth and influence in the world. Surveying his own and his friends' late adolescence, he said that what they had done was to overlook and even repudiate "customary morals, conventions and traditional wisdom . . . we recognised no moral obligation upon us, no inner sanction, to conform or to obey. Before heaven we claimed to be our own judge in our own case."

Leading the Memoir Club along these paths of the past, Maynard invited it to ask itself whether Bloomsbury, in its early meliorism and optimism, had not overlooked the fact that there were "insane and irrational springs of wickedness in most men. We were not aware that civilization was a thin and precarious crust erected by the personality and the will of a very few, and only maintained by rules and conventions skillfully put across and guilefully preserved." Keynes concluded: "I can see us as water spiders, gracefully skimming, as light and as reasonable as air, the surface of the stream without any contact at all with the eddies and currents beneath." Such had been early Bloomsbury.

IV

They sat, the originals of Bloomsbury, in easy chairs and on sofas, in their characteristic postures. So they had sat together long ago in those first hesitant gatherings. We see them now, some stockier, larger, faces more set, each a distinctive character with an achieved existence: Maynard and Leonard, the two "activists" concerned with human development; Virginia and Lytton, the imaginative writer and the historian seeking to describe the "eddies and currents" of which Maynard had spoken; the two critics, Desmond in literature, Clive in art; the three painters, Roger the aesthetician, and Vanessa and Duncan in full possession of their visual memories and feelings, now inscribed on canvas or wall or panel. The group memories encompassed those early days of idealism, when, young and questing, they had tried to break the barriers of reticence and sex, to this postwar time, when they looked back upon recent ravage, personal disaster and daily struggle. Bloomsbury had paced its twenty years in ever-increasing awareness of the life process. It had never espoused "art for art's sake" as the preceding generation had. The friends had created and lived and loved and hated, and done silly things. They had their moments of arrogance and mischief: but as a group they were a particular and unusual elite, singularly powerful through the gifts they had cultivated in the world and the particular radiance of their personalities. They had refused to accept the received ideas of the Victorians. They had moved far from those early beliefs illuminated by Maynard. Roger Fry had brought them, at an ideal moment, his sense of inner and outer experience, his new definition of art as essentially the expression of the artist. They were nearly all touched by the new psychology. Maynard had alluded to this in his coupling of Freud and Marx. They possessed something else, which some of their peers in Cambridge did not have: they had learned from their painters that aesthetic values reside not only in ideas of the mind but in visual beauty. This awareness of beauty as idea and beauty as vision had been superimposed upon Cambridge intellectuality.

Behind them lay the centuries of British history and learning which had formed them; and the heritage of Greece and Rome—something Greenwich Village lacked at this same moment on the other side of the sea. They were high products of a civilization soon to be shattered by another war. And within their ranks were the two sisters, Virginia and Vanessa, who among the first had proclaimed their freedom as women, their parity with the Bloomsbury males.

Something deeper had bound them together. They were connected by love, a linked chain. Leonard Woolf had originally loved Vanessa's beauty at a distance and Virginia's mind as well as her beauty. Clive had loved and married Vanessa and had wooed Virginia. Vanessa had loved Roger and then Duncan. Duncan had been loved by Lytton and then by Maynard and had in turn loved both Keynes and Vanessa. Lytton and Virginia had had that curious love which springs up between a homosexual and a woman because they are comfortable with one another in a nonsexual way. Bloomsbury had broken barriers and had discovered for itself the nature of androgyny; above all, it had understood the relationship between love and sex, where the Victorians had tried to bury sex as if it didn't exist. They had shown that sex could be freed of its Victorian guilt and shame. And they had shown that private lives need not interfere with public lives. The two hedonists, Desmond, who tended to be asexual, and Clive, who tended to exaggerate his masculinity, might have been thought to be voluptuaries and epicureans, but something within impelled them to work hard in the margin of their pleasures. Lytton had disciplined himself in spite of his amatory nature and had produced three singular books. Virginia had a lifetime of discipline, she who outside the linked chain of Bloomsbury's loves needed more love than she could give. In their work as in their affections, they believed in the individual and in freedom—the freedom to create one's own life. Even in their egotism they lived in awareness of their fellows and their humanistic world.

Twenty years of creation lay ahead of Bloomsbury. Virginia Woolf was at the threshold of her experiments in fiction and her struggle for women's rights. In her fiction she worked her way into new forms as her artist-sister had done in painting, and she sought through verbal iridescence to emulate Vanessa's pictorial iridescence and Roger's "vision and design." Maynard was now ready to write his masterly *Treatise on Money*, and he had developed his plans for deficit spending which would help lift Britain out of its depression and aid Roosevelt in launching his New Deal. Lytton was absorbed in what would prove his least satisfactory and yet in certain ways most remarkable recreation: his attempt to recover the Elizabethan world, a task more difficult than reviving the recoverable Victorian world. The painters would continue to look through their emotions at the colors of reality around them; at times they were admirable colorists, but always admirable craftsmen. Roger was gathering in the strands of his long and energetic life. Clive would write a book on the civilization Maynard had sought to define. It would not be Maynard's kind of civilization, but it expressed Clive's own enjoyment of the immediate things of his life, linked to his ideal of pacifism, and a belief in the Age of Reason. Desmond would continue to allow the humane play of his mind to grace Mayfair and Bloomsbury.

The club of memories sat in rooms in which they had met so often, in Gordon Square, in Wellington Square, in Duncan and Vanessa's studio in Fitzroy Street. Or they dined in restaurants—a group that espoused the very essence of "modernism"; that is, the relation of the artist's feelings to what he created and the fusions of form and feeling. They seemed at this time in excellent health, and their minds had the full vigor of their maturities. It would be Virginia who would seek to record their complicated inner worlds in her novel *The Waves*, touching the delicacy of Desmond's world of words, Lytton's homosexuality, Leonard's self-discipline, Vanessa's aloofness, finding a thousand poetical phrases for her friends in their fictional disguises, and demonstrating how a novel can become a poem. And in its pages she showed how Bloomsbury, in spite of faults and vanities, defeats and errors, had always belonged to the party of life. In its own way it had demonstrated how individuals can free themselves to enjoy evanescent immediacies, without divesting themselves of responsibilities.

Quentin Bell, in his little book on the characteristics of Bloomsbury, has admirably stated the criticisms his generation raised in its close intimacy with the Bloomsbury of the later years. In art the new generation found that Bell and Fry had stressed form at the expense of content. Bloomsbury had also "allowed Post-Impressionism to degenerate into something wholly frivolous and fashionable." In its politics and economics it "acquiesced in a social system which it knew to be wrong and allowed itself to become a part of the Establishment." And finally it failed to see the new world implicit in the Marxian revolution (regardless, one assumes, of the immediate and historically tentative forms which this revolution took). The criticisms were on the whole valid; they were those of a younger group, including the children of Clive Bell, drawing away from what had become obsolete in the old generation. But to take a historical view of Bloomsbury is to see that its originality lay in the ground it broke and the changes it achieved; and history would say that it was up to the next generation to make further changes. Quentin Bell gives us the historical position when he says that Bloomsbury was "conscious, deeply conscious of the dark irrational side of life but absolutely convinced of the necessity of holding fast to reason, charity and good sense." In this view the friends were not far from the Fabians or the general British upper-class dislike of revolution, its desire for an evolutionary change in society—this representing the chasm between the sheltered optimistic upper-class society in which most of the Bloomsbury friends grew up as distinct from a working-class society which formed a writer such as D. H. Lawrence.

"Everyone in Gordon Square has become famous," Virginia Woolf wrote her friend Jacques Raverat in 1922 when the Memoir Club was two years old. "Inwardly," she wrote, "one still feels young and arrogant and frightfully sharp set. Still, we have grown a little mellow." She gave a gossipy picture of the friends. "Clive has taken to high society. I assure you, he's a raging success, and his *bon mots* are quoted by lovely but incredibly silly ladies. Really they give parties to meet Clive Bell! Maynard of course scarcely belongs to private life any more, save that he has fallen in love with Lydia Lopokova, which is, to me, endearing. Nessa and Duncan potter along in extreme obscurity." Her quip about her sister and Duncan contradicted her claim that Gordon Square was "famous," but then she always felt herself in competition with the painters. Of Bloomsbury she also wrote, this time to Gwen Raverat, "Where they seem to me to triumph is in having worked out a view of life which was not by any means corrupt or sinister or merely intellectual; rather ascetic and austere indeed; which still holds, and keeps them dining together, and staying together, after twenty years; and no amount of quarreling, or success, or failure, has altered this. Now I do think that this is rather creditable. But tell me who *is* Bloomsbury in your mind?"

Many years lay ahead for most of the Bloomsbury friends; only a handful for Lytton and Roger, and just two decades for Virginia; and not too many more, after the Second World War, for Maynard Keynes, who by then was a peer, as Desmond would become a knight. Virginia refused honors and insisted that her work alone speak for her. Leonard, Clive, Vanessa, Duncan and Desmond lived into old age.

But all this was of the future. In 1920 they sat together at the Memoir Club having struggled and survived—how intensely their words alone can tell us today—and gave themselves over periodically to the happiness of remembering. They understood very well how man constructs his world out of memories.

ACKNOWLEDGMENTS

NOTES

BIBLIOGRAPHY

A BLOOMSBURY CHRONOLOGY
1885–1920

INDEX

Acknowledgments

Of the Bloomsbury personages dealt with in this book, I knew Leonard Woolf during the last decade of his life, when he was writing his autobiography. I had a number of talks with him both in Monks House and in the home of a friend, Dr. Octavia Wilberforce, at Backsettown in Sussex. She had been Virginia Woolf's last doctor.

In 1962, through the kind offices of Mrs. Ruth Simon, later Lady Hart-Davis, I was fortunate to meet Clive Bell in Menton on the Riviera, where he was wintering. I also met, at Clive Bell's villa, Angelica Garnett and Barbara Bagenal, both of whom I encountered again in England. In 1973 Mrs. Garnett very kindly invited me to visit Charleston Farm and also took me to see the decorations in the Berwick Church nearby. On this occasion I spent a delightful morning with Duncan Grant, the easiest and most graceful octogenarian I have ever encountered. He was eighty-nine. He still painted and went to London exhibitions and the theater. In that year I visited Barbara Bagenal's little house in Rye, a stone's throw from Henry James's Lamb House. She showed me many paintings, photographs and memorabilia. A few years earlier I had met Roger Senhouse, Lytton Strachey's friend, and had examined that portion of Strachey's library which Senhouse inherited. I had several long talks with Senhouse about Strachey during a long weekend in Rye. I had met David Garnett still earlier in London. His son Richard Garnett, whom I first knew at Rupert Hart-Davis Limited, was and remains one of my editors, and he has been of considerable help to me. I had in addition the benefit of talks with Octavia Wilberforce.

Quentin and Olivier Bell have shown me great kindness and hospitality and have answered all my inquiries. I am grateful to George Spater for access to his Hogarth Press Collection and for his profound knowledge of the life of the Woolfs. Trekkie and Ian Parsons have been extremely helpful, Mrs. Parsons in particular giving me much first-hand information about the literary and artistic backgrounds of Bloomsbury. I discussed this book long ago with Sir Harold Nicolson during his last visit to New York and with Sir Rupert Hart-Davis, who published most of my books in England. Simon Nowell-Smith very kindly put me in touch with the late William Plomer, shortly before his untimely death. And I want to thank Professor S. P. Rosenbaum of Toronto for help with the illustrations.

At King's College I had an opportunity to talk with George (Dadie) Rylands, whom I had met some years earlier. He showed me paintings and decorations by the artists of Bloomsbury and their friends. Thanks in particular to Angelica Garnett, I saw many canvases, unframed and unrestored, in Vanessa Bell's studio at Charleston. Others with whom I have had some opportunity for talk about the Bloomsbury Group have been John Lehmann, J. H. Plumb, Janet Adam Smith and Lord David Cecil.

In the world of the libraries I am especially in debt to Lola Szladits, curator of the Berg Collection (New York Public Library, Astor, Lenox and Tilden Foundations). At Berg in 1973 I read Virginia Woolf's unpublished journals, now emerging under Olivier Bell's editorship. At Cambridge the late A. N. L. Munby and his assistant, Mrs. Penelope Bulloch, proved very helpful in the King's College Library. I have also used materials from many other libraries, including those of the University of Texas, the Houghton Library at Harvard, the Bancroft Library at Berkeley, and the National Library of Britain.

At Cassis-sur-Mer in Provence, the present owners, Joe and Lillian Maffei, generously allowed me to visit La Bergère and took me over the vineyards and orchards of Fontcreuse, where Vanessa Bell and Duncan Grant often painted between the wars. Unfortunately, their decorations in the little house have been effaced by subsequent tenants.

I wish in particular to thank Marjorie Sinclair, Professor

of English of the University of Hawaii and formerly of the San Francisco Museum of Art, for the opportunity to draw upon her extensive knowledge of modern painting. The University of Hawaii Foundation generously provided travel funds during my work on this book, and Genie Wery gave me considerable secretarial help.

Notes

In a work of this kind, composed as a mosaic of facts and interpretations, every sentence could carry a footnote of interest to the specialists in Bloomsbury and its personages. But how many footnotes does the general reader need? I have decided in this instance to offer only the briefest kind of indication; the experts will, with this guidance, know where to look. Moreover, the recent Bloomsbury volumes have splendid indexes and are carefully documented. Allusions to Harrod, Quentin Bell (QB), Holroyd, Shone, Spater-Parsons (SP), Garnett and others refer to the basic works by these writers listed in the ensuing Bibliography. Initials are used for the Bloomsbury nine who are the subject of this book. Other works in the Bibliography are usually referred to here by their author's name.

I

THOROUGHLY
  LW *Sowing, Growing.* Author's talks with subject.

THE HUNTER'S EYE
  Quentin Bell described to me CB's shooting skills. See also CB *Old Friends; Art; Civilization;* VW *Letters* I, II; Holroyd; Bywater; Shone.

CALIBAN IN DIFFERENT VOICES
  Holroyd; *Old Friends;* Marie Souvestre, in Edel, *The Master;* Sanders; Egyptian diary in *Strachey by Himself.*

VERY SERIOUS YOUNG MEN
    LW *Sowing, Growing; Old Friends;* Holroyd; SP; Moore, *Principia Ethica; JMK Two Memoirs;* Harrod.

HANDS
    Harrod; JMK *Essays in Biography; Economic Consequences;* author's talks with George Rylands, J. H. Plumb; SP.

A FIRST-CLASS CARRIAGE
    DM *Memories,* "Memoir of Youth" and "Bloomsbury"; "Edith Wharton," in *Sunday Times* 21 Sept. 1947; Holroyd; Forster and Pritchett, *Listener* 26 June 1952.

THOBY'S ROOM
    Readers will recognize the portion of this chapter which is a pastiche created out of *Jacob's Room.* VW *Letters* I; LW *Sowing;* Annan.

II

A HAUNTED HOUSE
    Moments of Being; James to Mrs. Clifford (Harvard); "A Haunted House" in *Monday or Tuesday.*

THE SANITY OF ART
    Conversations with Quentin Bell, Angelica Garnett, Barbara Bagenal, DG and LW; the VW-VB correspondence (Berg); LW *Growing;* Rothenstein I; Clark; *Moments of Being;* Shone; *Mausoleum Book;* VW *Letters* I; QB.

THE OTHER FACE
    Moments of Being; QB; *Mausoleum Book; Mrs. Dalloway;* VW *Letters* I; VW *Diary* (Berg); Helen Lewis.

46 GORDON SQUARE
    VW *Letters* I; QB; *Moments of Being;* Thoby and sisters' photo, see *N.Y. Public Library Bulletin* 80:2 (winter 1977).

CLIVE IN PARIS
CB *Old Friends;* Buchanan; Bennett, *Journals* I; VW *Letters* I.

LEONARD IN CEYLON
Author's talks with LW; *Growing;* LW *Ceylon Diaries; Village in the Jungle; Tales of the East.* SP draws on hitherto unpublished LS-LW letters.

LYTTON IN CAMBRIDGE
Holroyd; Harrod.

BLOOMSBURY: FISRT PHASE
LW *Sowing; Moments of Being;* Holroyd; Harrod; QB; VW *Letters* I; Shone; Molly MacCarthy; Boyd.

THOBY
VW *Letters* I; QB; Holroyd; LW *Growing;* Annan.

III

RESURRECTIONS
VW *Letters* I; QB; *The Waves; Jacob's Room;* Edel; Shaw *Letters* I (ed. Laurence); Shone.

THE EDUCATION OF DUNCAN GRANT
Shone; Holroyd; VW *Letters* I; Lawrence, *Lady Chatterly;* Garnett; Harrod; Blanche. The decorations in Keynes's rooms at King's were hidden from view during my visit in 1973. Dr. Munby kindly supplied color photographs. There are two sets of decorations: those of 1910–11, "Grape-Pickers," are preserved behind the later panels of 1919–21 by Vanessa and Duncan.

PHASE TWO: FITZROY SQUARE
VW *Letters* I; *Moments of Being; The Voyage Out;* VB "Notes on Bloomsbury" in Rosenbaum; Adrian Stephen's diary in QB; Ottoline *Memoirs;* CB and VW in *Letters* I and in QB; CB *Poems* (1921); SP; VW's aviary: these quotations are not given in VW *Letters* II. They have since been published in *VW Miscellany* (California State College).

VISION AND DESIGN

RF *Letters;* Holroyd; QB; VW *Roger Fry;* RF *Last Lectures* (ed. Clark, 1939); Dickinson, *Autobiography;* RF *Vision and Design; Cézanne; Transformations;* Shone; DM *Memories,* "RF and the Post-Impressionist Exhibition of 1910"; Sickert *A Free House* (ed. Sitwell, 1947).

A JOURNEY TO BYZANTIUM

RF *Letters;* VW *Fry;* Shone; QB.

BLOOMSBURY: THE THIRD PHASE

QB; Shone; Harrod; VB "Notes"; VW *Letters* I; LW *Beginning Again;* Rosenbaum.

PERICLES AND ASPASIA

LW "Aspasia" document is one of George Spater's illuminating finds in the Woolf papers at Sussex. A section is quoted in SP. LW *Principia Politica; Beginning Again; The Wise Virgins;* LS courtship in SP; VW *Letters* I; QB; Shone.

IV

A CRYSTAL MOMENT

VB "Notes"; LW *Beginning Again;* the Duncan Grant murals are in the Tate Gallery and are reproduced in Shone; Garnett; Plomer *Celebrations;* RF *Letters;* VW *Fry;* QB.

BETWEEN THE ACTS

LW *Beginning Again;* Helen Lewis; LW dates VW's breakdown as 1915, SP show it began shortly after the marriage; *The Years;* QB.

THE WAR

Russell; Ottoline *Memoirs;* LW *Beginning Again;* Harrod; Holroyd; VW *Letters* I; RF *Letters; Old Friends;* DM *Experience;* Edel.

DESMOND IN FRANCE

DM *Experience;* DM's war reports in *New Statesman* 20 Feb.; 13, 20 March; 3, 10, 24 April; 1 May 1915; VW *Diary* I.

LOVE AMONG THE ARTISTS

Charleston Papers; VW-VB letters (Berg); VW *Letters;* RF *Letters;* Shone; QB; Darroch; Garnett.

EMINENCE OF LYTTON

Holroyd; Garnett; Carrington letters, diary; VW *Diary* I; VW *Letters* I; LW *Downhill;* Gertler, *Letters.* The Freud letter is in Holroyd II.

MAYNARD AT VERSAILLES

Harrod; Ottoline *Memoirs;* VW *Letters* I; VW *Diary* I; Duncan Grant told me the story of the Paris auction; it can also be found in Shone and Garnett; Shone: JMK *Economic Consequences;* LW *Beginning Again;* SP; "Dr. Melchior" in *Two Memoirs.* George Spater showed me the memorandum to Colonel House.

HOUSES OF LIONS

Shone; VW *Letters* II; Garnett; LW *Beginning Again; Downhill; Night and Day; Diary* I; Plomer; Fry *Letters;* VW *Fry; Old Friends;* Garnett; Carrington; Holroyd; Boyd; Charleston Papers; Whitall; conversations with LW.

THE MEMOIR CLUB

Fry, *Letters.* I saw VB's unfinished Memoir Club painting at the d'Offay Couper Gallery in 1973; QB showed me the completed painting of the club. Boyd; VW diary notes (Berg); Garnett, preface to JMK *Two Memoirs; Moments of Being;* QB *Bloomsbury;* VW *Letters* II, III; VW *Diary II;* Rosenbaum.

Bibliography

BLOOMSBURY GROUP WRITINGS

CLIVE BELL

Art (1914); *Pot Boilers* (1918); *Since Cézanne* (1922); *On British Freedom* (1923); *Civilization* (1928); *Landmarks in Nineteenth Century Painting* (1927); *Old Friends: Personal Recollections* (1956).

ROGER FRY

Giovanni Bellini (1899); *Vision and Design* (1920); *The Artist and Psychoanalysis* (1924); *Art and Commerce* (1926); *Transformations* (1926); *Cézanne* (1927); *Flemish Art* (1927); *Henri Matisse* (1930); *Characteristics of French Art* (1932); *Reflections on British Painting* (1934); *Last Lectures* (ed. Clark, 1939).

JOHN MAYNARD KEYNES

Indian Currency and Finance (1913); *The Economic Consequences of the Peace* (1919); *A Treatise on Probability* (1921); *A Revision of the Treaty* (1922); *A Tract on Monetary Reform* (1923); *The Economic Consequences of Mr. Churchill* (1925); *A Short View of Russia* (1925); *A Treatise on Money* (2 vols., 1930); *Essays in Persuasion* (1931); *Essays in Biography* (1933); *The General Theory of Employment, Interest and Money* (1936); *Two Memoirs* (ed. Garnett, 1949); *The Collected Writings of John Maynard Keynes* (25 vols., Royal Economic Society).

DESMOND MACCARTHY

The Court Theatre (1904–7); *Remnants* (1918); *Portraits* (1931); *Criticism* (1932); *Experience* (1935);

Leslie Stephen (1937); *Drama* (1940); *Shaw* (1951); *Humanities* (1953); *Memories* (1953); *Theatre* (1954). (It should be noted that there is considerable duplication of material in these volumes.)

LYTTON STRACHEY

Landmarks in French Literature (1912); *Eminent Victorians* (1918); *Queen Victoria* (1921); *Books and Characters* (1922); *Elizabeth and Essex* (1928); *Portraits in Miniature* (1931); *Characters and Commentaries* (1933); *Spectatorial Essays* (ed. Strachey, 1964); *Lytton Strachey by Himself* (ed. Holroyd, 1971); *The Really Interesting Question* (ed. Levy, 1972).

LEONARD WOOLF

The Village in the Jungle (1913); *The Wise Virgins* (1914); *International Government* (1916); *Cooperation and the Future of Industry* (1918); *Economic Imperialism* (1920); *Empire and Commerce in Africa* (1920); *Socialism and Cooperation* (1921); *Fear and Politics* (1925); *Essays on Literature, History, Politics* (1927); *Hunting the Highbrow* (1927); *Imperialism and Civilization* (1928); *After the Deluge* (*Principia Politica*, 3 vols., 1931, 1939, 1953); *Barbarians at the Gate* (1939); *The War for Peace* (1940); *Quack! Quack!* (1953); *Autobiography*; *Sowing* (1960); *Growing* (1961); *Ceylon Diaries* (1963); *Beginning Again* (1964); *Downhill All the Way* (1967); *The Journey Not the Arrival Matters* (1970).

VIRGINIA WOOLF

The Voyage Out (1915); *Night and Day* (1919); *Kew Gardens* (1919); *Monday or Tuesday* (1921); *Jacob's Room* (1922); *Mrs. Dalloway* (1925); *The Common Reader* (1925); *To the Lighthouse* (1927); *Orlando* (1928); *A Room of One's Own* (1929); *The Waves* (1931); *The Common Reader: Second Series* (1932); *Flush* (1933); *The Years* (1937); *Three Guineas* (1938); *Roger Fry* (1940); *Between the Acts* (1941); *The Death of the Moth* (1942); *A Haunted House* (1944); *The Moment* (1947); *The*

Captain's Death Bed (1950); *A Writer's Diary* (1954); *Woolf-Strachey Letters* (1956); *Granite and Rainbow* (1958); *Contemporary Writers* (1965); *Collected Essays* (4 vols., 1967); *Mrs. Dalloway's Party* (1973); *Letters* I–III (ed. Nicolson and Trautmann, 1975–78); *The London Scene* (1975); *Freshwater* (ed. Ruotolo, 1976); *Moments of Being* (ed. Schulkind, 1976); *Books and Portraits* (ed. Lyon, 1977); *The Pargiters* (ed. Leaska, 1978); *The Diary of Virginia Woolf* I, II (ed. Olivier Bell, 1977, 1978).

BLOOMSBURY

Bell, Quentin, *Bloomsbury* (1968); *Virginia Woolf* (2 vols., 1972); *The Bloomsbury Group* in *The Word and the Image*, VII (National Book League, 1976).

Blomfield, Paul, *Uncommon People* (1955).

Boyd, Elizabeth French, *Bloomsbury Heritage* (1976).

Fry, Roger, *Letters* (2 vols., ed. Sutton, 1972).

Gadd, David, *The Loving Friends* (1974).

Harrod, Sir Roy, *The Life of John Maynard Keynes* (1951).

Holroyd, Michael, *Lytton Strachey* (2 vols., 1968).

Johnstone, J. K., *The Bloomsbury Group* (1954).

Leavis, F. R., *The Common Pursuit* (1964).

Noble, Joan Russell (ed.), *Recollections of Virginia Woolf* (1972).

Partridge, Frances, *A Pacifist's War* (1978).

Rosenbaum, S. P. (ed.), *The Bloomsbury Book, An Anthology* (1975).

Shone, Richard, *Bloomsbury Portraits* (1976).

Spater, George, and Ian Parsons, *A Marriage of True Minds* (1977).

RELATED WORKS

Annan, Noel, *Leslie Stephen* (1951).

Askwith, Betty, *Two Victorian Families* (1974).

Baron, Wendy, *Miss Ethel Sands and Her Circle* (1977).

Beerbohm, Max, *Lytton Strachey* (1943).

Bennett, Arnold, *Journals* I (1932).

Brenan, Gerald, *South from Granada* (1959); *A Life of One's Own* (1962); *Personal Record* (1974).

Buchanan, Donald, *James Wilson Morrice* (1936).

Bywater, William G., Jr., *Clive Bell's Eye* (1975).

Clark, Kenneth, *Another Part of the Wood* (1974).

Darroch, Sandra Jobson, *Ottoline* (1975).

Dickinson, G. Lowes, *Autobiography* (ed. Procter, 1973).

Donahue, Delia, *Virginia Woolf* (1977).

Edel, Leon, *The Modern Psychological Novel* (1955); *Literary Biography* (1957); Henry James, *The Master* (1972).

Forster, E. M. *Goldsworthy Lowes Dickinson* (1934); *Virginia Woolf* (1941); *Two Cheers for Democracy* (1951).

Fry, Roger, *Duncan Grant* (1930).

Gaither, Mary E., and J. Howard Woolmer, *Checklist of the Hogarth Press* (1976).

Garnett, David, *The Flowers of the Forest* (1955); *The Familiar Faces* (1962); (ed.) *Carrington, Letters and Diaries* (1970).

Gertler, Mark, *Selected Letters* (ed. Carrington, 1965).

Hamnett, Nina, *Laughing Torso* (1932).

Heilbrun, Carolyn G., *Toward a Recognition of Androgyny* (1973); *Lady Ottoline's Album* (1976).

Kirkpatrick, B. J., *A Bibliography of Virginia Woolf* (1957).

Lawrence, Frieda, *The Memoirs and Correspondence* (1964).

Lea, F. A., *The Life of John Middleton Murry* (1959).

Lehmann, John, *In My Own Time* (1969).

Lewis, Helen Block, *Psychic War in Men and Women* (1976).

Lewis, Wyndham, *Letters* (ed. Rose, 1963); *On Art* (ed. Fox and Michel, 1969).

MacKenzie, Norman and Jeanne, *The Fabians* (1977).

Majumdar, Robin, and Allen McLaurin, *Virginia Woolf: The Critical Heritage* (1975).

Mansfield, Katherine, *Journals* (1927); *Letters* (2 vols., ed. Murry, 1929).

Merle, Gabriel, *Lytton Strachey* (3 vols., 1976), University of Paris thesis, offset.

Moore, G. E., *Principia Ethica* (1903).

Moore, Harry T., *The Priest of Love, A Life of D. H. Lawrence* (1974).

Morrell, Lady Ottoline, *Ottoline, Early Memoirs* (1963) and *Ottoline at Garsington* (ed. Gathorne-Hardy, 1974).

Mortimer, Raymond, *Channel Packet* (1948); *Duncan Grant* (1948).

Nicolson, Nigel, *Portrait of a Marriage* (1973).

Pippett, Aileen, *The Moth and the Star* (1955).

Plomer, William, *Celebrations* (1972); *Autobiography* (1975).

Quennell, Peter, *The Marble Foot* (1976).

Raverat, Gwen, *Period Piece* (1952).

Rothenstein, William, *Men and Memories* (2 vols., 1931–32); *Since Fifty* (1940).

Russell, Bertrand, *Autobiography* (1967).

Sanders, Charles R., *Lytton Strachey* (1957).

Sassoon, Siegfried, *Siegfried's Journey* (1955).

Sickert, Walter, *A Free House* (ed. Sitwell, 1947).

Sitwell, Osbert, *Laughter in the Next Room* (1949).

Spender, Stephen, *World Within World* (1951).

Stansky, Peter, and William Abrahams, *Journey to the Frontier* (1966).

Stephen, Leslie, *Mausoleum Book* (ed. Alan Bell, 1977).

Swinnerton, Frank, *The Georgian Literary Scene* (1938, 1951).

Whitall, James, *English Years* (1935).

BLOOMSBURY PAINTERS

The most comprehensive history is Richard Shone's *Bloomsbury Portraits* (1976). In addition to other works mentioned above, a list of catalogs, exhibitions and principal articles about the painters can be found in the Rosenbaum anthology of the Bloomsbury Group. Reproductions of Carrington's work can be found in *Carrington* by Noel Carrington (1978). An Arts Council Exhibition of Roger

Fry's work took place during 1966 and the catalog was prefaced by Quentin Bell; a Vanessa Bell memorial exhibition was also staged by the Arts Council in 1964 and the catalog has an introduction by Ronald Pickvance. There have been several recent Duncan Grant retrospectives, including one in 1972 at the d'Offay Couper Gallery, the catalog carrying a note by Stephen Spender; and one of Vanessa Bell's work at the same gallery in 1973, the catalog prefaced by Richard Morphet.

A Bloomsbury Chronology 1885-1920

1885 Roger Fry at King's College, Cambridge.

1894 Desmond MacCarthy at Trinity.

1895 Death in Kensington of Julia Jackson Stephen, wife of Leslie Stephen, mother of Vanessa and Virginia, who are educated at home.

1899 Clive Bell, Lytton Strachey, Leonard Woolf, Thoby Stephen enter Trinity, meet and found Midnight Society.

1900 Vanessa and Virginia in Cambridge for May week encounter their brother Thoby's friends, Clive, Lytton, Leonard.

1901 Roger Fry writes art criticism for *Athenaeum*, has been painting since 1892; Vanessa Stephen at Royal Academy Schools.

1902 Duncan Grant at Westminster Art School; Leonard Woolf and Lytton Strachey elected "Apostles" in Cambridge secret society, Desmond and Roger being earlier members; Maynard Keynes arrives at King's.

1903 Keynes elected Apostle; Desmond critic for *Speaker.*

1904 Virginia Stephen writes book reviews; Leslie Stephen dies; daughters move with brothers Thoby and Adrian from Kensington to Bloomsbury, 46 Gordon Square; Clive Bell in Paris learning about art; Leonard goes to Ceylon as colonial civil servant; Lytton lingers in Cambridge in hope of a Fellowship.

1905 BLOOMSBURY, the first phase: Thoby Stephen invites to Gordon Square his Cambridge friends for Thursday "at homes," where they also find Vanessa and Virginia; Vanessa organizes Friday

Club, an arts club; Strachey leaves Cambridge without becoming a don.

1906 Desmond marries Mary (Molly) Warre-Cornish; Duncan Grant studies art in Paris; Keynes in India Office as civil servant; Thoby dies of typhoid after trip to Greece.

1907 BLOOMSBURY, the second phase: Clive and Vanessa marry; Virginia and Adrian move to 29 Fitzroy Square; Thursday evening "at homes" now alternate between Gordon Square and Fitzroy Square; Lytton writes for *Spectator*.

1908 Julian Bell born; Leonard Woolf attains post in Ceylon of Assistant Government Agent at Hambantota.

1909 Keynes elected Fellow of King's; Duncan paints at 21 Fitzroy Square.

1910 Roger Fry meets Clive and Vanessa and is introduced to Bloomsbury, stages first Post-Impressionist show at Grafton Galleries with Desmond as secretary; birth of Quentin Bell.

1911 BLOOMSBURY, the third phase: Virginia, Adrian, Maynard, Duncan and, shortly after, Leonard, returning from Ceylon on leave, move into 38 Brunswick Square; Roger and Vanessa fall in love.

1912 Leonard Woolf resigns from the Ceylon Civil Service, woos and marries Virginia Stephen; second Post-Impressionist show, with Bloomsbury participating and Leonard as secretary, staged by Roger; Keynes editor of *Economic Journal*.

1913 Leonard reviews for the *New Statesman*, writes *The Village in the Jungle;* Keynes publishes *Indian Currency and Finance;* Roger founds Omega Workshops; Virginia has breakdown and long illness; Desmond becomes drama critic of *New Statesman*.

1914 Clive Bell publishes *Art;* Leonard Woolf publishes *The Wise Virgins,* a novel about Bloomsbury; with advent of war, Desmond goes to France as ambulance driver; Keynes accepts post in Treasury.

1915   Clive Bell's *Peace at Once* publicly burned; Virginia attempts suicide; her first novel, *The Voyage Out*, published.

1916   Leonard's two reports on "International Government"; Lytton and Leonard exempted from service for reasons of health; Clive, Duncan and young David Garnett farm in lieu of service; Vanessa moves with Duncan to Charleston Farm, where they henceforth reside.

1917   Woolfs buy printing press and establish Hogarth Press at Hogarth House, Richmond, where they live; Leonard becomes adviser to Labour Party on imperial and international questions; Virginia Woolf begins to keep a diary; Lytton Strachey sets up house with Dora Carrington at Tidmarsh, Berkshire.

1918   Angelica Bell born at Charleston; Lytton brings out *Eminent Victorians*.

1919   Keynes at Paris Peace Conference as principal representative of the Treasury, criticizes treaty and resigns, writes *The Economic Consequences of the Peace* at Charleston.

1920   With peace, Bloomsbury individuals, publishing, writing, painting, active in economics and politics, exercise wide influence but are unaware of collective power, which is considerable; Bloomsbury establishes a Memoir Club and meets regularly to reminisce. The friends, now middle-aged, will go on to large achievements during the next twenty years "between the wars."

Index

HENRY
JAMES

THE COMPLETE BIOGRAPHY
BY LEON EDEL

*Winner of the National Book Award.
The Pulitzer Prize Biography*

THE UNTRIED YEARS: 1843-1870

THE CONQUEST OF LONDON: 1870-1881

THE MIDDLE YEARS: 1882-1895

THE TREACHEROUS YEARS: 1895-1901

THE MASTER: 1901-1916

Available individually, or in a boxed set for $14.75

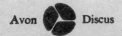

Avon   Discus

HJ 10-78

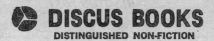

DISCUS BOOKS
DISTINGUISHED NON-FICTION

A SELECTION OF RECENT TITLES

DRT 1-80

GREAT READING
FROM AVON ⬡ BOOKS

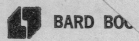 **BARD BOOKS**

distinguished modern fiction

A SELECTION OF RECENT TITLES

ANAIS NIN READER Philip K. Jason (Ed.)	36624	2.50
BETRAYED BY RITA HAYWORTH Manuel Puig	15206	1.65
BILLIARDS AT HALF-PAST NINE Heinrich Böll	47860	2.75
THE CLOWN Heinrich Böll	37523	2.25
THE EYE OF THE HEART Barbara Howes, Ed.	47787	2.95
FERTIG Sol Yurick	21477	1.95
FLIGHT TO CANADA Ishmael Reed	35428	2.25
THE GREEN HOUSE Mario Vargas Llosa	15099	1.65
HERMAPHRODEITY Alan Friedman	16865	2.45
HOPSCOTCH Julio Cortázar	36731	2.95
HUNGER Knut Hamsun	26864	1.75
LEAF STORM And Other Stories Gabriel Garcia Márquez	35816	1.95
THE MORNING WATCH James Agee	28316	1.50
ONE HUNDRED YEARS OF SOLITUDE Gabriel Garcia Márquez	45278	2.95
NABOKOV'S DOZEN Vladimir Nabokov	15354	1.65
PRATER VIOLET Christopher Isherwood	36269	1.95
THE RECOGNITIONS William Gaddis	49544	3.95
62: A MODEL KIT Julio Cortázar	17558	1.65
THE VICTIM Saul Bellow	24273	1.75
THE WOMAN OF ANDROS Thornton Wilder	49460	2.25

Where better paperbacks are sold, or directly from the publisher. Include 50¢ per copy for postage and handling; allow 4-6 weeks for delivery.

Avon Books, Mail Order Dept.
224 W. 57th St., New York, N.Y. 10019

BDF 5-80